HOW TO HUNT
THE WHITETAIL DEER

HOW TO HUNT THE WHITETAIL DEER

New and Revised Edition

TOM HAYES

South Brunswick and New York: A. S. Barnes and Company
London: Thomas Yoseloff Ltd

© 1960, 1966, 1977 by A. S. Barnes and Company, Inc.

Library of Congress Catalogue Card Number: 65-20343

A. S. Barnes and Co., Inc.
Cranbury, New Jersey 08512

Thomas Yoseloff Ltd
Magdalen House
136–148 Tooley Street
London SE1 2TT, England

ISBN 0-498-06277-5 (Hardcover)
ISBN 0-498-01979-9 (Paperback)

Printed in the United States of America

FOREWORD

My wife accuses me of spending all my time hunting. This is not true. I spend some of my time fishing—which goes to show how unfair a woman can be. But I can not deny that deer hunting has been for many years the supreme interest, aside from my family, of my misspent life. To compound my guilt, I infected my two sons with this virus at very tender ages, which placed the almost intolerable burden of three rabid deer hunters on one poor defenseless woman.

Deer hunting, to the dyed-in-the-wool deer hunter, is much more than a healthful sport and relaxing pastime; it is a burning obsession. When opening day rolls around, all ailing deer hunters crawl out of their sickbeds and stagger into the deer coverts, where they rapidly recover. No genuine deer hunter will allow himself to die until he has made one more hunting season, and, as there is always another season coming up, it is quite obvious that all true deer hunters will live forever.

Most of you readers will be veterans of several campaigns against Mr. Whitetail Buck and will have become respectfully impressed with his ability to avoid becoming venison. Rightly refusing to believe that your success must depend in large portion on fickle fortune, you are seeking ways and means of

5

reducing the element of luck in your chosen avocation. The completely green first-timer will seldom waste money on a hunting book; he knows that shooting a deer is such a simple operation that, were any instructions necessary, they would have been placed on the rifle at the factory in the form of a tag reading, "Aim at deer through sights (A) and pull trigger (B)."

The purpose of this book is to help you to become more successful in your pursuit of the whitetail buck. Perhaps you have never hunted whitetails before, but for this book to be of much benefit to you at least a little knowledge of guns and gunning will be necessary. You may be a moose and grizzly hunter, a varmit hunter, or a squirrel and rabbit hunter, but unless you are a competent rifle shot and have established some sort of hunting background I do not believe this or any book will in itself turn you into a top whitetail hunter. It is my firm belief that the futile attempt to transform the completely innocent pavement-pounder into a finished deer slayer is the principal failing of the average treatise on this subject.

To you would-be deer hunters who are completely unfamiliar with rifled arms I offer the following advice, which should be worth more to you than the price of this book: your first rifle should be a good quality .22 rimfire and its purchase should precede by two or three years the purchase of a deer rifle. These years should be spent in learning to shoot quickly and accurately, in becoming familiar with the operation and feel of a rifle, and in spending as much time as possible in squirrel and rabbit coverts. Unless you are now an accomplished rifle shot, a free booklet on the art of rifle shooting will be of vastly more immediate value to you than all the books on hunting ever published.

The consistently successful whitetail hunter is thoroughly aware of his own temperament and reactions, his capabilities and limitations. He knows his rifle thoroughly and intimately —its potential, its operation, its feel, heft, and balance. He knows his hunting ground intimately—its roads, paths, and game trails; its thickets, rivers, meadows, and water holes; its hills, valleys, draws, and fences. He also knows the appearance, habits, temperament, and reactions of his game. Lack of knowledge of the habits of whitetail deer, or failure to take advantage of this knowledge, is the primary reason for lack of success among reasonably experienced hunters. Read that last sentence twice and then we will discuss our quarry.

T. H.

CONTENTS

ILLUSTRATIONS

1 ———————————— THE GAME

From rump to nose the average whitetail buck measures five feet or a little over and stands about thirty-two inches at the shoulder. Size varies considerably from one section of the country to another—and between individual animals—but the above dimensions and a field-dressed weight (guts only removed) of 135 pounds are about right for a national average. The doe does not stand quite so tall, is more daintily built, is somewhat shorter in proportion to her height, and averages about 30 per cent lighter in weight.

The summer coat of the whitetail is quite reddish, being replaced in the fall by the heavier tannish-gray winter coat. Most books on the whitetail state that there is no difference in the color of the two sexes; but after you have seen enough deer you will learn to detect a slight variation of shading, when viewed in good light, that can sometimes make the difference between success and failure of your hunt, when quick identification of sex becomes necessary. The doe often appears more bluish and the buck more rusty and somewhat darker along the back. This darker streak along the back becomes more pronounced as the buck grows older, and accounts for the origin of the term "mossback." Under direct sunlight the buck often appears distinctly reddish, even in the winter coat. When standing back in the shadows, all deer seem to become colorless and all but invisible. Fawns are born in the late spring and come into the world with a coat liberally dappled with large white spots, which usually disappear by the time the hunting season opens.

The tail is rather long for a member of the deer family and is broadly spade-shaped, with a white edge-band distinctly visible from the top side. The under side of the tail is pure white, as is the area covered by the tail. The under-belly and the inner sides of the legs are also white, and there is a large white throat-patch at the juncture of the neck and jaws. The ears, though somewhat smaller than those of other American deer, are fairly large and the eyes are large, dark, and round, with a surrounding white band.

The hooves have pointed toes and the heart-shaped tracks— about three inches long—are not easily confused with those of any other animal after you have studied and familiarized yourself with their appearance. The two dewclaws at the rear of each hoof are not prominent, and under normal conditions will show only on snow or soft ground. The heavier the animal, and the faster it is traveling, the wider will be the spacing between the toes and the more plainly will the prints of the dewclaws show. There are two scent glands on each hind leg which are known as the tarsal and metatarsal glands. One appears as a slit about an inch long on the outer side of each shank, and the other is located on the inner side of each hind leg near the point where the haunch and shank join. This is a dirty brown swirl of hair surrounding a small opening in the skin.

The maximum life span of whitetails seems to be about fifteen years, and only the bucks have antlers. The latter are shed every year in midwinter and start to grow out again by early spring. While growing, the antlers are soft and rubbery and are covered with fine short hair which is called "velvet." They are fully grown and hardened by late summer, and the buck will then rub off the dead skin on small trees and saplings. In the first summer and fall of its life, a buck fawn has two little black knobs on the top of his head and is called a "button spike." The following autumn he will be as large as his mother and will sport a pair of sharp, goatlike antlers of from three to five inches long. He is now called a spike-buck or plain "spike." The following year will find his antlers forked and normally about eight to ten inches in overall length. He is now a four-point buck or "forkhorn." After this year he will develop a set of antlers with probably as many points (or tines) as they will ever have and unless drought conditions exist which will result in a marked reduction in both size and quality, the antlers will increase in both length and beam until about the seventh year. After about the tenth year the antlers will progressively decline in both size and symmetry. A very old buck may wear only a scraggly miniature set of antlers. After the third year, the number of points is no indication of a buck's age, the number and condition of the teeth becoming the more reliable means of age determination. It is customary to count the total number of points on the whitetail rack instead of only the points on one antler, as is usual in the case of blacktail and mule deer. The definition of a point is somewhat debatable, but a projection one inch long is a generally-accepted minimum.

The above description of the whitetail deer is by no means complete, but it should suffice to enable you new deer hunters to identify what you are shooting at. I suggest that you make a thoroughly-detailed study of your first trophy.

All deer possess highly-developed senses of smell and hearing, and the whitetail is generally credited with having these senses developed to their highest degree. I know that they also have a well-developed ability to feel vibration, and a heavy tread, even though silent, can be "felt" by a deer at a considerable distance. A deer can hear a watch tick at twenty feet and can hear a loud swallow or heavy breathing up to twenty yards—so always breathe through the open mouth when close to a deer.

A deer's eyesight is usually described as poor. This is not quite true. A deer has excellent vision except for resolving power. His vision is by no means weak, for he can see even a small movement or any clearly outlined object at a great distance. Regardless of what you may have been told, if you stand motionless in a bare clearing a deer can see you from the next mountain top. He can't tell what you are, but he knows you were not there yesterday, and if he has plans for crossing that clearing he'll remember to find out exactly what you are before exposing himself. Should you be walking, the deer will instantly and correctly identify you. The hunter must never forget that any deer within the range of his vision will probably see him if he makes any quick movement, no matter how small. I believe that deer see much better at night, relatively, than they do in the daytime. A deer's visual weakness is limited solely to his inability to clearly distinguish a motionless object which fails to contrast sharply with its immediate background. "Contrast" means the degree of shading, because all deer are color-blind and see everything as either black, white, or some shade of gray in between. The deer's eyes, however, are quite sensitive to light reflections, and the animal can quickly determine between objects which are glossy and those which are dull, even if both have the same degree of shading.

You are doubtless familiar with the extrasensory "sixth" sense so ably described by Colonel Jim Corbett in his classics on man-eaters. This can best be described as a "feeling" of impending danger which puts us on guard when no evidence of danger has been conveyed to us through any of our recognized senses of perception such as sight, smell, or hearing. The whitetail possesses this sixth sense to a high degree.

The whitetail possesses such remarkable powers of scent that it relies principally on the sense of smell for detecting and identifying its enemies. This sense is also depended upon almost exclusively in selecting food and locating feeding areas, and is the sole means by which a buck is attracted to a rutting doe. I have watched unsuspecting deer walk into my scent stream and leap violently backward with an involuntary snort, exactly as if they had run their noses into an electrically-charged fence. A deer may pause to argue with its eyes or its ears, but never with its nose.

High wind renders a deer's senses of sight and hearing much less reliable, so that it becomes doubly vigilant, wary, and suspicious. Moving and feeding as little as possible, the deer will stand and strain every faculty against the possible approach of enemies. Deer are most difficult to approach under high wind conditions, and hunting them at such times is usually a lost cause. As has been stated by one leading authority, it takes the hunter many seasons to fully comprehend the vastness of the sensitory gulf that separates him from his whitetail quarry.

The tail, though nervously twitched at regular intervals, is normally carried close against the rump when the deer is standing, walking, trotting, or on the seldom-observed dead-run. The tail seems to rise automatically whenever the flitting, bounding gallop is employed—the gait most often observed by the frustrated hunter. This snow-white organ waves from side to side as the animal bounds away, as though taunting the hunter for being so clumsy.

A walking deer takes such long, effortless strides that his rate of progress is often much greater than it appears to be. When stepping along with a purpose his speed is often close to six miles an hour, and, where the footing is good, he may slide into a fast, effortless, gliding, twinkle-legged trot which has no perceptible up or down motion. Unalarmed deer normally carry their heads well forward, pausing at frequent intervals and thrusting the head high in an incessant search for possible enemies. Whenever a deer becomes suspicious and decides to ease out of an area, it will hold the head rigidly high and walk away with a haughty, high-stepping gait which is virtually soundless—a picture of poise, grace, and acute alertness. Mature bucks will sometimes emerge from cover at twilight in this manner.

When really startled at close range, a whitetail will stretch out and dig like a racing horse until he has put a little distance between himself and the booger. If you happen to be the booger, you will often hear him grunt with each drive of those powerful hind legs. After forty or fifty yards, provided you are not chasing him, he will probably hoist his white flag and drop down to that gay bouncing gallop which you observed on the very first whitetail you ever saw. Quite often, as a precautionary measure, a deer will flee from an object which has neither offered a direct threat nor been positively identified. Then, having run a reassuring distance without detecting any sign of pursuit, the deer will very often pause at the last point of visibility, turn either broadside or head-on, and stand for a brief moment watching his back trail.

Where the opportunity exists and circumstances seem to warrant, a deer may suddenly drop behind a log or into high grass or a slight depression, and be erased instantly and magically from your sight. Then, while flat on its belly, the deer is able to move a great distance in an incredibly short time. If this ever happens with a deer you are watching you will feel like the sucker at a circus shell game as the earth seems to swallow up your deer. When a deer soars over a fence he makes a bird appear clumsy, and he flits around brush, over rocks, up mountains, and through timber like a creature detached from the earth.

Whitetails thrive in all temperate and semi-tropical zones and at all altitudes. They are as much at home in low-lying swamps and river bottoms as on mountain tops, and they will take to water almost as readily as will a beaver. Deer have hollow hairs which make them very bouyant, and they often cross even large bodies of water to escape persecution or to reach an attractive feeding area. Deer swim tirelessly and rapidly, their normal rate of progress through the water being equal to the normal pace of a walking man. Deer have been known to cross bodies of water ten miles wide.

The whitetail has often been described as an "edge" animal—one which prefers country that is a mixture of dense cover and open patches. Although most hunters accept this description, few fully realize its accuracy. In this instance, the term "edge" means the *very* edge, as most of the animals in a given area will be found concentrated in a narrow belt of cover, seldom more than a quarter-mile wide, immediately adjacent to open meadows, fields, and parklike terrain. Most veteran hunters do not consider large, unbroken tracts of solid timber, dense brush, or open meadow to be likely whitetail range, and few of them will bother to hunt such places unless they are definitely known to harbor deer.

Whitetails will readily come up to human premises, accepting the presence of people there as a minor annoyance in the same category with dogs, house cats, and flies. They understand that humans live and belong there, that they chop wood, play radios, draw water, plow the fields, mend their fences, and whoop and holler. They may sometimes jump into a field within a hundred yards of where you are working, and calmly begin their feeding; but the moment *you* pass beyond the limits of *your* homestead and enter *their* domain, the deer's attitude completely changes and you immediately become booger number one. It's strictly a one-way street as far as the deer are concerned. This becomes especially true when you surprise a deer in his own habitat at close quarters; he will instantly suspect that you are there to do him in. The deer, knowing that men normally make so much noise while walking that you could not likely have approached so close without sneaking, will correctly conclude that your sudden appearance bodes him no good. Whitetails become much more self-assured during the hours of darkness, and will boldly invade a backyard garden which they would not dare to come near during daylight.

Where deer live close to civilization and no natural enemies exist in their habitat, they will, if no poaching takes place, become amazingly tame and trusting. Under this condition, with the exception of the older mossback bucks which probably have had several close escapes from hunters, deer can often be taken with ridiculous ease during the first day or so of hunting season. Like turkeys, however, deer catch on very quickly, and after a few days of hunting they will become as wild and wary as any animal can possibly be. This book presupposes you to be hunting late-season animals which have become thoroughly aware of your intentions.

Deer usually snort (or "blow") to warn other deer in the vicinity of the intrusion of a booger. A description of this sound, an explosive blast of air from the lungs, will be necessary only for the benefit of the man who is planning his first whitetail hunt. This discouraging sound is all too frequently heard by even the most experienced of us, and it has the same significance to the hunter as has the sound of the gong to the contestant in an amateur-hour program.

When whitetails discover an intruder in their area they seem to assume that the latter will have quitted the area within two hours of his discovery. It is very important, therefore, that the hunter arrive at his selected stand, if in the afternoon, early enough that, in the event he is discovered while going in, there will still remain more than two hours of shooting-light. Whenever you are discovered with less than two hours of light remaining, the only deer you will have any reasonable hope of killing will be one that was out of hearing when the alarm was sounded. Incidentally, those men who hunt only in the mornings and evenings are doe hunters who luck onto a buck occasionally. Buck hunters, for reasons soon to be unfolded, hunt all day in suitable weather.

Whitetails use their vocal cords very sparingly and a person might spend many autumns in the deer coverts without ever being made aware that they have vocal cords at all. In mortal fear or agony, a whitetail has been known to bleat much in the manner of a sheep, and a doe will occasionally call to her fawns with a *very* soft bleat inaudible a few feet away. Needless to say, few men are ever this close to an unsuspecting doe at one of these rare times; so you will probably have to accept my statement for this occurrence.

Whitetails, like all the higher animals except civilized man, instantly recognize the alarm sounds of all other creatures native to their habitat. This includes all species of domestic animals which use the area, as well as all migrants which regularly pass through. Squirrels are probably the hunter's chief betrayers, but jays, crows, and turkeys all contribute heavily to his downfall. However, it does happen occasionally that a squirrel will also announce the approach of a deer; so the little blabbermouth sometimes repays the hunter in some small measure for the harm he has done. A few lumbering strides of a milch cow startled by your unexpected appearance can warn all the deer in the vicinity as effectively as a doe's snort, and the alarm sneeze of a domestic goat or the "pert" of an alarmed turkey will herald your approach as effectively as a brass band.

All ruminants in general, deer in particular and whitetail deer most of all, are governed in their behavior to a considerable extent by the position of the moon. Go ahead and have your belly laugh and then we will proceed with our casting of pearls. Except for a brief early-morning and late-evening feeding period, the whitetail normally gets up with the moon and lies down with the moon. Man and turkeys, for example, are creatures of the day; coons and possums, on the other hand, are creatures of the night. Deer, being lunar creatures, are somewhere in between; but the whitetail is much closer than any other American deer to being a night rather than a day animal. Unless food is scarce or a storm is either ending or impending, the whitetail will ordinarily feed up in the day only after the moon has risen or is about to rise, and he will dispense with most midday feeding at the slightest sign of hunting pressure. Under heavy or prolonged hunting pressure, the whitetail will normally cease all midday feeding and may drastically shorten—or even entirely dispense with—the early-morning and late-evening feeding periods as well.

Though hunting is generally poorest at the time of the full moon and is generally best when the night is totally dark, at all times—during favorable weather—when the moon rises during the daylight hours the days will be above average for hunting while at those times when the moon rises during the hours of darkness hunting will produce below average results. The lunar month contains one excellent hunting week, one good week, one fair week, and one poor week for hunting, although weather conditions and food scarcity can cause marked variations in the whitetail's activity levels, as previously noted. Any man who refuses to regard the moon's position when planning his strategy is not now and never will be a top whitetail hunter. Yes, this includes you.

There are times when all wildlife is active—birds, squirrels, armadillos, hawks, and even insects. Deer also can be expected to be active at such times. At other times, the covert gives the impression that it has been extirpated of every living animal and that you are all alone in a lifeless world. The answer often lies in the position of the moon. Just before moonrise a hush seems to fall over the woods and all nature is still. Then, as the moon rises, all living creatures seem to come vibrantly alive and all wildlife becomes exceptionally active and vocal. Civilized man has lost his awareness of the profound influence of the moon, but those who commune with nature can readily sympathize with the moon worship of our primative ancestors. Whenever sheep, goats, or cattle are lying around and chewing their cuds, you may be certain that old Whitetail is setting the example.

The whitetail grazes less than other American deer and probably eats a much higher percentage of forbes (weeds) and browse. He seems interested in eating grass only while it is young and tender, and he dearly loves winter oats when they are two to three inches high. Deer have a passion for nearly everything grown on a farm, especially grains, legumes, and vegetables, and they will regularly travel many miles to raid a garden.

Most whitetail country is hardwood country, and nuts and acorns are the main staple of their autumn diet. Though primarily a leaf and twig browser, a weed, mast, and berry eater, the whitetail has a goat's ability to adjust his stomach to anything edible in the vegetable kingdom, and he can survive hard winters as well as any herbivorous animal except his larger cousins. When food becomes desperately scarce, whitetails abandon their lifelong feeding habits and scrounge for food each waking moment. In the north, deep snow forces the animals to herd together in sheltered patches of timber, where they trample the snow into what is called a "deer yard." When the winter is long and the snow is deep, these places might better be called graveyards.

Where food is well scattered throughout an area, the deer will usually be well distributed, also. Where concentrations of preferred foods occur, such as fields of grain or alfalfa, the cover adjacent to these fields may harbor such a vast deer population as to astound the hunter, while more distant areas may be virtually drained of deer. Excessive hunting of such concentrated areas or exhaustion of the food will again cause the deer to disperse more evenly over the covert.

Whitetails have a like-mindedness in feeding tastes which prompts them to gang up at concentrations of currently preferred food. For example, when a certain choice berry ripens, the deer will all feed almost exclusively at patches of these berries until the supply is exhausted. The same applies to other foods and feeding places, such as fields of grain, mesquite flats, or acorn ridges. What one deer feeds on, all deer feed on, and it is utterly useless to seek deer where luscious acorns lie knee-deep if they happen to be feeding on stinkweeds at the time.

Regardless of the moon's position, a deer will stuff himself night and day immediately preceding and after a storm, and he will forego feeding for as long as two or three days during a spell of bad weather, while he "holes up" in the best piece of cover that his range provides. This windbreak may be a patch of dense timber or brush or, whenever available, a sheltered creek or canyon bed. Standing motionless and alert, a deer is not easily taken during a storm, especially by anyone stupid enough to be deer hunting in duck weather.

The end of the season's first snowstorm will really bring the deer out. The younger ones will often romp and play in the new-fallen snow, and even the oldsters seem to enjoy it. After a storm has passed, especially one of long duration and great severity, whitetails really feed and move about. This is your time to hunt, and if the weather turns beautifully fair and bright you will never have it better. This is particularly true when another storm is destined to follow quickly.

Deer seem to pay no attention whatever to light misting rain, or even moderately heavy rain as long as it is warm. A cold, penetrating rain which drives the hunter to cover will do the same to the whitetail, and I doubt that any other warm-blooded creature can stand motionless under a tree, hour after hour, for such long periods of time as a deer can. They will seldom lie down on cold soggy ground, preferring to take their rest while standing. The warm rain of Oregon's September is quite different from the November rain of Maine, Michigan, or even Texas. If you are ever out in whitetail coverts and catch yourself saying, "Only an idiot would be out hunting in this kind of weather," you will probably be making an observation of remarkable astuteness.

Though deer appear to suffer much less than do human beings under extremes of temperature, they best like the temperature and weather conditions which we ourselves prefer. A still, frosty dawn that sets your blood to tingling with anticipation of a glorious autumn day will often find the whitetails loitering around the edges of open, grassy meadows and awaiting the warming rays of the rising sun. You'd better be there, too. The best hunting weather is presaged by the conditions of the preceding night, which are characterized by a subsiding wind and clearing skies, and which may be summarized by the old jingle, "Clear as a bell and cold as hell, and the dangdest frost that ever fell." When such weather occurs during the dark of the moon, and especially following stormy weather, whitetail hunting conditions are absolutely ideal. Any time the temperature is cool enough to drive you into the sunshine, whitetails will be sunning themselves, too; and whenever you are inclined to seek the cooling shade, old Whitetail will be similarly disposed.

In normal weather the whitetail will retire in the morning to a patch of cover on the top of some mound or hillock, or to the brushy slope of a higher hill or mountain. There is an old saying that deer go up in the morning and come down in the evening. This is generally true, being modified somewhat by the topography. Around lakes and swamps, the shore line becomes the "down," while the somewhat higher surrounding ground becomes the "up." In flat country, the meadows and more open stands of brush and timber become the "down," while the thickets and denser stands of brush and timber become the "up." The normal relationship of up and down becomes completely reversed in those areas where all the higher ground is open cultivated fields or pasture and the only cover is found in lower-lying valleys.

Deer travel over definite, established trails. All whitetail country is criss-crossed with deer trails, and before beginning to hunt in strange territory the hunter should locate as many of the major trails as possible. Whatever method of hunting is employed, knowledge of these trails will be essential to consistent success. Many of the trails will be used by all the larger species of game animals in the area, as well as by domestic horses, cattle, sheep, and goats. Horses and cattle will use only those portions of the trail that wend through the more open terrain as these much larger animals will be forced to detour many windfalls and thickets which offer no obstacle to the agile deer.

All animals employ the route to their destination which requires the least possible expenditure of energy, and regardless of the fact that a game trail which you may be following is very twisting and circuitous you may be absolutely sure that it's the best route for a deer which must travel this way to follow. Where the footing is good and the land is fairly flat and open, deer trails will often be quite broad and so indistinctly defined as to escape detection by the casual observer. The hunter should be on the constant lookout while scouting along the edges of thick cover for evidence of these broad trails, or "crossings." These are often indicated by the mouth of a well-worn trail which emerges from the heavy brush and then seems to evaporate into the more open terrain. Even these broad, indistinct trails will roughly follow the more easily traveled portions of the terrain, possibly curving slightly here and there to take advantage of patches of cover. Deer trails will spiral and zigzag up steep hills and mountains at exactly the proper angle to allow the climber to top out with the least possible exertion.

Many, and perhaps most, of the major game trails in an area can usually be located very quickly. The only likely exception that comes readily to mind is in the case of flatland areas, which may require considerable leg work because of the limited visibility. In all whitetail country you may reasonably expect to find main game trails along the foot of every brushy hill and skirting, just back in the brush, all fields, meadows, and extensive openings of every sort. Wherever open uplands or hillsides meet brushy valleys or timbered swamps, there will be a major trail just back in the cover and skirting the more open ground. Every tongue of cover which juts out into an extended opening will be a potential deer crossing because it offers the shortest *exposed* route to any deer wishing to cross the stretch of open ground.

All saddles, cuts, and low passes through hilly and mountainous country will have a deer trail running through them, and, if the hilltops offer any appreciable cover, there will be a main trail running down the ridge line. All timbered creeks will have a main trail winding along their edges, often crossing and recrossing to take advantage of the better side for walking. Deer are practical opportunists and will readily use all or part of any tote road, fire track, or cindera that will ease their journey from one part of their range to another.

Any natural avenue of travel which connects two distinct areas, such as adjoining valleys, will be a deer crossing, and virtually nothing will stop the deer from using it. A railroad or a highway built across such an avenue will not deter the deer in the least nor make them change their route. This is the reason for the *Deer Crossing* signs to be seen at various places along all highways that cut through deer country. These signs protect the motorists as well as the deer. Deer trails resemble the veins and arteries of the circulatory system in their manner of branching and rebranching into lesser and lesser trails at both the bed ground area at one end and the feeding ground areas at the other.

Up to this point, we have called your attention to several minor differences between the habits and characteristics of the whitetail and those of other deer species. Now, here is a major difference—one which opens a wide chink in the whitetail's almost impregnable armor: he has a permanent home, a small piece of real estate that he considers his very own and which he will never willingly abandon. Mule deer migrate periodically, blacktails migrate regularly, but old Whitetail will probably die within two miles of the thicket in which he entered this world.

With the fall of night, whitetails become great travelers, making forage raids and watering trips of distances as great as eleven miles, but time themselves to be back on the home range by the first faint streaks of dawn. Only destruction of their home range or a severe and prolonged drought will move whitetails to new ranges, and many will return even after an absence of several years, when the drought has broken. They will temporarily camp in the vicinity of an abundant food supply, but only until the supply is exhausted. A cougar moving onto their range or excessive hunting by man will often temporarily move the deer to another range. This is especially true when they are being hunted on their bedding ground. In any event, however, they will soon return to the home range when conditions become more nearly normal. Unless misfortune overtakes him in the meantime, the huge old mossback that made a monkey out of you last fall will be waiting on the same old stamping ground to match wits with you again this coming season.

Since the beginning of time the whitetail's enemies have attacked principally from the rear; so deer constantly anticipate an attack from the direction of their back trail. Their perennial enemies have been the larger cats, which hunt by sight but usually strike their victim from behind, and the larger members of the canine family, which generally strike a hot trail and follow it to their quarry. Therefore, deer continually watch their back trail with which they seem more concerned than with any possible danger that may lie ahead or on either side of them. This trait precludes the probability of their being taken by a trailing hunter, but repeated failure fails to discourage the bulk of hunters from the popular practice of following fresh deer tracks in the snow. This method of hunting becomes even less productive in areas where only bucks may be taken, because, except in the case of truly outstanding old mossbacks, no hunter can positively distinguish between the track of a large doe and a young buck.

Deer soon become aware of anything following their back trail, either through one of their recognized senses or that "sixth" sense we have spoken of. At the least suspicion of being followed, a deer will lay a "trap" by standing motionless behind a thick screen of brush and watching a length of back trail, or by circling and cutting his back trail for evidence of pursuit. A whitetail will play hide-and-seek all day with you if you follow his tracks, and five will get you fifty that the deer is the better at playing this game.

Deer depend principally on their noses to warn them of any danger which lies ahead; so to avoid blundering into an unseen enemy they travel into the wind whenever it is practical for them to do so. Deer invariably approach their bedding ground with noses to wind, and will often circle the feeding ground so that it, too, can be entered from down-wind.

Deer are very reluctant to travel down-wind for any appreciable distance, and whenever they feel compelled to reach a rather distant place that lies directly down-wind from them they will usually employ a tacking "vee" course. This mode of

traveling will virtually eliminate the possibility of being surprised by a following enemy, but the deer's nose will be of no
service in detecting a waiting one. However, the deer's constant quartering of the down-wind will prevent his own scent
from beaming-in a hungry predator.

Except during times of steady or prevailing winds, there
occurs a twice-daily air current reversal in fair normal weather.
This reversal generally takes about half an hour to complete
and manifests itself by the calm and stillness you have noticed
at the times between dawn and sunrise and again in the evening
between sundown and dusk. Under the rays of the rising sun
the chill air of the low-lying ground is warmed. This warmer
air has a tendency to rise, which produces currents that sweep
upward along the rising ground. At sunset, when the source of
heat is removed, the warm air will rise straight up from the
lower ground and replace itself with cooler air drawn down
from the surrounding higher ground. Therefore, the normal
trend of the air currents or breezes is from down to up in the
daytime, and from up to down at night. This phenomenon is
generally termed the diurnal wind-reversal, and deer know all
about it; in fact, they make the best use possible of it. They
depend on the morning wind-reversal to warn them of the approach of enemies on their back trail after they have bedded
down for the day.

Deer, being weather wise, will know in advance whether or
not the morning reversal will take place and will choose their
bedding procedure accordingly. If a lowering sky or strong
prevailing wind will prevent the normal upward flow of air,
deer will pass to one side of, and thirty or forty yards beyond,
the spot they have selected for their bed. Turning at right
angle and crossing over to a point directly up-wind from the

chosen bed, the deer will then turn and follow the down-wind to the spot where they will bed down.

The bed will have been chosen so that a portion of the back trail will be visible, and any following enemy which might escape detection as it passed this point in the trail would be scented instantly as it made that last up-wind turn. Whenever the morning wind-reversal is to take place, the deer will travel directly to their chosen bed and have little worry of being surprised by a following enemy, whose scent would be carried ahead of it to the ever-vigilant deer. Deer always lie facing away from the direction of the wind, depending on their sensitive noses to protect their rear. A moderate breeze will deliver a man's scent to a deer fully a mile away, and it would be difficult to conceive of a less rewarding way to spend your time than watching cover over which your own or other man-scent is blowing.

The whitetail has been described as a solitary animal. Well, it is and it isn't. A deer seems to prefer a companion or two while traveling, probably because of the mutual security offered, and he likes to feed in the company of other whitetails, probably for the same reason. But on that certain piece of brushland or hillside he regards as home, old Whitetail likes to keep strictly to himself. Even as you and I, he definitely likes neighbors but not close ones. Although most of the deer in a local area will be found bedded in the same general vicinity, it will be because of the desirability of the bed ground rather than any craving for companionship.

The doe lives in company with her fawns; the buck fawns through their first year and the doe fawns for at least two years. When several deer are seen traveling together, you may be reasonably sure that the group comprises an older doe, her this-year's fawns, and her last-year's doe fawn or fawns. The circumstance under which a buck will be seen with such a family group, or with a single doe, will be discussed later. Even these family groups open up on the bed ground, each deer selecting a resting spot at a distance from, and overlooking an avenue of approach not visible to, any of the others.

Although the whitetail deer is somewhat of a rugged individualist, his like-mindedness in choosing a general bedding area, coupled with his propensity to dine in company, often results in much the same effect as though whitetails were dedicated herd animals, traveling and living together constantly. These traits, collectively, often have the effect of giving two hunters, operating at a distance apart, widely differing opinions as to the number of deer in the area. One hunter, not stationed near an active feeding ground or along a trail connecting with one, may become convinced that there are few if any deer in the area. The other hunter, operating in a currently active area, may see so many deer as to conclude that the covert is swarming with whitetails. Both hunters are usually wrong because each has received a lopsided picture of the true situation.

Methods of hunting whitetail deer will be discussed in subsequent chapters, but the reader is counciled to reflect on the fable of the goose which laid golden eggs and refrain from molesting the deer on their bedding ground. When whitetails are hunted on their bedding ground the normal yield is not worth the time and effort involved. Nothing will so quickly cause deer to remove to another range as an invasion of their resting place. Contrary to the results obtained by some of our leading rifleman-authors in the case of blacktail deer, hunting whitetails on their bedding ground is by far the least productive method of taking them. It is also the most challenging type of rifle shooting offered by any game anywhere in the world.

The foregoing information on deer behavior has been necessarily brief and sketchy, but as we progress in our instructions for hunting whitetails we will discuss thoroughly, and describe in detail, all behavior characteristics and mannerisms which could have even the slightest effect on the outcome of our hunting effort.

Up to this point in our discussion, the terms "whitetail," "deer," "he," and "it" have applied, in at least a general sense, to both sexes of the whitetail deer except where the sex has been clearly indicated by the word "buck" or "doe." However, there are so many marked differences in the behavior of the two sexes that, as one astute authority has pointed out, the hunter might do well to consider them as two entirely different *species* of animal. Recognition of this difference, and the realization of its magnitude, is the first long step in making a *buck* hunter out of a *deer* hunter.

2 ———————————— BUCKS AND DOES

Does normally give birth to a single fawn as a result of their first mating. Subsequent matings most often produce two fawns, usually one of each sex, but something seems to happen to many of the male fawns and in unhunted whitetail ranges the sex ratio is about one buck to three or four does. Where the does are completely protected but the taking of bucks is allowed, the ratio of bucks to does will be smaller. If you are lucky enough to be hunting in good areas which are little hunted, or in those states which have not been blighted by so-called "buck laws," you should experience no particular difficulty in putting a buck under your sights if you follow the instructions laid down in this book.

Complete understanding of the buck and his behavior, plus a good, properly-loaded rifle and the ability to use it, plus patience and determination, plus common sense and close attention to detail add up to a good buck within two or three days, providing the weather holds favorable and other hunters in the area do not spoil your plans. In any good whitetail territory reasonably free of other hunters, I will be willing to bet even odds that I can produce three men who will bring out three legal bucks in three days.

35

The main breeding season for whitetails, better known as the "rut" or "rutting season," is a long one. There *may* be a few local exceptions, but throughout the bulk of the whitetail ranges the beginning of the rut will coincide very closely with the autumnal equinox, and will be practically completed by the time of the winter solstice—a period corresponding quite closely to the entire autumn season. The rutting season starts with a rush and ordinarily reaches its peak in late October, with activity dropping off sharply after Thanksgiving. There is always a minor late-season flurry in December when the does which failed to conceive at their earlier mating indulge in a second honeymoon—or perhaps a *third*. Latest findings by an eminent biological survey team indicate the whitetail doe's conception periods are 28 days apart. The buck's latent libido is aroused by the autumnal shortening of the daylight hours.

A young doe reaches puberty at about seventeen months of age and will continue, unless impregnated, to come into heat each fourth week thereafter for the remainder of her fruitful life. The gestation period is seven months and the doe will come into season about five months after giving birth, thus completing the twelve-month cycle. You will note that the rutting (or running) season roughly coincides with the hunting season, and this is a most fortunate circumstance for us buck hunters. As we delve more deeply into the buck's behavior, you will learn why this is so.

Bucks venture much less often into open ground during the daylight hours than do the does, particularly the mature or trophy bucks. Their normal procedure is to abandon the feeding grounds to the does, spikes, and fawns at the first hint of dawn, and to head for their home bedding-ground where the first rays of shooting-light will find them well hidden and placidly chewing their cuds. The does and fawns will follow these older bucks by a period ranging from about fifteen minutes to several hours, the time delay depending largely on the position of the moon and the prevailing hunting pressure. The younger bucks will follow the does, who usually travel quite leisurely, by distances ranging from several yards to several hundred yards. Since does most often just amble along, nibbling juicy tidbits and pausing long and often to search for boogers, the buck, should one be following, will sometimes be as long as thirty minutes in making his appearance. If the does show the least alarm or uneasiness as they pass you, you will never lay eyes on the buck.

Does will cross a road, fire-track, or *cindera* in a causal manner, but a buck will more often cross with a quick rush which seldom offers a shot. All deer will pause and take a good look around before stepping from cover into open ground, but the buck is a fanatic on this subject and will often stand for upward of twenty minutes while he meticulously scrutinizes every leaf, twig, and blade of grass within the limit of his vision. Keeping his body well screened by brush, the buck will very slowly extend the tip of his nose and gradually ease the head forward until the eyes can take in the entire length of the opening. The head is often held quite close to the ground while executing this maneuver, and the watcher will detect no movement—only the amazing growth of a black spot into a deer's snout. Does may amble placidly across an extensive opening but a following buck, if he crosses at all, will hurry across. Much more often than not he will circle the opening, while keeping well back in the brush, and join the does on the other side without once having exposed himself to the hunter.

The does are the first to come out in the evening, always departing the bed ground before the evening wind-reversal if there is to be one. The bucks will follow at some later time but generally put in their appearance during the slack period of the wind-reversal, depending on the does ahead to warn of any danger. The older trophy bucks seldom venture out of the brush until shooting-light has faded. They come so slowly, so quietly, so cautiously, and so alertly that few hunters, quitting their stands at darkness, ever know that a huge old buck was standing just back in the shadows, an easy rifle shot away.

The old hunter with whom I began my whitetail hunting career used to say that a buck deer is born "scared." He also claimed that deer possess ears in their feet, and pointed out the metatarsal glands as conclusive evidence. This type of advice and instruction is quite typical of the hunting "lore" which has been passed down from generation to generation, and is in no small degree responsible for the large numbers of both deer and luckless deer hunters presently to be encountered. A great deal of misinformation regarding deer and deer hunting is not confined to word of mouth, the printed page often being a major disseminator.

Bucks are not born in the least "scared," but they are born with the instinct to be everlastingly wary for every remaining moment of their lives. If they lived in a constant state of fear and apprehension they could easily be stampeded into rash and heedless actions which could be readily exploited by the hunter, but whitetail bucks usually do exactly the right thing when the chips are down. Their composure under fire is usually greater than that of the shooter, and their refusal to panic under even point-blank fire, fleeing only after they have located the direction of their enemy, can be a valuable lesson to the hunter.

A deer becomes immediately interested in anything which strikes it as being strange, unusual, or alien to the covert. With the exception of an intrusion into his bedding or home grounds, however, a mature buck exhibits very little of the curiosity that most writers ascribe to him. Does are the sentinels for the deer herds and curiosity is their middle name. If anything attracts a doe's attention, she will rarely rest until she has satisfied herself as to its identity. A doe will frequently go completely out of her way and travel an astonishing distance to investigate an unidentified movement or object. Spike bucks will often demonstrate much feminine curiosity, and even forkhorns will demonstrate a slight amount on occasion. The mature buck would like very much to know exactly what you are, but is not curious enough to risk his neck in finding out.

Deer rely heavily on their eyes and ears for identification but absolute reliance is placed on their noses, and one whiff of you will answer all their questions in a blinding flash. The hunter will, of course, be down-wind or cross-wind from any deer exhibiting interest in him. A nosey doe will ease gently closer for a better look. If she becomes suspicious, but not certain, that you are a potential enemy, she will strive to conceal the fact that she is aware of you. Putting on an act that merits the award of an Oscar, she will stay at a distance from you which she considers will be safe, should you prove to be a cougar, and will try to feint you into making a move toward her which will establish your identity. Assuming that you will attack the moment you have her at a disadvantage, she uses two tricks to lure you into making a move. Pretending to be feeding, she will thrust her head deeply into a clump of high grass or a handy bush, then instantly withdraw an eye with which to catch you in the act. If this fails to elicit movement, she will then step nonchalantly behind a screening bush, as though casually feeding. If you look closely at the bush you will detect a big brown eye frozen on you through some tiny opening.

If a curious doe is rather more of the opinion that you are

something harmless, she will often approach you quite closely and stamp her foot and jerk her head in an effort to panic you into precipitous flight which would reveal your identity. In any event, she will find out what you are, and as a last resort she will circle you until she cuts your scent stream. The first breath of you which she inhales will be instantly expelled in a violent whoosh of air, and this sound will usually be followed by drumming hoofbeats which will quickly fade into utter silence. Whenever you realize that you have drawn a doe's attention, you had better ignore her and begin straining your eyes for a possible buck in the background because your hunting in that area is just about over for the time being. The finding of does is usually a small problem with a good hunter; his big problem is to prevent the does from finding *him*. I have had other whitetails come by within a few minutes of my firing a heavy rifle, but just one alarm snort from a deer will put you out of business in that area for at least two hours.

Quite often a doe will detach herself from her companions and come a surprising distance to investigate you if she has seen you move. She may sneak, if she considers herself undetected, but will usually approach rather boldly if she believes her presense to be known. Often she will walk back and forth a time or two while trying to figure out a suspect's identity, though never openly indicating interest. This procedure failing of result, she will ordinarily pretend to feed quite closely, then step behind a screen of brush and proceed to wait the suspect out. Having once seen you move, a doe may devote an exasperating length of time to finding you out, but find you out she will. Her companions, meanwhile, will demonstrate an equal disregard for the passage of time, and will wait patiently and indefinitely for her report.

Once in a while, and only when she is not being followed by

a buck, a single doe accompanied by small fawns may detour quietly around a suspicious object—but not if she has seen that object move. I have learned, through several failures, that a leisurely traveling doe will sometimes spot a motionless man sitting with back to tree, if she happens to pass nearer than fifty yards of him. For this reason, I always make a special effort to place myself at least fifty yards from where I expect my deer to pass, although occasionally, because of heavy brush or unfavorable wind direction, I sit much closer than I would like, especially when I feel that there is a better than even chance that a buck will come by. In such cases I realize that the first deer to pass will probably spot me, but I gamble on that first one being a buck whose belated discovery would do him little good.

When a buck sees something which arouses his suspicion, he will rarely take another step until he becomes convinced that the thing under suspicion is harmless. If up to twenty minutes of intense scrutiny—with perhaps an occasional tail-twitch to encourage movement—has not completely removed all doubt as to the identity of the suspected object, the buck will stealthily withdraw provided he does not think himself discovered and in immediate jeopardy. A buck that has come upon you at close range but is not sure of your identity will often give you the same stand-and-study treatment, but in these circumstances upon realizing your identity, he will *not* employ a silent, stealthy departure. He will swing his head around rather deliberately and pick the spot on which his first jump will land him. By the time his head has reached the end of its swing, the buck will have selected the first contact point for his feet and the inevitable leap comes instantaneously with the completion of the head-turning.

Did I forget to say that the buck turns around before jumping? No, I didn't forget, but the buck seems to. By some miraculous secret shared only between a deer and his Maker, Mr. Buck seems both to turn around and leap in the same motion. Honestly, I have had a deer give me the distinct impression that it turned wrong-side-out in a flash. Until you have seen a boogered whitetail in action you will be completely unable to visualize such a large animal demonstrating the blinding speed of a striking rattlesnake.

Several times I have stood eye-to-eye, sometimes as near as fifteen feet, with a buck which had come up behind my back. For some reason which defies explanation the hunter, under these circumstances, will seldom be able to see the antlers. He may see the face, the legs, the belly, or even the entire deer except the top of his head, which will almost invariably be hidden by leaves or branches. The antlers will first be seen as the buck makes that triggering turn of the head, but this belated discovery will seldom change the course of events. From the sitting position, I cannot twist my body around and bring my rifle into play before the deer has made three jumps. This leaves a deficit of half a jump, as any buck approaching so closely will rarely be more than two and one-half jumps from cover. My son Tom once took a buck under these circumstances with an almost incredible shot, but I have never yet been quite fast enough to pull it off. Incidentally, I can kill most of the quail that flush back over my head, and have met few men who could have prevented my taking birds from under their guns; so you can see that I'm not exactly slow with a firearm. If you ever become aware of an unidentifiable deer which is watching you from a close distance, I advise you to swing your rifle on him as fast as you possibly can and try to beat him to the jump. You will have plenty of time to withhold your shot if the animal turns out to be a doe.

Whenever a buck is following, the does will depend on him for the protection of their back trail, and they seem to know exactly where he is at all times, regardless of the distance he may be lagging. At regular intervals they will pause and look back over their shoulders in his exact direction, instantly tipping off the hunter that a buck is trailing. Both the leading does and the following buck are dedicated to each other's protection, and each will go to great lengths to warn the other of any danger. If the buck is following closely and the does become aware of you to one side of the trail, they will usually freeze and point you almost like a bird dog points a pheasant. The buck will soon join them with a rush, and his arrival will trigger the motionless does, all scattering in the same general direction like a covey of quail. You must shoot the instant the buck appears, as it is only a forlorn hope that he will pause and arrange himself beside the standing does.

Should the buck be following at a considerable distance, the does will probably walk warily past you—or scamper if they are sufficiently boogered—then stop and blow when out of your sight. Should the does discover you before drawing well abreast, they will more likely turn and flee in the direction of their back trail. The hunter must take care that his scent will reach no part of the trail, as it would avail him little to be passed undetected by the does only to have them catch his scent a little distance down the trail.

When not trailed by others of their own kind, deer watch their back trail continually. However, in this event, they do their watching in an unobtrusive manner intended to bait a stalking foe into betraying himself through overhaste and carelessness. Danger, either known or suspected, on their back trail will be easily detected by the hunter. The deer will appear nervous and agitated, show no interest in feeding, and will stop often to scrutinize the back trail with deep concentration.

I have read that only bucks snort. Other writers, more astute, have said that does snort, also. The longer I hunt whitetails, the more I become convinced that 98 per cent of all snorts heard in the covert are made by does. Does always blow when there are other deer in the vicinity which might be in need of warning, and I am quite convinced that when a doe gives the alarm snort two or three times in quick succession it indicates that a buck is trailing. This statement would be difficult to prove, because no buck would put in his appearance after having thus been warned. All deer will snort violently upon being startled at close range. This seems to be an involuntary reaction, and this snort will be especially violent if their first indication of an enemy is a great snootful of close-by scent. The mature buck's alarm snort is normally identifiable at a moderate distance because of its greater volume and more explosive quality. The listener receives the impression that the buck first builds up super lung-pressure against blocked nostrils then suddenly lets go with the effect of a tire blowout. The doe's snort is somewhat less explosive, and varies with the meaning which she wishes to convey.

If a buck is the first deer to discover you, he will usually give the alarm snort only once and then turn all future blowing chores over to the does. By their manner of blowing, deer can convey at least four pieces of information, namely as follows: (a) General alarm! I've just discovered a booger! (b) The enemy is motionless, but I'll watch and tell you if he moves. (c) The enemy is advancing. (d) The enemy is withdrawing.—All these different meanings are accomplished by variations in the length and volume of the snort, frequency of repetition, and sometimes by the sequence. A somewhat softer, long drawnout blow, often repeated at intervals, indicates (b) above. By shortening the length of the snort and increasing both the volume and tempo, the watching deer indicates that the enemy has begun to stir. Should the enemy now proceed in the known direction of other deer, the watcher will again give the loud, sharp alarm snort. If the enemy begins a retreat from the covert, the sentinel deer will announce this turn of events with a moderate, defiant type of snort which clearly indicates "good bye and good riddance."

Every whitetail is dedicated to the protection of all his fellow kind, and seldom will a deer be derelict in his duty. Whenever deer are detected scampering away soundlessly from your approach, you may safely conclude that there are no other deer in the immediate area. At those times when deer are moving between bedding ground and feeding ground, the first deer to discover you will retreat to a safe vantage point and blow repeatedly at frequent intervals until the trail movement has been completed and all other deer have safely detoured your position. At times, the hunter may be "pinned down" in this manner for fifteen or twenty minutes, and he'll see no deer moving at all. The moment I'm certain that a deer is blowing at *me*, I immediately remove to another area regardless of the time, place, or circumstance.

Whenever at a great distance you see a deer running across an opening as though he were scalded by the devil's cauldron, it will be a buck which was very close to you but which has sneaked out. He knows exactly where you are, and when his escape route takes him across this opening he will dash over it at his utmost speed in order to discourage you from attempting pursuit. Just as soon as he is out of your sight he will drop back down to a walk, but you can probably chalk up a hunting error to yourself on such an occasion.

You frustrated hunters who have lost a series of humiliating rounds to old Whitetail Buck should be feeling better now that you are beginning to fully realize what you have been up against. The longer I hunt whitetails and the more I learn about them, the more I wonder that the average hunter manages to kill a mature buck. If they were not so plentiful and if there weren't so many hunters to spook them over each other's guns, I doubt that many would be taken. Bucks, like people, are not infallible, and sometimes even the wisest ones will make mistakes. However the majority of trophy bucks photographed beside their smugly grinning slayers are purely the victims of downright hard luck. The first day or two of hunting season is unquestionably the best because the deer are unsuspecting, but, believe me, they sure smarten up fast.

I have done a lot of still-hunting, which means moving slowly and quietly through deer coverts, and am convinced that very few deer are ever closely approached unawares. Except under extraordinary circumstances, a deer is aware of your approach, and only at those rare times when you are mistaken for another deer—or some other harmless animal—are you permitted an easy shot. Practically speaking, you just can't slip up on a deer.

You have been hunting an animal which feeds and travels almost exclusively at night and lies up in inaccessable thickets during the day. He will detect any hunter that enters his bedding ground and will either sneak out undetected or will burst out behind screening brush which rarely offers even a gambling shot. He makes very little noise while traveling at ease, and none at all when he suspects trouble. When he needs to travel in daytime, he is usually well protected by an alert advance guard, and his coloration makes him difficult to see even when you look directly at him. He emerges from cover so late that you probably can't see your rifle sights even if you *should* happen to spot him. Then how do you find him? You don't. How do you hunt him? You don't.

You hunt a *place* to kill a buck, and then you let the buck come to *you*. How do I know that he will come? Because he has a fatal weakness, an Achilles heel which will be his undoing— the same weakness that has been the undoing of many bucks and many men before him and will be the undoing of many bucks and many men still unborn—the overpowering urge of sex. To enable us to take advantage of the buck's sex urge, we will discuss the buck's behavior just prior to and during the rut.

Sometime during late summer or early fall, the velvet, that fuzz-covered membrane filled with blood vessels which enveloped and developed the antlers to full growth and hardness, having fulfilled its mission, begins to dry up and annoy the buck. He will begin rubbing off this now-useless velvet on saplings, stout bushes, and small trees. He will work diligently at this chore until every shred of clinging tissue has been removed, and usually completes this task within forty-eight hours of its beginning. Sometimes the buck will begin this rubbing before the velvet has completely dried, and he will look a bloody mess with ragged strips of tissue dangling from his antlers. But if you should see him again a day or two later, his antlers will be shining like new money and his neck will have begun to swell.

From now on, he will be spending a lot of time fighting small trees and bushes and polishing his horns. As he travels about his range he will pause occasionally to hook a bush or polish his antlers, but most of his "rubs" will be made along the main trail which passes by his home bed ground and the side trail which leads directly to his private bedding spot. The greatest concentration of any given buck's rubs will be directly at and in the very near vicinity of the point where his "private" road intersects the main trail.

Each locality has its favored varities of rubbing trees, but willow and cedar are used to a certain extent everywhere they grow. Any soft-barked tree is suitable, and live oak and persimmon are used extensively in certain areas. The hunter must develop a sharp eye for rubs, and this is assisted by a knowledge of the preferred trees in his area as well as a "sense" for locating preferred places. Rubs normally extend from about a foot above the ground to a height of three or four feet, and they rarely encircle the tree. Usually, there will be at least one direction from which the rub will not be visible, so the hunter should keep a sharp eye to either side and behind him while scouting a game trail for rubs. Many rubbing trees are used rarely, some only once, but a few strategically located trees, especially the larger ones, are used repeatedly throughout the rutting season and often for several successive seasons until either killed by excessive rubbing or grown too large for use.

Deer rubs are unmistakable, as elk rubs will normally be higher than a man's head while a tree used by bears will have their hairs sticking to it and generally will be larger than any a deer would choose. Deer will often rub a spot until the sap flows, and it is not difficult to tell when a rub has been used quite recently, a week ago, a month ago, or last season. A rub made last season will be completely healed, but any rub made this season, if well used, can be easily spotted from a considerable distance, especially if the sunlight falls on it. A quite recently used rubbing tree will often have a small pile of "sawdust" at its base. Trees with diameters of from two to four inches are most often chosen for rubbing, but many one-inch saplings as well as some fairly large trees will be used. I doubt that even the largest whitetail buck will use a tree much more than eight inches in diameter, and you can bet that even a six-inch rubbing tree will be used by a mighty big buster of a buck.

Bucks will often rub on any other "rub" they may come across, so the greatest number of rubbing trees, as well as the largest and most used ones, will be either on or *very* close to a major trail. A buck likes to make a chain of several rubs, placed at convenient intervals, on all trails that he uses regularly. These rubs are frequently spaced in such a manner that each is just visible from the next one. We have named these chains of rubs "buck runs," and this term will be applied hereafter in this book. If autumn is well advanced and you have located and scouted the major deer trails, and there are no rubs to be found, then there are no bucks in the area unless they have recently drifted in. An ordinary tree that shades a smoking-hot buck track only indicates a place where a buck *was*. A freshly-used rubbing tree indicates something far more important—a place where a buck is *going to be*. The man who refuses to attach any great significance to whitetail rubs is not now and never will be a competent whitetail hunter.

With his antlers all freshly cleaned and polished, Old Buck now sets up for business and there is plenty of "doe" involved. He selects a spot directly on or very close to the main trail, in the vicinity of the point where his private trail converges, and makes a "scrape." He goes in business by the simple expedient of pawing away all small stones and rubbish and exposing a bare spot of soil ranging in size from less then a foot to several feet in diameter. This is his love trap, and he baits it by urinating on this bare spot and pawing the mud. Until the rutting season is well past, Old Buck will haunt the vicinity of his scrape during idle moments when the moon is up, and will even leave his bed several times daily during moondown to visit his scrape for evidence of business or to renew the love potion. During the highly active period of the rut, he will even deny himself the luxury of dining out at choice feeding areas, barely pausing to snatch an occasional few bites of local browse. Where the terrain permits, the buck will often lie where he can watch his scrape—a possibility to be well considered by the hunter.

When the mating urge comes upon the doe, she will find a scrape and then browse and loiter in its vicinity in the hope of the buck making a prompt appearance. If he doesn't show up within a length of time the doe considers ample, she will drift over to another scrape and repeat the performance, but often she will urinate in the scrape and trample in it before proceeding about her business. Unless old Romeo Buck is currently engaged in bringing connubial bliss to a prior candidate, he will probably be right on the ball and make a prompt appearance. He will walk directly toward the brazen temptress, who will ordinarily allow him to approach to within ten yards or so before wheeling and dashing away. The buck responds with a full burst of speed and the race is on. The doe may be young and streamlined and the buck old and fat, but somehow he manages to overtake her and the honeymoon is begun.

The doe's conception period is about seventy-two hours, and the buck will stay with her constantly and follow her anywhere she may lead him until her passion cools. Her fawns will continue unconcernedly about their business and will pay absolutely no attention to their mother when she and her consort dash away on a frequent love chase. The yearling does seem to honeymoon completely away from the family group, rejoining it when the fling is over.

As soon as one affair is over, the buck will make a beeline back to his scrape with undiminished ardor. If he discovers that his scrape has been visited by a love-smitten doe in his absence, he has been known to be so overcome with love lust that he would drop his shoulders into the scrape and scoot himself along by his hind feet. Then, like a Plott hound on a cat trail, he will put his nose to the doe's scrape-moistened tracks, and he won't stop for wood, water, or coal until he comes up to her. When the trail is very hot, he may become so excited as to engage in a series of comical, stiff-legged hops, grunting delightedly each time his feet hit the ground. The doe may have circled and be standing quite close to her back trail, but the buck will rarely look up unless his eye is attracted by movement; he'll just stay exactly on her footprints until he comes up to her or she breaks and runs.

Sometimes the buck is so tardy in returning to his love trap that the impatient doe, after leaving her calling card, has offered her favors to another buck, and then the stage is set for drama. When Old Buck discovers another buck's track overlapping that of his amorata, his hair will rise up and turn forward, which makes him appear much larger and quite formidable. His walk and his manner become truly menacing, and bucks in this mental state have been known to advance threateningly upon, or even charge, a man who was mistaken for a rival. Two bucks following the same doe seldom fight unless they are quite evenly matched, the lesser buck almost invariably giving the doe over to the more powerful rival, though occasionally hanging on the flanks of the lovers throughout the honeymoon. Oddly, this seems to disturb the honeymooners not at all, and they are as completely uninhibited as though their fellow traveler didn't exist. Most always these kibitzers are either old bucks past their prime or young spikes or forkhorns. The dispossessed mature buck will return to his scrape and hope for another doe.

Though whitetail bucks fight somewhat less often and less determinedly than the other American deer, this is most likely due to the plethora of willing does rather than any lack of courage and spirit. Elk, Sitka deer, mule deer and blacktails all rut in a manner different from whitetails. Among these species, the strongest males round up a harem and all other males are denied a chance at a doe. It becomes a case of all or nothing, so every male must fight grimly to give himself a reason for living. Whitetails get along well with civilization because they themselves are much more civilized than any other American deer species.

Both in their manner of rutting and their addiction to a permanent home range, whitetails are completely different from all other species. The consistently productive pursuit of the whitetail buck requires an entirely unique method of hunting. Anyone who tells you that the accomplished hunter of any one species will experience no difficulty in taking any other species is probably quite mistaken. Do not be taken by the common platitude that a deer is a deer is a deer. For instance, if whitetails, like elk, immediately put several miles between themselves and one whiff of human scent, no living man could hunt them profitably.

Though the whitetail buck becomes much less wary when trailing or running a doe, he is still no setup which can be taken with ridiculous ease, as has been so often stated. The doe is never so overcome with libido as to lower her guard materially, and she is not inclined to lead the buck into places or situations which she normally avoids. Except for her love-impelled mating flights, which consist of somewhat reckless dashes of a hundred yards or so, the doe continues to conduct herself during the rut exactly as she does at all other times. Whitetails are fully aware of their vulnerability during their mating act and there-

fore confine the honeymoon to the most remote and unmo-
lested portions of their range. Relatively few hunters ever become aware of this facet of whitetail behavior because most
hunters haunt the more open areas of the range which the deer
avoid while mating. If you want to take whitetail bucks you
must get right in the brush with them.

One of our party was watching a pretty little glade which
contained a number of rubs and four scrapes which roughly
formed a square. A doe with a buck at her heels came bounding
into the small clearing and led the buck a merry chase from
scrape to scrape, turning sharply as she touched each scrape
and heading for the next one exactly like a batter running
bases. As they passed our hunter at fifty feet, he put a 30-30
slug squarely through the buck's heart. Neither deer flinched
or faltered at the shot, but continued the mad chase from
scrape to scrape, the buck's nose seemingly glued to the doe's
tail. The hunter could clearly see the placement of his shot,
and, knowing for a certainty that the buck was his, he just sat
back and watched. The stricken buck matched the doe stride
for stride for three more complete laps before he failed on one
of the quick right-angle turns and ploughed straight ahead a
few steps, then piled up in the brush. This is as good an example of the single-mindedness of rutting deer as I can think
of.

I know of no whitetail seasons in the eastern part of our
country which are set to open before the rutting season, and
few which are set to open after its close. However, most hunters
are of the mistaken opinion that the rut is completely over by
the time their hunting season is opened. Also, most people
wrongly suppose that the deer rut earlier in their more north-
erly ranges. You can very closely determine the peak of your
own region's rutting season by observing the appearance of the

spring fawns and then counting seven months backward. It can be readily seen that, should the latitude be a factor, southern deer would be more likely to rut earlier than northern deer because spring comes earlier to the southland. One of my finest whitetail heads was taken at dawn on the twenty-eighth of December in the famed Texas hill country. The tremendously swollen neck of this old mossback, and the circumstances under which he was taken, indicated that he was returning home after a rutting binge.

Incidentally, that hunting trip will always be remembered as my first arctic expedition. It was colder than a witch's kiss and the ground was frozen and crusted over with ice. When I heard this buck crunching toward me, I thought surely it was one of our hunters staggering back to camp to die, frozen like myself beyond the point of recovery. Recollection of this incident reminds me to tell you that large deer seen traveling alone are usually bucks.

Bucks run themselves nearly to death during the rut, and the immense drain on their sexual reservoir, coupled with their loss of appetite, causes them to lose weight quite rapidly once the run has begun. All wild animals put on a lot of fat during the autumn in order to be able to survive the famine of winter, and even an old buck will be reasonably tender if taken while in good condition. But an old trophy buck with swollen neck and wasted flanks, taken late in the rut, will usually provide strongly-flavored meat so tough that you won't be able to fork the gravy. A young spike or forkhorn will usually make good venison for the double reason that he is still a young animal and because the older bucks keep him pretty well chased away from the does. But the big old tough mossbacks are the harder to come by, and the ones which make the finer trophies for snapshot album or den wall.

One of my best heads came from the largest-framed whitetail I ever saw. He hung two feet lower on the meat pole than any of the several average-size deer hanging beside him. My dreams of a record deer for the vicinity went glimmering when, after a long haul into town next day, the ice house scales showed only a few pounds over a hundred. Had that deer been in good condition he would have easily hog-dressed two hundred pounds, and he could have gone two-fifty if really fat.

We have found many rubs where there was no sign of a scrape, but, except where deer are temporarily camped as previously noted, we have seldom found a scrape more than a few steps from a rub. Also, the status of both scrapes and rubs may change from time to time throughout the season, heavily used ones falling into disuse and vice versa. This condition is caused by two occurrences—a shift in the bedding grounds where the covert affords the game a choice, caused by a drastic food or weather change, or, after the peak of the rutting season, lulls in activity caused by the tardy coming into season of various does in the area. Sometimes a brand-new scrape will appear where there was none yesterday, sometimes a long-disused scrape will become suddenly active, and sometimes a new scrape will appear just a few feet away from an old disused one. Excessive hunting, especially on the bedding grounds, exhaustion of the local food supply, or a cougar moving in— each can cause whitetail activity to come to a grinding halt.

In proportion to their great numbers and accessibility, mature whitetail bucks are the most difficult to bag of all hooved game on this continent when hunted by the usual methods employed on other deer species. By the same token, they are the most certain of being taken during the autumn when hunted properly by a person who understands their behavior.

The most productive method for taking whitetail bucks is by watching a fresh scrape.

Whenever the hunter finds a well-used scrape, he should mentally make a big "X" to mark the spot where some buck will meet an end he hasn't planned on. Hope springs eternal in the buck's breast, and he will continue to make regular, though less frequent, daytime visits to his old scrape long after the last flaming doe has had her ardor quenched. Even on the last day of a late season, there is no better place for the hunter to watch than an old scrape. It will be located not only where its maker normally hangs out but along a main trail used regularly by most of the deer in the area. In some red-hot spots, generally where two or more great crossings converge, several bucks may make their scrapes so close together that the resultant activity soon churns them into a sort of huge community scrape. We have taken as many as three bucks each season from some of these scrapes.

Though the battle is more than half won when you have located a fresh scrape, many things can go wrong and rob you of success. Aside from hunting technique, taken up in a later chapter, shooting a buck standing in the open at very close range is not always a gut-cinch. In all big-game shooting, nerve control, a proper weapon properly loaded, confidence in and familiarity with your rifle, and good shooting-habits are essential to success.

3 ——————————— THE DEER RIFLE

All dedicated hunters develop a feeling toward a trusted rifle which is seldom bestowed on a shotgun. This sentiment is most difficult to put into words, but it grows through long and close association with a thoroughly reliable arm—one that has seen us through a number of tense and vivid hunting adventures without ever once letting us down. Before we get started on the relative merits of deer rifles, let me tell you this: if you own a rifle in which you have such abiding faith that, every time you draw a bead on a deer, you *know* you will soon have a gutting job on your hands, then that is the right weapon for you. Regardless of its weight, balance, sights, appearance, or ballistic properties, you should not be persuaded to discard such an arm in favor of another.

Perhaps the basic factor in determining the relative merit of a deer rifle is the cartridge it chambers. Actually, the rifle is only a launching devise for a missile—the bullet which wounds or kills our game. The powder contained in the cartridge case provides the propelling force that starts the bullet on its way, and the type and amount of this powder chiefly determines the velocity at which the bullet leaves the muzzle of the arm. Strictly speaking, the term "caliber" should refer only to the diameter of the hole through the barrel, but it has become standard practice to designate each cartridge of differing case measurements as a particular caliber. All currently made American rifles having caliber designations of 30, 300, or 308 use, or can use, identical bullets. Let us now list the requirements of a good whitetail bullet.

The bullet must not be easily deflected from its course by leaves, twigs, or even small branches. It must have sufficient diameter to insure a good blood trail from the entrance wound *only*. This is of great importance when the bullet fails to exit from the animal and the latter, though well and fatally hit, is able to travel out of the hunter's sight. This occurs much more frequently than the inexperienced hunter probably realizes. I will go so far as to say that this is the normal result in whitetail brush shooting. The bullet must be so constructed that it will expand uniformly and reliably upon striking flesh but will not disintegrate if it happens to strike a small tree limb nor blow up on contact with game shot at very close range. Penetration must always be deep and reliable—sufficient even to reach the frontal chest cavity from an entry in the ham, if the deer should happen to be going away when hit. The bullet should exhibit pronounced shock or numbing effect—sometimes called knock-down power—when a solid hit is made on neck or body.

Much has been learned about bullets through close observation by experienced hunters and through tests and experiments by ballisticians. With all other factors remaining equal, the following facts are known about bullets: the larger the bullet's diameter, the larger the entrance hole and the greater the knock-down power; the more blunt the nose shape, the less the bullet will be deflected by contact with brush and the greater the shock effect produced; the greater the bullet's weight, the less it will be deflected by brush, the deeper it will penetrate, and the greater will be the resultant shock and killing power. The faster the bullet is driven, the less reliable becomes its action upon striking flesh, the more easily it is deformed and deflected upon striking brush, and the greater the recoil induced in the weapon from which it is fired. Recoil is roughly proportional to the *square* of the muzzle velocity.

Now, knowing our requirements and working with the above facts, let's imagine ourselves cartridge designers. Maybe we can come up with a super-duper cartridge for whitetail hunters. We know that we want a large-diameter, heavy-weight, blunt-nose bullet that will get through brush well, exhibit good shock effect, give deep and reliable penetration, and always produce an easily-followed blood trail. Let's try a blunt 200-grain bullet of .35 caliber. Now, how fast do we want to drive this bullet? To keep noise, muzzle blast, and recoil to a minimum, and brush-bucking ability to a maximum, we want no more velocity than that necessary to still allow us dead-on aiming to the greatest distance at which we may be likely to obtain shots in the brush and timber of typical whitetail cover.

A 200-yard shot will probably be the longest one we are likely to get at a standing whitetail—or blacktail for that matter—and a little experimenting will determine that a muzzle velocity of 2,200 feet per second will give us this range. What about recoil? Reviewing the published reports of exhaustive army tests, we learn that practically all soldiers can easily handle a recoil energy of fifteen foot-pounds, but, that as recoil energies are increased, there is a progressive deterioration in the average soldier's marksmanship. A measurement of the recoil energy of our load gives a figure of fourteen foot-pounds, well within the tolerance limit of any healthy teen-ager, so we are all set to try it on deer.

To our delight and amazement we find that our bullet tears through brush like Irish confetti, penetrates to the boiler-room from any angle, and often knocks a deer down, if una-larmed, with even a poorly-placed gut-shot. When we track a well-hit deer we usually find a blood trail that a beatnik could follow at a dead lope. And last, but not least, the short length and low working-pressure of our cartridge allow it to be chambered in any modern rifle action. But when we rush to the patent office with our super-duper deer killer we will receive startling news. One of our major arms makers devel-oped an identical load about fifty years ago; it's called the 35 Remington and it's still going strong.

All modern center-fire sporting-rifle calibers of larger bore than .22 inches, when loaded with proper bullets, are generally conceded to be powerful enough for the shooting of deer-size animals. We will go into the question of how much power is "enough" power a little later on. No serious hunter is inter-ested in borderline tools, and we will waste no time in dis-cussing the relative merits and demerits of marginal calibers. Today, practically every state has regulations defining the min-imum loads and calibers which may be legally used for taking the larger species of game within its borders; so we will discuss only calibers more powerful than those generally prohibited.

The following is a list of calibers which could be considered adequate for deer-size game and for which sporting arms are now available: 243 Winchester, 6mm Remington, 257 Weatherby Magnum, 264 Winchester Magnum, 270 Win-chester, 270 Weatherby Magnum, 280 Remington, 284 Win-chester, 7x61 Sharpe & Hart, 7mm Weatherby Magnum, 7mm Remington Magnum, 30-30 (30 WCF), 300 Savage, 30-'06, 300 H&H Magnum, 300 Winchester Magnum, 300 Weatherby Magnum, 308 Winchester, 308 Norma Magnum,

32 Winchester Special (32 W.S.), 338 Winchester Magnum, 340 Weatherby Magnum, 35 Remington, 350 Remington Magnum, 358 Winchester, 358 Norma Magnum, 375 H&H Magnum, 378 Weatherby Magnum, 444 Marlin, 458 Winchester, and 460 Weatherby Magnum. The excellent 348 Winchester has been removed from this list by the discontinuance of the equally excellent Model 71 Winchester —the only rifle to which it was adapted. This was quite possibly the best load-and-rifle team that has ever been available to the American brush and timber hunter, and its passing has left a void in the rifle line-up—as well as in the hearts of veteran hunters—which has yet to be filled.

The 378 Weatherby, the 458 Winchester, and the 460 Weatherby are elephant cartridges. Frankly, I see no practical use whatsoever for the 340 Weatherby Magnum caliber although its originator recommends it for the taking of large game at long ranges. Any of these, however, would be ridiculous in whitetail coverts, all being generally characterized by excessive weapon weight, power, and recoil. In fact, *no* caliber which includes the word "magnum" in its name is suited to typical whitetail hunting in typical whitetail coverts. This statement includes the 7x61 Sharpe & Hart which is a true magnum caliber although this fact isn't generally publicized.

The currently popular 243 Winchester caliber—like the 250 Savage (250-3000), the 244 Remington, and the 257 Roberts of yesteryear—is primarily intended for long-range varmint shooting. All of these calibers are satisfactory deer killers out to moderate ranges, but, contrary to popular belief, none is reliable on deer-size animals at distances much greater than 250 yards. Lacking adequate killing power at truly long game ranges, and lacking the ability to buck brush or to leave a sufficiently large entrance wound, these "pea-shooters" are not the wisest choice for the dedicated hunter. Because only carbine-length barrels are currently provided for the 6mm Remington, this fine new caliber is doomed to the "pea-shooter" classification also unless a 26-inch barrel is installed by a custom gunsmith, or handloads deveolping excessive pressures are employed. But either practice results in still greater velocity which makes the weapon even less suited to brush and timber hunting. Initial bullet velocity of 2,550 feet-per-second is the universally accepted maximum for reliable brush-bucking ability, and each and every one of these light-bullet small-bores starts even its heaviest bullet at a velocity in excess of 2,800 feet-per-second.

Truly satisfactory *long range* calibers—for our lighter big game—begin with the 257 Weatherby Magnum and the 264 Winchester Magnum as currently available in over-the-counter rifles. For a short time following Winchester's introduction of the 264 it appeared likely that this caliber would quickly obsolete the venerable 270 Winchester, but this hasn't come to pass; the 270 is simply too good a caliber for its intended purpose—which is the long-range shooting of mule deer, antelope, sheep, and goat—to be easily knocked off by *any* caliber. The 264 exceeds the 270 very slightly in the matters of range and killing power, but with a heavier rifle, costlier cartridges, a bigger "bang," greater recoil, and a *much* shorter barrel life. And though touted as such, the 264 hasn't proven itself to be an entirely adequate elk caliber; it is now trailing (in popularity) the newer and better 7mm Remington Magnum caliber which is entirely adequate for elk-size game.

For all practical purposes, the 270 Winchester, the 280

Remington, and the 284 Winchester can be lumped together; although none are interchangable, all perform similarly, and all use bullets of about the same weights. The
only notable difference between the 270 and the 280 is
six one-thousandths of an inch in bullet diameter although
the latter is a trifle longer at the shoulder. The 284 Winchester is simply the 280 Remington in a shorter but fatter
case—of equal capacity—which will work through the actions and magazines of Winchester and Savage rifles of non-
bolt-action persuasion. The 280 Remington cartridges are
factory loaded to somewhat lower pressures than are those
of the 270 so that extraction will be better in Remington
autoloading and slide-action rifles. All three of these calibers
are frequently encountered in the whitetail coverts, and
even on the elk ranges where they are equally out of place.
All are excellent for the long range shooting of deer-size
game in open, unobstructed terrain, but even their heaviest
available bullets are a trifle shy in both diameter and weight
(and travel a bit too fast) to be ideal for brush and timber
shooting. The 270 as factory loaded is probably a bit the
better of the three, but the 284's case design is more modern
and efficient. Unless *very heavy* handloads are employed,
none of these are suited to elk, and *no* loading will make
them suited to close-range brush shooting. However, the
arms press has convinced the public that these calibers are
satisfactory "all-around" propositions.

All high-power, center-fire calibers below .30-inch bore,
for which sporting rifles are currently manufactured, are
intended either for long-range big-game shooting, varmint
shooting, or both. This is as it should be; these small-
diameter bullets, when they fail to exist, can't be depended
upon to leave a satisfactory blood trail from the entrance

wound until the stricken animal may have traveled a considerable distance. In open country, a wounded animal can usually be kept in sight until it either falls or finally begins to bleed, but a blood trail beginning only 50 yards from the spot of shooting will lose you many a head of game in thick cover.

Personally, when my quarry is big game in thick brush, I prefer to hunt with calibers not smaller than .30, and I won't choose a load which starts its bullet faster than 2,700 feet per second. I am further convinced that .30 caliber bullets of less than 165 grains in weight lack sufficient sectional density to insure adequate penetration. This should be a sufficiently broad set of limitations to satisfy almost anyone, as it doesn't exclude any of the following calibers currently available to the new rifle buyer: 30-30, 30-'06, 300 Savage, 308 Winchester, 300 H&H Magnum, 32 Winchester Special, 338 Winchester Magnum, 35 Remington, 358 Winchester, 375 H&H Magnum, 44 Remington Magnum, and 444 Marlin. Now, let's add to this list other calibers in popular use that meet these requirements, but for which no sporting arms are now being produced by domestic factories: 351 WSL, 401 WSL, 405 Winchester, 35 Winchester, 30-40, 38-55, 8mm Mauser, 303 Savage, 303 British, 33 Winchester, 348 Winchester, 45-70, 30 Remington, and 32 Remington. All these calibers, with proper loading, rate from fair to excellent for our purpose; but many are completely obsolete, and, at least in this country, all are obsolescent.

We will now eliminate from further discussion the following calibers for which factory-loaded ammunition is no longer available: 33 Winchester, 35 Winchester, 405 Winchester, and 401 WSL. The 351 WSL and the 38-55 are marginal calibers and will not be discussed. The 45-70 is thoroughly reliable, but its point-blank range of only about 125 yards is well below present-day standards. The 8mm Mauser (8x57) is a pretty good whitetail caliber with domestic loading, and with imported Swedish Norma ammunition it can be one of the very best obtainable. The currently available loadings for the 303 British are practically identical to those provided for the 30-40, and all are superlative whitetail loads and calibers.

In the event that you may be interested in comparing any of these obsolescent calibers with current-production numbers, here is a close enough guide. The 303 Savage is virtually identical to the 30-30, differing only in case shape. The 30 Remington is simply the 30-30 except for the case head which is rimless. The 32 Remington is a rimless counterpart of the 32 Winchester Special; this latter so nearly resembles the 30-30 that the head-stamp must usually be examined for positive identification. All of the above are so nearly identical ballistically that they are considered as one and the same in all generalized discussions pertaining to the "30-30." The lighter (180 grain) load for the 30-40 slightly exceeds the power of the 300 Savage load using the same bullet weight, but the 30-40's power—when 220-grain bullets are employed—more nearly approximates the power of the 308 Winchester's 200-grain loading although it doesn't shoot quite as "flat."

The 348 Winchester is quite similar to the 358 Winchester both in power and in available bullet weights although it is even better than the latter for brush shooting, and that's saying a great deal. However, the 358 "holds up" better than the 348, and the newer caliber is better at all ranges beyond 100 yards. The 358's 200-grain bullet, by comparison, has a more streamlined nose and a better form factor which permits it to be used with moderate success in open-country shooting. Both calibers are highly recommended for all American big game from whitetails to moose and Alaskan brown bears. The great savage Models 99-R and 99-RS— now discontinued—were made to order for the 358 Winchester cartridge, and for the 308 Winchester cartridge, too. But neither caliber is recommended for use in an iron-sighted *featherweight* rifle.

Returning to our list of current calibers, the 30-30 and the 32 Winchester Special—when loaded with 170-grain bullets—make very reliable whitetail (and black bear) killers, and countless thousands of hunters are quite satisfied with their performance. Both of these calibers are a trifle shy on shocking power, however, and penetration isn't always sufficiently reliable to justify their indiscriminate use on raking or rear-end shots. Actually these calibers would be fine for our use if better ones were not available.

The large magnums—the 300 H&H, the 338 Winchester, and the 375 H&H, in particular—have considerably more power than is necessary for deer except at extremely long ranges. Their heaviest available bullets get through brush fairly well but are too strongly constructed to expand with certainty on animals the size of small deer. They will kill whitetails reliably, but usually less spectacularly than will many less powerful though more appropriate calibers. Although quite satisfactory for use on whitetails, these calibers should never be acquired strictly for this purpose; the noise, muzzle blast, ammunition cost, and weight of the associated weapon are all excessive, which precludes our listing these calibers among the best available for our needs. Unless handloads were employed in the other big magnum calibers currently available—the 300 Winchester, the 300

Weatherby, the 308 Norma, the 340 Weatherby, and the 358 Norma—these would be *very* inappropriate selections for *any* type of brush or timber shooting; all—as presently loaded—are strictly long-range propositions.

The 300 Savage caliber, when loaded with blunt, 180-grain bullets, is an excellent whitetail cartridge. Considerably more powerful than the 30-30 class of cartridges, the 300's recoil is mild; about like that of the 35 Remington's. Results have always been uniformly reliable with the 300 Savage, and if you have a good rifle in this caliber, you don't need a more powerful weapon for the brush and timber shooting of deer and black bear. But the 300 *isn't* an elk rifle. Except in the matter of recoil, however—which definitely favors the 300 Savage—the newer, more versatile 308 Winchester will do everything the 300 Savage will do, and do it better.

The 308 Winchester closely approaches but doesn't quite equal the power of the 30-'06. This difference in power will not likely be detected by the deer hunter, but it will become more pronounced when both calibers are turned on larger game. This will be particularly true if heavy handloads are employed in the 30-'06, thereby generating power equal to the factory-loaded 300 H&H Magnum ammunition. At present, there is no safe way of boosting the 308's power; therefore, the rifle buyer should always choose the 30-'06 over the 308 Winchester whenever the desired type of action allows him this choice. The 308 Winchester should be substituted for the 30-'06 *only* when the lever-action rifle is selected, or *only* if the user is a small woman, a frail man, or a young lad who wishes to avoid the handicap imposed by a "pea shooter" but to whom every bit of saving in recoil is of paramount importance.

The 44 Remington Magnum is a pistol cartridge—a rip-snorting pistol cartridge, I will admit, but still a *pistol* cartridge. Currently available Marlin and Ruger carbines chambered in caliber 44 Remington Magnum have been hailed by numerous "experts" as the deer-hunter's dream-come-true. With few exceptions, these selfsame "experts" have castigated the "old fashioned" 35 Remington as "archaic" and "obsolete." Any person who may support these *combined* views is no more qualified to give advice in the sporting arms field than I am qualified to be head choreographer for the Ballet Russe. Compared to the 44 Remington Magnum, the 35 Remington is a smashing, devastating powerhouse—a flat-shooting, ultra-modern cartridge of incomparably more advanced design. The 44 Remington Magnum bullet retains reliable deer-killing power to only 100 yards; exactly *half* as far as does the 35 Remington's 200-grain bullet. If I were assigned the task of designing the most inefficient deer rifle in existence—the shoulder-supported firearm most conducive to hunting failure—I would, of course, be at a temporary loss concerning many of the construction details. But I am absolutely certain regarding *two* features that would be incorporated; a *very* short barrel and a weapon-weight of 5-3/4 pounds. And, Oh yes! The weapon would be chambered for a pistol cartridge. The 44 Remington Magnum's "rainbow" trajectory limits the dead-on deer-hitting range to 160 yards; the 35 Remington outranges it by 30 yards or more. Also, there is a very unpleasant surprise awaiting the innocent purchaser of a featherweight 44 Remington Magnum carbine who anticipates mild recoil from his weapon.

The more recent 444 Marlin cartridge is similar to the 44 Remington Magnum but the case is quite a bit longer and holds considerably more powder. This is a *rifle* cartridge, however, and it is currently chambered in the fine lightweight Marlin Model 336 *rifle*. The slow-spinning, large-diameter, 240-grain bullet is a terrific brush-cutter—the best one currently loaded. Excepting the matter of the 444's *substantial* recoil, which is *quite* noticeably greater than that produced by the 30-'06, this is an otherwise splendid whitetail rifle/caliber combination. Contrary to popular opinion, however, the 444 Marlin is *not* an entirely suitable elk, moose, and big bear caliber; the stubby, blunt-nose bullet sheds its velocity so rapidly that reliable elk-killing power is retained to only about 150 yards. At ranges exceeding 200 yards, the 35 Remington cartridge demonstrates a flatter trajectory coupled with greater remaining energy.

To the serious hunter planning to acquire a whitetail rifle, I heartily recommend that he choose an arm which chambers one of the following calibers: 35 Remington, 358 Winchester, 308 Winchester, 300 Savage, or 30-'06. These are all splendid calibers for our use, and when loaded with *blunt, soft-nose* bullets weighing not less than 180 grains, performance of all is so uniformly reliable that the purchaser's personal preferences as to brands, actions types, and models, may well be the deciding factor. Most unfortunately, however, satisfactory rifles chambering satisfactory whitetail calibers have practically disappeared from the market. This is a truly astonishing circumstance in light of the fact that more big-game rifles are acquired for whitetail hunting than are sought for all other purposes combined. With the sole exception of the splendid Remington Model 742 autoloader, there is in my opinion *no* other completely satisfactory whitetail rifle in current production. What brought about this deplorable drought?

Until the beginning of World War II, the design of hunting rifles and their ammunition had always reflected the consensus of highly experienced veteran *hunters;* men who had arrived at their opinions and convictions after long and frequently painful periods of trial and error. Then, following the war and the subsequent industrial and economic revolution a host of newly interested shooters suddenly appeared on the scene. Gun stores were stormed by an army of arms-ignorant but eager buyers who pawed over the stocks of rifles, and then selected almost unanimously those particular weapons featuring the lightest weight, the shortest barrels, the gaudiest trimmings, and the "hottest" flat-shooting calibers. Almost over night, the arms industry learned a new fact of life: arms ignorant rifle buyers now outnumber their arms-wise counterparts about ten to one, and economic necessity dictates that the industry cater to the whims, fancies, and desires of the buying majority.

The arms press, which is supported principally by the arms industry's advertising budget, has furthered and perpetuated this pamper-and-please-the-novice campaign by not only subscribing to the movement but by appointing itself the *avant-garde.* Those writers, editors, and publishers who have been reluctant to reflect the tyro's opinions, prejudices, and desires, have in the majority of cases been gradually eased out of the picture in favor of eager replacements whose tastes, opinions, and interests are more closely geared to those of the buying public.

The arms industry's "planned obsolescence" movement, which has been patterned after that of the automative industry, has finally resulted in a continual parade of new (and frequently bizarre) weapons and calibers, plus many weird and off-beat combinations of the same. The majority of these are launched with little or no expectation of their continued survival; their purpose is to skim off that quick hunk of folding money which seems ever eager to surrender itself in exchange for anything new and different that will go "bang"—provided, of course, that the device somewhat resembles a firearm, and that it could also be described as "cute," light, short, flashy, and "handy."

There are much more important things to consider when choosing a deer rifle than the caliber or action type, so long as both are satisfactory for our purpose. Good sighting equipment, a clean trigger-pull, proper weight and balance of the weapon, and the proper fit of rifle to shooter, are all of vital importance, and collectively outweigh all other considerations. The *effective* recoil must be taken into consideration when selecting our shooting combination; an otherwise "perfect" rig can prove worthless if it punishes the user with every shot. The weight of our rifle should be in keeping with the power developed by our selected cartridge, although good stock design, and a rubber recoil pad, will do much to reduce the recoil effect of any arm. Also remember that short barrels increase muzzle blast, which, in turn, definitely increases *recoil effect*. To those of you who are deeply interested in hunting rifles—rifles for all game, for all types of terrain, and for all shooting situations—I respectfully recommend my book, *The Modern Hunting Rifle*.* All matters touched upon herein, and a great many other matters related to rifles, loads, and bullets, are discussed at length in this up-to-date rifle book.

In rifles of reasonable weight and modern stock design— and having barrels of normal length—none of our recom-

* Obtainable from your local book dealer, or from the N.R.A. Book Service, 1600 Rhode Island Ave., N.W., Washington 6, D.C.

mended calibers is considered to be a hard kicker. Here are the approximate recoil energies of each: 300 Savage and 35 Remington, 14 foot-pounds; 308 Winchester, 17 foot-pounds; 30-'06, 19 foot-pounds; 358 Winchester, 22 foot-pounds. By choosing our lightest rifles for the least powerful loads, and adding weapon weight as we go to the more powerful calibers, the effective recoil can be kept down to a figure which permits pleasant shooting with all. The newly announced 444 Marlin caliber develops a recoil energy of about 26 foot-pounds in a 10-pound rifle, which—in the 7½-pound Marlin Model 336 rifle—is generally considered to be a *quite* substantial back-thrust. With this direct warning regarding the recoil that can be anticipated, I will now recommend this Marlin rifle/caliber combination as a most effective whitetail proposition.

By way of camparison, the 375 H&H Magnum develops 34 f.p. of free-recoil energy, which is approximately double that of the 308 Winchester. The free-recoil of the 375 is again doubled by that of the 458 Winchester whose free-recoil energy of 70 f.p. is typical of other big stopping-rifles used as tools of the trade by African white hunters. Anyone desiring to experience the feel of firing a thirteen-pound elephant rifle, but having no opportunity for obtaining one, may readily duplicate the recoil effect by firing an over-the-counter, 6½-pound featherweight rifle in calibers 30-'06 or 358 Winchester. I kid you not—but maybe I'm just sensitive to recoil. A hefty English gentleman of African fame, Sir Samuel Baker, once used a tremendous muzzle-loading rifle that he called "Baby," and which developed a free-recoil energy of one hundred and fifty foot-pounds. We will have more on recoil in a later chapter.

Now, let's take a look at the various rifle actions available, and determine which of them chambers calibers of our choosing. The 358 Winchester caliber is available only in imported bolt-action carbines—in which we aren't interested —and in hammerless lever-action rifles. There are two current candidates in this latter category: the Savage Model 99 series, and the Winchester Model 88. Both are ridiculously underweight, and their recoil—even when the rifle boasts a recoil pad—is truly gut-jolting. This statement is particularly true when iron sights are employed. A scope and mount would add another pound of recoil-reducing weight, but the 358 caliber isn't well suited to scoped rifles. And aside from their weight deficiency, both brands exhibit other shortcomings; the Model 88 is *not* noted for having a clean, crisp trigger, and the Model 99 lightweights are *not* noted for outstanding accuracy.

I highly recommend the now-discontinued Savage Model 99-R in caliber 358 Winchester. If you can find a good one floating around, offer its owner a brand-new 99-DL in exchange if necessary and equip your prize with a recoil pad, a Redfield M-375 Sourdough front sight, and a good quality, micrometer-adjustable, receiver aperture-sight unless this latter feature is already present. Choice of receiver sights would lie between the Redfield Tr-LS, the Lyman 57SA, or, if installation of a scope is never contemplated, the fine Williams FP 99.

The Savage Model 99 lends itself particularly well to dual sighting (the optional, alternate use of iron or scope sight). If dual sighting is wanted on the 99-R, I recommend that in addition to the suggested iron sight combination either a two-piece Weaver Q.D. top-mount (with base numbers 14 and 19) or the similar Leupold Detacho-Mount (with base numbers 206 and 306) be added. If scopesight only will be employed, I recommend a sturdy one-piece bridge mount such as the Redfield Jr. 99 R, or the Williams TM 99. An "Ace-In-The-Hole" peep sight is available for the Williams mount; it makes a fine emergency rear sight in the event that scope failure or lens-blotting rain should befall you on a hunt. Only 200-grain bullets, incidentally, should ever be used in the 358 Winchester on deer.

The 308 Winchester caliber is available in most makes and models of bolt-action rifles, including a model for left-handers, and in every other action-type except the exposed-hammer lever action. The Model 760 Remington pump-action rifle chambers the 308, but this otherwise excellent firearm is a congenital "rattler." It not only rattles while being carried, but it may often rattle audibly while being raised into shooting position. I know of no way to eliminate the rattle, so I can't recommend this weapon to you. Among autoloaders chambered in 308 Winchester, the Model 100 Winchester is moderately satisfactory. Outstanding, however, in my opinion is the fine Remington Model 742. Compared to any other hunting rifle of this type, the Model 742 has a better trigger, a better stock design, a higher more nearly correct sight-line, a somewhat handier safety, a less disturbing recoil, a more nearly ideal weapon-weight, and is better adapted to use with *either* aperture or telescope sight or *both* (dual sighting). *Any* 308 Winchester-caliber rifle, unless permanently scope sighted, should be fitted with a recoil pad; this caliber in a hard-butted weapon develops sufficient recoil to require the unloaded combination to weigh at least 8 pounds.

The only other 308 Winchester-caliber rifles I can recommend to the serious whitetail hunter are certain Savage lever-actions which are no longer made: the previously discussed Model 99-R (RS), and those early production 99-E models having a basic weight of *not less* than 7¼ pounds, and barrels *not less* than 22 inches long.

At this writing, the only rifles still chambered for the 300 Savage caliber are the 99 series of Savage lever-actions. However, none of the current offerings possess *all* the characteristics which I deem essential to a *first class* whitetail rifle, so the person seeking a good rifle in this caliber is referred to the used-gun department of his sporting goods store. Recommended rifles include those models suggested in the paragraph above plus the Model 99-EG and the now-discontinued Remington Model 81 autoloader (or the earlier Model 8). All of the recommended Savage 99 models should be equipped with recoil pad, and the sights should be modified as suggested for the Model 99-R in caliber 358 Winchester. Although the Model 81 Remington is *not* adaptable to telescope sighting, and is somewhat lacking in esthetic appeal, it is, nevertheless, one of the most reliable and effective venison producers ever made. I suggest that the 81's open rear sight be removed and replaced with a Lyman "Remington Special" slot blank, and that a recoil pad be installed. The front sight should be exchanged for the correct Redfield Sourdough, and a Williams FP SSM aperture sight should be attached to the rear of the receiver.

The splendid 35 Remington cartridge is currently chambered in the pump-action Remington Model 760, which has already been discussed, and in the underweight Marlin Model 336 carbines. The Model 600 Remington bolt-action —a featherweight carbine—is also chambered in caliber 35 Remington, but this stubby-barreled 5½-pound weapon has nothing to recommend it to experienced hunters. With deep regret, I must again refer you to your used-rifle dealer if you are in the market for a truly satisfactory "woods" rifle chambering this, the finest whitetail caliber that has ever been available to the average hunter.

The recently discontinued Marlin *rifles*—the models 336-A and 336-ADL (deluxe)—having *24-inch* barrels, are superlative whitetail propositions in 35 Remington chambering. The "A" model has fixed-type sling swivels which should be removed and replaced with Jaeger Q.D. type, and a recoil pad is definitely in order. The equipment front sight should be removed and replaced with a Redfield M-437 Sourdough, the open rear sight replaced with a Lyman 12 S slot blank, and a Lyman 66 LA or Redfield Tr-OM receiver sight installed. All Marlin lever-action rifles lend themselves to scope-sighting, and all of recent manufacture come with tapped holes for standard mounts.

The pump-action Model 141 Remington—forerunner of the current Model 760—is also a most excellent bet in caliber 35 Remington. Like its present counterpart, however, the Model 141 is also subject to rattling; but unlike the Model 760, the Model 141 can usually be successfully de-rattled by an experienced gunsmith. Suggested modifications include removal of the open rear sight and its replacement with a Lyman slot blank #12 S, and the installation of a recoil pad, a Redfield W-375 Sourdough front sight, and either a Redfield Tr-B or a Lyman 66-A receiver sight.

The now-discontinued Remington Model 81 autoloader, which has been previously discussed, is truly outstanding in caliber 35 Remington. Both this rifle and this cartridge are particularly well suited to each other, and each has contributed about equally to the enviable reputation enjoyed by the other.

The recommended modifications relative to this model/

caliber combination are identical to those outlined for the Model 81 in caliber 300 Savage.

Although calibers in the 30-30 class are not included in our list of recommended whitetail cartridges, the present dearth of suitable lever-action rifles revives our interest in those particular arms which offer otherwise outstanding qualifications. One such weapon is the discontinued Winchester Model 64 "Deer Rifle" which in either 30-30 or 32 Winchester Special chambering has always been highly regarded. The 30-30 caliber is preferable, but the 32 W.S. is quite acceptable. A good hunting rifle, such as the Winchester Model 64 or the Marlin Model 336-A(ADL) in 30-30 chambering, makes an excellent whitetail arm for a young lad, a frail man, or a small woman. The Winchester, however, isnt' adaptable to proper telescope sighting. The open rear sight should be removed and the slot filled with a Lyman #12 S slot blank, and the factory front sight should be replaced by a Redfield N-260 Sourdough. A Williams FP 94 is the recommended receiver sight.

There are other excellent whitetail rifle/caliber combinations from the past which I won't recommend to you because their ammunition now sells so slowly that it may soon disappear from dealers' shelves. One exception might be a Winchester Model 95 in calibers 30-'06 or 303 British, but *good* Model 95s are being priced out of the hunter's reach by arms collectors. Also, these weapons have such poorly designed stocks that an expensive restocking job is almost a necessity. The loudly lamented Winchester Model 71 was probably the best lever-action hunting rifle ever made, but 348 Winchester ammunition may become non-existent by 1975. Such cartridges as 30 Remington, 32 Remington, 303 Savage, and even the fine old 30-40 are becoming increasingly hard to find, and the remaining days of each—as concerns factory-loaded ammunition—are definitely numbered.

This brings us to the remarkable 30-'06 caliber, and to the types of rifles currently available in this chambering. The previously discussed Remington Model 760 is offered in this caliber, but a quite undesirable feature of this pump (or slide) action weapon has already been brought to your attention. The 30-'06 caliber is currently featured in the Remington Model 742 autoloading rifle, and *this* is the rifle/caliber combination I wholeheartedly recommend to every whitetail hunter who is in the market for a new rifle. I am talking about the Model 742 *rifle—not* the cute little underlength muzzle-blasting carbine version which is so eagerly sought by the press-indoctrinated beginners. Although the Model 742 *rifle* has astonishingly low recoil because of its gas-operated action, a recoil pad should be added to insure pleasant shooting with the iron-sighted weapon. A spare magazine should be purchased, and this should be carried fully loaded while hunting.

The Model 742's open rear sight should be removed, and the two small screw holes filled with tiny, headless filler screws which are available from any gun shop. The front sight should be replaced with a Redfield M-375 Sourdough, and two holes for a standard receiver sight should be properly located, drilled, and tapped, by your gunsmith. The recommended receiver sight is the Lyman 66 RH, although the Redfield Tr BR is quite statisfactory.

The Model 742, like its near-identical forerunner, the Model 740, is perfectly adaptable to the installation and use of a telescope sight; the receiver is drilled and tapped at the factory for quick and easy scope mounting. My own

742/30-'06 is equipped with a Weaver Q.D. top mount (base #56) and I can change from receiver peep-sight to telescope, or vice versa, in less than one minute. The commendably high iron-sight-line in conjunction with the correctly high-combed stock not only places my aiming eye in proper position for telescope sighting, but also permits the iron sights to be employed easily and effectively *right over the top* of the scope mount's base. This rifle is not only the *last* of the truly satisfactory "woods" rifles, but it may well be the over-all *best* one we have ever known.

Like the majority of today's weapons, the Model 742 is a mass-produced firearm which reflects a few disadvantages associated with this production method. For one thing, the detachable magazine isn't individually fitted to the weapon; this may result in an audible click each time the rifle is gripped about the receiver, or at each jolt incurred while the weapon is being carried in the "trail" position. To eliminate this slack-induced clicking, the punch-pressed locking lip, which projects from the front of the magazine, must be lengthened a bit. By slightly *out*-flaring the metal edge immediately *below* this lip, a snug magazine fit can easily be effected. Using a light hammer and a screwdriver for a "flaring tool," it took me about two minutes to correctly position my magazines' locking lip. Now, when the magazine is inserted, and then slapped smartly with the butt of my palm, it locks firmly into place with little or no remaining slack.

Another source of rattle is the loosely fitted bolt-release lever, an integral part of the detachable magazine. I completely eliminated this looseness in my own magazine by slipping a reshaped bobby pin (inserted from the top) over the hinge-pin between the follower and the finger-lever. A split, nylon washer, however, would be a better solution. Another fault is the *non-silent,* hard-to-operate safety; its indent spring, whose purpose is to retain the safety button in the desired position, and to prevent its inadvertant release, is so powerful that *silent* release is impossible even when the button is bucked by an opposing finger. I snipped two turns from this coil spring, and now my safety works smoothly and quietly. All these adjustments and improvements took about 30 minutes of my time, and I was rewarded with a sleek, smoothly working, and deadly efficient woods rifle which satisfies me completely, and suits me to a "T." Regarding this rifle's accuracy, each of my first three sighting shots—fired from 100 yards—would have cut a dime.

The working parts of *any* newly acquired firearm should be removed from the weapon and *thoroughly* degreased by washing in gasoline or commercial solvent. The working parts should then—and forever thereafter—be lightly oiled with Anderol, or an equivilent synthetic oil which positively won't gum or thicken at any earthly temperature. This procedure is particularly essential in respect to autoloading weapons. A clean, rust-free chamber is particularly necessary to an autoloader's functioning reliability. A special chamber-cleaning brush is supplied with every new Model 742; use it. Never use dirty, dented, or corroded ammunition in your autoloader, and, if handloads are used, the cases should have been no more than once fired, and full-length resized prior to loading. The reloads should never exceed factory loads in either pressure or velocity.

Old hands with autoloading weapons know how to avoid functioning failures, but a few beginners experience trouble. Excepting gummed oil failures in cold weather, about 99 per cent of the beginner's troubles stem from his ignorance regarding the proper loading procedure for his weapon. Almost invariably, the tyro will chamber the first round by *gently* lowering the bolt on the cartridge. This is a *big* mistake. The bolt should be let fly—from its extreme rearward position—and *slammed* home on the cartridge. Also, the experienced hunter will periodically check the position of his autoloader's bolt handle while hunting and assure himself that the handle hasn't been pushed back even the tiniest bit by passing brush. We have used autoloaders for more than 20 years, and never have we experienced a malfunction in the field.

At about this point, in books of this nature, it is customary for the author to make a carefully detailed analysis of the relative speed with which succeeding (or follow-up) shots can be made with rifles designed around the different types of actions. I personally believe that—so far as the average once-a-year hunter who practices little if any on running game is concerned—the rapidity with which succeeding shots can be delivered is of quite secondary importance. When pitted against a fleeing whitetail buck, here is how they usually stack up: the fleeing buck, the autoloader, the pump-action, the lever-action, the bolt-action, then the shooter, and lastly, the profanity. All joking aside, however, there really are a few men who can do a bang-up job on a running whitetail. Some men actually prefer to hunt while on the move so they can take their deer as it careens away through the timber. But few such men use bolt-action rifles, and I've never known one who uses a telescope sight. However, such men will tell you that they rarely get more than one good shot at a departing whitetail, and none of these fellows would even *consider* a volume-of-fire technique. But, without a doubt, the ability to get off a quick follow-up shot will get you an extra deer now and then, and will also secure a few wounded animals which might otherwise escape.

If you are determined on using a scopesight, exclusively, then get yourself a bolt-action rifle, If you are determined on getting yourself a bolt-action rifle, then equip it with a telescope sight. The Model 742 autoloader is a most excellent choice for the man who wishes to make optional use of *both* iron and telescope sighting. The bolt-action rifle should have a basic weight of not less than 6-¾ pounds—if chambered in 308 Winchester caliber—and it should weigh not less than 7 pounds if the caliber is 30-'06. A recoil pad is highly recommended for either caliber, and unless the rifle comes with quick detachable sling swivels, Jaeger ⅞-inch Q.D. swivels should be provided. The rifle's stock should have a high, telescope-intended comb, and the weapon should boast a light, crisp, single-stage trigger, preferably one which is adjustable.

The south-paw whitetailer seeking a bolt-action rifle has a single, simple solution: the Model 110-MCL Savage in caliber 308 Winchester. For a youngster, or a slight woman, I suggest the same caliber in the Model 110-MC Savage, which is the right-handed version of the same rifle. Another excellent choice in caliber 308 Winchester is the fine Remington Model 700, in either the standard (ADL) or the deluxe (BDL) versions. For the normally robust (and right-handed) man, I strongly suggest the 30-'06 caliber in a somewhat heavier rifle such as the Colt Hi Power Coltsman, the Sako Finnbear, the F.I. Musketeer, or the Winchester Model 70. A barrel shorter than 22 inches, is *out.*

If a *dual-sighted* bolt-action whitetail rifle is wanted, I know of but one weapon I can recommend at this writing:

the fine F.N. Supreme in caliber 30-'06. Have your gunsmith add a recoil pad, Jaeger $\frac{7}{8}$-inch Q.D. sling swivels,
a Redfield M-313 Sourdough front sight, a Griffin & Howe
Double-Lever side mount, and a Lyman 57-FN (or 48-FN)
receiver sight.

The recommended scopesight is a good quality, fixed-
power 4x instrument of American make, and having a
medium-heavy cross-hair reticle. I recommend that the
scope have internal adjustments, that it be mounted in a
rugged bridge mount such as the Redfield Junior or the
Conetrol, and that it be positioned just as far forward as its
construction will allow without depriving its user of the
full field of view. This will minimize the very real possibility
of the shooter ever being struck about the eye when the
rifle recoils from a hasty shot, or a shot fired from an
unorthodox position.

How much should the whitetail rifle weigh? Beginning
with the fifteenth-century matchlocks, and continuing to
the present day, shoulder-supported firearms intended for
game shooting have weighed in the neighborhood of eight
and one-quarter pounds. There must be a reason for this
particular weight, and there *is* a reason—the best reason in
the world. In millions of miles of hunting, and millions of
shots at game, millions of hunters, trying rifles of every
possible portable weight, have proved to themselves time
and time again that weapons of this weight are the most
effective. In other words, this particular weight is the best
overall compromise between a burden to be carried, an
object to be pointed quickly, and a mass to be supported at
arm's length without tremor and very steadily for exact aim.
This optimum weight for rifles evolved in exactly the same
manner as did the present weights of the ax and the base-

ball. With the progressive increase in both the power and recoil of modern rifles, there is now even less reason to cut rifle weight than existed in times past. Only because of extra-heavy recoil or the necessity for extra-exactness in bullet placement on stationary targets should the weight of the rifle exceed nine pounds; this is about the upper weight limit for a rifle which is to be carried, and used effectively on close, fast-moving game.

A hunting rifle of any caliber, if lightened below seven and one-half pounds, will have lessened effectiveness on any game—including squirrels—except possibly in the hands of an invalid or a child. Even this qualification will be entirely removed in the case of a rifle delivering substantial power and recoil. The persons most likely to get acceptable performance from a powerful featherweight rifle are those big, hairy-chested bruisers who are least in need of shaving a few ounces of needed rifle weight. The featherweight craze was started unintentionally by some of our top arms writers, who kept pointing out the real need for a good bolt-action rifle which would be about a pound lighter than the conventional eight-pound-plus rifles then solely available. This was for the very good reason that a scope plus mount weighs about one pound, and thus the lighter rifle, when so equipped, would be returned to optimum weight. The rocking-chair experts, nuts, and irresponsible extremists swarmed onto the bandwagon, and the rat-race was on. Where it will end, I do not know; but at this writing there are better deer rifles in the second-hand department of many gun stores than are to be found among their new merchandise.

The featherweight fanatics are responsible for the current, fallacious belief that lightness in itself is a highly desirable virtue of the hunting rifle. Their conception of the perfect rifle is one which has no weight at all, and they strive continually to sell their argument by promising the user of an underweight weapon that he will come in less tired after a hard day of mountain tramping. Unless I am able to dissuade you from trudging over mountains all day in your whitetail hunting, it will make little difference what you carry. A very light walking-stick, substituted for the rifle, will tire you even less, and will normally produce the same amount of venison.

Except in mule deer country, where whitetails are seldom deliberately hunted, whitetail hunting in the United States is very rarely wilderness hunting. Except those deer in parks and sanctuaries, 95 per cent of all whitetails east of the Rockies can be approached within one mile by automobile, canoe, or boat. You will normally have little excuse for coming in tired from a whitetail hunt unless you tote one back with you.

I cannot disagree more with those writers who; professing to speak for us whitetail hunters, maintain that we are in dire need of featherweight rifles for our hunting. Ours is the most leisurely hunting in the world, and, if done properly, is much harder on the bo-hind than the feet. Of all the world's big-game shooters, the whitetail hunter is least in need of reducing the optimum rifle weight at the inevitable price of lowered performance, and most in need of the stability and more precise aiming ability provided by a standard-weight weapon. If all deer were shot while unalarmed, I would place no upper limit on the rifle's weight, but very often the need for deliberate speed is encountered.

It is my opinion that the extreme weight variation of the whitetail rifle should be no more than one-half pound either under or over the ideal weight of eight and one-quarter pounds. Seven and three-quarters pounds is about the lowest permissible weight limit for the complete rifle which chambers an adequately powerful cartridge, unless maximum efficiency is to suffer. This weight includes the sight (or sights) and recoil pad, if any. The Marlin Model 336-A(ADL) will run a little underweight—even with recoil pad and micrometer-adjustable receiver sight—but the stock is well designed, and the 35 Remington cartridge is low enough in recoil to permit this rifle to be used quite effectively.

In calculating the completed weight of a projected rifle/ sight combination, we take the maker's published weight of the weapon and add the weight of all accessories we intend to install. We can safely figure on 14 ounces for a scope and mount, and 2 ounces for a quality receiver sight. A recoil pad will add another couple of ounces. Therefore, when selecting our deer rifle, we must first decide on all accessories that will be added before final decision is reached on the rifle, and the total weights of all items must be known before the overall decision is finalized.

The 30-30, 300 Savage, and the 35 Remington calibers will probably be highly effective in rifles weighing as little as 7-3/4 pounds. The 308 Winchester, however, requires a full 8 pounds of weapon weight to prevent the recoil from becoming excessive. The 30-'06 and the 358 Winchester will be better at a full quarter-pound more, and I am perfectly happy with an 8½-pound rifle which chambers either cartridge.

Always remember that the carrying ease and fractionally increased handling speed that is bought with needed rifle weight will be paid for with less reliable shot placement and slower follow-up shots, caused by the greater disturbance to the hunter's equilibrium due to increased recoil effect. Very light rifles may be fine for mountain hunters when equipped with scopesights, but these are not suitable to the iron-sight user. Unfortunately, the scope-everything craze has practically driven standard-weight rifles off the market, leaving the iron-sight users pretty much out in the cold.

What barrel-length should the rifle have? There is nothing wrong with a 24-inch barrel that I can discover; this is the length I prefer, and recommend to you. A 22-inch barrel is acceptable for the woods rifle, but you will needlessly penalize yourself if you use one shorter than that. There is no sense or reason for any hunting rifle having a barrel longer than 26 inches or shorter than 22 inches. I have yet to hear a valid argument in favor of either longer or shorter barrels. No one is currently plugging for barrels longer than 26 inches, but our highly vocal "progressive" arms press keeps yammering for shorter and shorter barrels for the hunting rifle, claiming that these can be pointed faster, and that they are "handier" in the brush, and also in the saddle scabbard. They seem to lose sight of the fact that pointing and *aiming* are not exactly one and the same thing.

The effectiveness of the rifle should always be the hunter's chief concern, and handiness, although a greatly desired attribute, should be incorporated only to the point where it ceases to contribute to the overall effectiveness. If quick pointing and extreme handiness were our only objectives, and precise aiming were not a consideration, then we could all discard our rifles and arm ourselves with pistols, which are the ultimate arms development in handiness and quick pointability. The whitetail hunter is seldom concerned with the horseback hunter's problems, but any standard-length hunting rifle can be carried in a properly fitting saddle-scabbard with negligible inconvenience, as we have often demonstrated in both Mexico and the American Rockies. A very flat carbine with a short barrel is the logical choice for the man who works in the saddle, and carries a rifle as a tool of his trade, but the serious hunter has arms available which are much better suited to his purpose.

Completely aside from the barrel's mass (or weight, if you prefer), the dynamic stability inherent in longer barrels due to increased inertia demonstrably reduces the angular deviation (wobble) while aiming, which allows a more precise let-off of the shot because the frequency as well as the magnitude of the wobble is reduced. In plain words, brother, you can *aim* faster and shoot better with a 24-inch-barreled rifle than you can with its 20-inch-barreled twin. Velocity, power, and trajectory will also be better in the longer-barreled version. These may be unimportant to the whitetail hunter, but the shorter barrel's increased noise and muzzle-blast, which results in increased recoil effect, are *not* unimportant.

When only iron sights are to be used, there are few rifles available which have sufficient weight to be shot comfortably with a hard butt plate. Unless you are a better man than I am, which is no better than an even bet, a shot fired while prone or sitting from an unaltered, over-the-counter, six-and-one-half-pound 358 Winchester or 30-'06 caliber feather-weight rifle will give you the distinct impression that your eyeballs have exchanged sockets, and will leave you wandering around in a dazed search for your corner. The proper course of action for the luckless individual stuck with one of these booby traps, is to pass up no opportunity to extol its carrying ease—while continually badgering his companions for their senseless toting of "cannons"—but to carefully avoid any situation which might require discharge of his weapon.

The stocks supplied with factory-built rifles are nearly enough the correct length for normally built men of near-average stature. Shortening the stock, when required, is easily accomplished by slicing off a bit of the wood and refitting the butt plate, but when more than a very little *lengthening* is required, addition of a recoil pad is about the only practical solution. If you are well above or below average height, your stock may require alteration, but this is definitely no job for the home mechanic. If you have decided to equip your rifle with a recoil pad, you should first determine if there should be any change in the length-of-pull; if so, this can be easily made at the time the pad is installed. But, by all means, have this work done by a competent gunsmith.

The sights, and sighting combinations—both iron and telescopic—which I have recommended to you, are the best of their respective types of which I have knowledge. I once advised, and most arms authorities still do, the use of low (2½-3x) power scopes with post reticles for brush and timber shooting. I have gradually come to the opinion that *any* scope containing magnification will so badly handicap the shooter on all close-range running shots that the average scope user may just as well forget about running shots altogether. The 4x scope offers little additional handicap on such shots, while its larger, more clearly defined image will assist the shooter greatly on all standing shots attempted under conditions of poor visibility. Although somewhat less rugged—and also more expensive—the new *small* size, *moderately* powered (2x to 7x) variables such as recently introduced by Redfield and others might offer the hunter more advantages than will any scope of fixed power. If an aperture sight is selected for the whitetail rifle, the screw-in disc *must* be removed while hunting. The threaded hole into which the disc is screwed is of almost perfect diameter for all game shooting. If left in place, the disc's small aperture makes this type of sight utterly worthless for hunting. Some authorities urge you to throw this disc away, but I keep mine for sighting-in purposes; the tiny peep-hole sharpens the contrast between the black bullseye and its white background. If your rifle's front sight is provided with a removable hood, be sure to remove this useless appendage before going afield.

Open iron sights are a bit faster than aperture sights, but are not nearly so accurate. On dangerous game, which is prone to charge the hunter, open iron sights are strictly the ticket. Deer, however, are always *going,* never coming, so open iron sights have become the trademark of the tyro whitetail hunter. There are limitless combinations involving open iron sights, but all are so relatively inefficient for non-dangerous game shooting that we will waste no further time in discussing them. New rifles are provided with open sights because these are cheap, not because they are efficient.

When aiming the aperture-sighted rifle, the eye looks *through* the rear peep-hole, not *at* it, and the top edge of the front post is placed on the spot you wish to hit. The rear sight will be quite blurred, and will appear as a ringed halo surrounding the front sight which will seem to be floating all alone in space. Believe it or not, your eye will subconsciously center the front post in this halo; all you will have to do is place the top edge of the front sight on the spot you wish to hit, and press the trigger. Because you have only one sight to align instead of two, as in the case of open sights, this combination is not only deadly accurate, but lightning fast as well. A shooter accustomed to open sights, and looking through an aperture for the first time, will probably be aghast to see the front sight just floating in space; but a few get-acquainted shots will quickly make him a staunch disciple. This combination is the fastest known to me for getting an exact aim; definitely more accurate than open sights, and definitely faster than any scopesight containing magnification. It is infinitely superior to the telescope sight for running game at short woods ranges. A person can get full use of these sights as long as his eye can focus the front sight sharply—long after his middle-aged eyes are useless with open iron sights.

Without question the scopesight is superior to all other sighting devices for long-range shooting, so much so that I will consider no other sight for my own open-country hunting. In fair weather, the scope surpasses any iron-sight combination for unhurried shots at standing or leisurely moving game up to any distance. Where spike bucks and does are not legal game, the scope will often reveal the exact status of the animal; this knowledge will not only result in a bonus deer now and then, but it should certainly prevent you from shooting something you'd prefer *not* to shoot. Accurate aim can be taken with a low (up to 5x) power scope in very dim light, thus adding at least 15 minutes to each end of the hunter's day. These last two features are the more important to the whitetail hunter, and offer the only worth-while arguments in favor of the scopesight's use by the brush and timber hunter.

Compared with the best iron-sight combinations, the telescope has certain drawbacks which tend heavily to cancel out its many advantages. Fortunately for you, I use both types of sights quite regularly (and about equally) and I am completely unbiased in this appraisal; it is almost impossible for the seeker of knowledge to get information from any but highly prejudiced sources. First then, the telescope has two minor disadvantages in addition to its much higher cost; a definite top-heaviness, which detracts noticeably from the balance and handling qualities of the rifle, and an increased bulkiness resulting in a pronounced tendency to snag on brush or clothing while the weapon is being carried or mounted to the shoulder. These faults, I repeat, are minor, and are a small price to pay for the increased clarity and target definition provided by the quality scopesight. But here comes the stinger.

Even *light* brush immediately in front of the shooter will often delay too long his ability to locate the target in the scope. Also, an animal standing plainly outlined behind screening brush may disappear completely when the hunter transfers his vision to the scope. This phenomenon is termed the "picket-fence effect," and it is even more troublesome when the target is moving rapidly. But the scopesight's greatest fault—when turned on close, fast-moving game—is its unpleasant property of increasing the *apparent* speed of the quarry to the same degree that the quarry's image-size is increased. This drastic difference between the target's *true* speed and its *apparent* speed makes smooth, accurate tracking with the rifle's muzzle a near impossibility—particularly when the target is racing *across* the shooter's field of view. This monumental failing, coupled with the telescope's always-restricted field of view, makes this instrument the poorest sighting device known to man when shooting must be done at short ranges on fast-moving game. Up to at least 50 yards, and possibly 75, a sightless, slug-loaded shotgun is far superior to any scope-sighted rifle for taking bounding deer in brush or timber. This statement is constantly refuted in print, but never in the deer coverts.

The scopesight is truly a fair-weather friend in the exact meaning of this term; dew-drenched brush, dripping tree limbs, or even light misting rain will foul up the lenses and occasionally cost you a chance. While mounting your rifle in cold weather, your warm breath may strike the ocular lens, and thereby render you temporarily sightless; few deer will linger obligingly while you wipe off your lens. And the telescope sight, though no cream puff, is more vulnerable to shock and abuse than is the aperture sight. For one reason, the scope's greater size and bulk causes it to intercept more knocks and bumps. For mechanical reliability—and permanence of adjustment—the telescope sight, with its two dozen threaded screws and collars, won't compare with the relatively simple and rugged aperture sight.

Up to this point, in our discussion of sights, I have limited myself to honest comparison and fair appraisal, while pointing out the optical and mechanical problems relating to the installation and use of each type. I have delayed as long as possible the serious responsibility of recommending a definite choice to you, hoping that you would make your own selection and thereby let me off the hook. If your eyes are not capable of near 20-20 vision, even with glasses, get a telescope. If you are developing symptoms of middle-age eyesight, get a telescope. But if you have the health, the eyesight, and the burning ambition to be a *master* whitetail hunter, then I advise you not to divorce yourself from the opportunity of using *aperture* iron sights whenever a situation suggests their use.

A great many hunters, including the Hayes clan, like to

take advantage of *both* types of sights, and this frequently poses a problem. The simplest solution lies in owning two rifles—one scopesighted, and one equipped with aperture sight—but perhaps few readers will be such rabid hunters as to follow our example and use the grocery money for a second rifle. A less expensive solution is a dual-sighted weapon, but very few of today's rifles are well adapted to the alternate use of telescope *and* good iron sights. The Remington Model 742 autoloader is a notable exception, as is the Fabrique Nationale "Supreme" model bolt-action rifle; detailed instructions for dual-sighting these fine weapons was given earlier in this chapter. Because of the optimum weight requirement of the satisfactory hunting rifle—7-¾ to 8-¾ pounds—and the one-pound weight difference between aperture and telescope sights, our choice of weapons is limited to those having a basic weight which lies between 7½ and 7-⅞ pounds. To justify the trouble and expense of dual sighting, the rifle should chamber a suitable all-around cartridge, and this specification further narrows our field of selection. Also, because the scopesight's sight-line is *always* relatively high, our chosen rifle must have either a *very* high iron-sightline or a compromise (all-purpose) stock. When our other requirements—which include 22-inch (minimum) barrel length, a clean, crisp trigger, and a non-rattling weapon —are added to the above specifications, the small remaining number of suitable candidates isn't in the least surprising.

To change quickly from receiver to telescope sight, you press the button on the frame of the aperture sight, lift out the sliding staff, and drop it in your pocket. This clears the top of the receiver for the telescope, which is now set in place and tightened, either by means of two levers provided for this purpose or a couple of large-headed knurled screws

containing wide slots designed to accept a coin to be used
for final tightening. The bulkiest part of the scope-mount
will be permanently attached to the scope, which may be
carried in a rucksack or a specially designed holster when
not in use. Only the receiver sight's frame and an unobtrusive base plate for the scope will remain permanently
attached to the rifle's receiver. The change-over from one
sighting device to the other can be easily made in sixty
seconds or less, coming or going.

A properly selected and fitted rig, such as just described,
will enable the user to give a good account of himself anywhere, any time, and under any shooting condition that he
is ever likely to encounter. This arrangement is the only
practical one I know for achieving good results when both
types of sighting devices are to be used on the same rifle.

For the one-gun man who hunts a wide variety of game
in all types of territory, the 30-'06 in a dual-sighted bolt-
action rifle is the best combination I can think of for the
average hunter. Though demonstrating its power peak on
animals weighing around six hundred pounds, the 30-'06 is
still the most versatile of all calibers for use on everything
from coyote to moose, in either open plains or brush and
timber. By carefully choosing the proper load and bullet
type from the many that are available, the 30-'06 can be
adapted to any shooting situation that may arise in the
western hemisphere. After more than fifty years it is still the
all-around champion caliber of America. It is quite easy
for the two-rifle owner, or the man who hunts but one type
of terrain, to avoid the 30-'06, but it is quite difficult for
the one-rifle shoot-everything-everywhere hunter to do so.

If your present rifle has a comb too low for the sights you
would like to install or for the ones you are presently using,

you will do well to get a higher-combed stock from either the rifle's manufacturer or from a custom stock builder. If neither source provides a practical solution, then you are well advised to seek an undiscriminating buyer, if one can be found. Or, as a last resort, you might attach a lace-on Monte Carlo-type check rest, but this unprepossessing appendage must be *cemented* on.

The greatest enemy of accurate shooting and the chief cause of ruinous flinching is a heavy, creepy trigger-pull. No hunter can do good shooting with a badly pulling trigger, and riflemen worthy of the name will flatly refuse to use a weapon having such a trigger. Experienced shooters demand a trigger that releases sharply and suddenly, with no detectable drag, thus giving what is commonly termed a "clean" let-off. This effect has been compared with the sudden breaking of a glass rod or icicle. Many writers wrongly advise the deer hunter to have his trigger adjusted to a pull of $2\frac{1}{2}$ pounds or so, but this figure should be doubled. The target shooter or the small-game hunter can profit by such a light trigger, but your strength doubles and your muscles grow taut under the intense excitement of big-game shooting, and premature discharges always frighten deer but rarely kill them.

The word "pull" should never have been applied to the act of releasing a trigger; triggers are pressed, never pulled. "Pulling" is a kissing cousin of "yanking," and both words are synonymous with "missing" in the shooter's lexicon. A jerked trigger can cause a pregnant elephant to be missed at twenty feet. A good trigger is one you are never conscious of pressing—the rifle just seems to discharge itself at the instant your eye tells your brain that all is ready.

Never buy a rifle until you have assured yourself that the

trigger is to your liking. Some rifles come from the factory with satisfactory trigger pulls, and most rifles can be given a good trigger pull in a few minutes by a competent gunsmith; but there are some models of rifles whose design incorporates an incurably hard, creepy trigger. Avoid such arms as you would the scurvy—and such arms can always be avoided by refusing to part with your money until the dealer has adjusted the trigger to your satisfaction.

If you hunt whitetails in a state which forbids the use of rifled arms but allows the use of a smooth-bore gun firing a single projectile, a Williams "Five Dollar" aperture sight affixed to the receiver of any repeating, single-barrel shotgun of 12 or 16 gauge will make an excellent substitute for the rifle. If the front sight is too low, the Williams Company can supply a clamp-on sleeve, which slips over the muzzle and furnishes a higher front sight—almost always necessary when a receiver sight is added. Be sure to carefully sight-in the gun at 50 yards with rifled-slug ammunition, and be sure to always use the same brand of ammunition for your hunting that you used when sighting-in. If the gun is equipped with an adjustable choke-changing device, best slug accuracy will usually be attained from the widest-open choke setting.

Repeating shotguns designed particularly for slug shooting are currently available. These have rifle-type open sights and special boring, but a five-dollar receiver sight is recommended to replace the factory rear sight. Accuracy of these guns, on deer, is claimed to be satisfactory to 100 yards when these weapons are sighted-in to be dead-on at 75 yards. The ordinary scatter-gun, with its barleycorn-type bead sight and its barrel containing more or less choke restriction, should be sighted-in to be dead-on at 50 yards. This sighting should give sure hits to about 75 yards, which will take care of about 90 per cent of the whitetail hunter's chances. The brush-bucking ability and killing power of the slug-loaded shotgun are truly superb—greatly superior to the buckshot-loaded weapon. Except where ranges in excess of about 80 yards are discussed, the slug-loaded shotgun will be considered as a rifle in this book. This is quite possibly the best weapon available for taking bounding deer in heavy cover.

A shooting sling is never used in brush and timber hunting, and the carry-sling, though a most important piece of equipment to the whitetail hunter, should always repose in his knapsack or pocket while he is actually engaged in hunting. A loose, looping sling is prone to catch on brush or clothing while the piece is being carried along, or when it is being mounted to the shoulder. Also, the side-to-side swinging of the loosely looped sling will spoil the shooter's aim. We have designed a sling for carrying, only, which makes swivels completely unnecessary for the woods rifle or shotgun; but if you *must* have sling swivels on your brush-intended weapon, be sure they are of the quick detachable type as made by Remington or Jaeger. These remove with the sling, and leave nothing attached to the weapon to catch on brush or to rattle as you walk.

An efficient, tight-loop shooting-sling, such as the Haye-sling, is a very important adjunct to the rifle used for long-range shooting. The owner of an all-around rifle, such as discussed earlier in this chapter, will do well to have such a sling on Q.D. swivels, but he should leave this somewhat bulkier sling at home while timber hunting, and take, instead, a light carry-sling which will normally repose in his pocket. A good carry-sling for swiveled arms is the very light

Guntoter, whose designer also fashioned the Hayesling. His identity will not be revealed for fear it would appear as though I were boasting.

The whitetail hunter must always be ready for instant action, and if the rifle is equipped with a sling the hunter will find it draped across his shoulder—and himself help-less—when a quick shooting opportunity presents itself. A light, compact carry-sling will come in mighty handy when there is a deer to be toted in, or if your companion should become ill or injured and require a helping hand back to camp. An ideal sling for this purpose is the afore-mentioned carry-sling which does not require the weapon to be equipped with swivels. It is called the Gunslinger Model 100, and it is available from your dealer or direct from the maker. This sling weighs only $3\frac{1}{2}$ ounces, occupies little more space than a pack of cigarettes, makes into a small, neat, self-contained package, can be attached or removed in 10 seconds, permits of emergency use of the weapon while attached, and it isn't expensive.

The purpose of this book is not to discuss all known white-tail rifles, sights, equipment, and hunting methods, but only the better ones. A precisely directed, unobstructed shot from almost any kind of rifle will drop a well-positioned white-tail—or grizzly bear for that matter—and you will meet men who regularly produce venison with arms and accessories which I have branded as inferior. This circumstance is mute testimony to their skill and patience; a manifestation of superior talent. Rembrandt could have painted a better picture with two bottles of shoe polish and a tooth brush than I could paint with a million-dollar art foundation at my disposal. You may be quite certain, however, that if you choose to follow my equipment recommendations, you will never be beaten at this game because of inferior armament. But the man holding the rifle is more important by far than the rifle held by the man.

4 — RIFLE SHOOTING AND SIGHTING-IN

Should you ask the average whitetail hunter what he will require to assure the success of his next hunt, he will answer emphatically and without the slightest hesitation, "Just show me a deer!"

However, comparatively few hunters fail because they have no opportunity for a shot. The majority are presented with sufficiently good chances but fail for one or more of several reasons. Aside from tactical blunders, the chief cause of failure is their inability to put a bullet into a vital spot on the deer which obliges them with a good shot. Failure is habit-forming, and hunters rapidly divide into two distinct groups—the smaller, which seldom fails, and the much larger, which seldom succeeds. I have made a serious study of a number of hunters who are chronic failures, and without exception they are lousy shots. Also, without exception, these men have little knowledge of firearms. And almost without exception, their rifles are never properly sighted-in.

The average hunter is unfamiliar with proper sighting-in technique, and this failing, coupled with pronounced lack of shooting ability, aggravated by loose sight screws and a bum trigger, and climaxed by a propensity to flinch, results in a combination having a killing range of about four feet—provided the user has a firm grip on the muzzle and is swinging the weapon with all his might. Under these conditions, Custer might have fired until his barrel melted without ever hitting an Indian. The rifle's owner is now caught in the toils of a vicious cycle; he can't do a better sighting-in job until he learns to shoot, and his shooting will rapidly worsen until his rifle is properly sighted-in. Each miserable failure automatically reduces this shooter's confidence until he reaches the point where his very first glimpse of game will panic him into a violent case of buck fever—a transient, but paralyzing seizure brought on by fear of failure.

Very seldom will the chronically unsuccessful hunter be armed with a cheap, worn-out, defective, or obsolete shooting combination. On the contrary, he most likely suffers from an overdose of ultramodernity, characterized by the super-long-range sniping equipment which is abundantly stocked and eagerly sought by the "well informed" disciples of the "progressive" arms authorities. In the case of the whitetail hunter, one man's meat becomes a thousand men's poison. There are probably a few people who would urge the forest firewarden to exchange his helicopter for a ram jet, and the carpenter to replace his wooden yardstick with a precision micrometer.

A gross misfit between a shooter and his rifle is not uncommon. The majority of big-game rifles made since 1960 have telescope-height stocks and *low-positioned* iron sights, an incredible circumstance considering the fact that higher sights, while costing no more, would add greatly to the weapon's versatility. The average hunter buys his rifle without a scope, perhaps intending to use the factory equipment sights. With most models of rifles, however, the new owner

will discover that he can't get his face down to the iron-
sight's level without twisting his head unnaturally and cocking it at an absurd angle, and that the poor shooting which
normally results from this head position is worsened by the
pain inflicted on the cheekbone by the rifles' recoil. So the
rifle's owner winds up with a scopesight whether it is wanted
or not, and regardless of whether it is suited to the particular shooting conditions or not.

On the other side of the coin is the low-comb-stocked rifle
which the owner is brain-washed into scope-equipping with
no concern as to the resultant misfit between himself and
his weapon, and with utter disregard toward the type of
terrain in which the hunting will be done. A man who
accuses his wife of being a moron for allowing herself to be
talked into a fifty-dollar permanent by a beautician will
solicit the advice of a sales clerk on rifles and rigs costing
several times as much money.

The better long-range open-country shooting rigs are
highly specialized instruments. Precisely the same is true
of the better brush and timber combinations, and neither
will adequately substitute for the other, especially where
each encounters the extreme conditions for which the other
is intended. Recently-compiled statistics indicate conclu-
sively that, even in the more open western states, the overwhelming majority of big game is taken at ranges well under
two hundred yards. This should convince the average hunter
that any error in choice of equipment should favor the near
game-taking ability of his combination.

The average hunter may be ignorant, but he isn't stupid;
he is honestly striving to give himself an edge in his whitetail hunting. With so little publicity on the brush-shooting
limitations of a sniping rig, and the continual ballyhoo on

its quarter-mile game-blasting ability, it is little wonder that the poorly informed whitetail hunter should select this type of equipment. Isn't it reasonable to assume that a 400-yard rifle would offer four times the area wherein game would be vulnerable compared with the area offered by the 200-yard rifle? A quite logical, but erroneous, assumption.

Many hunters, strangely enough, do not seem to realize that practice is necessary to good marksmanship. They cherish the odd notion that there is a knack to it, like riding a bicycle, and once they get the hang of it they will be on their way. All there is to it, they will assure you, is to put the sight on the target and pull the trigger. Well, it's almost that simple, but not quite. It's easy enough to place the sight on the target and release the trigger; but to *hold* the sight correctly aligned on the target until the trigger is released and to release the trigger in such a manner as to not disturb the aim, takes a bit of doing. No one would seriously say that all there is to playing a violin is sawing away with one hand while you finger around with the other.

Yet the rifle is mastered as the violin is mastered—by practice. There is no other way. High-power center-fire ammunition is so expensive that only a bureaucrat could afford to perfect his shooting eye by firing his deer rifle exclusively. The .22 rimfire rifle is the means for developing a good shooter, and is also the means by which he keeps himself in good form. It requires many thousands of rounds of ammunition to develop a master rifleman, and serious large-bore tournament shooters feel compelled to fire at least a thousand rounds of high-power ammunition each year to stay in sharp competitive form. They will also fire several times this number of .22 rimfire cartridges as a matter of course.

In addition to firing your .22 as often as possible—at targets, tin cans, or small game—you should run at least a hundred rounds through your deer rifle each year. Ten trips to the firing range, spaced throughout the spring and summer, at each of which you fire ten carefully-directed shots, will keep you in pretty fair readiness for your autumn deer hunt. Even after a man has become a master rifle shot, I would consider four ten-shot practice sessions an absolute minimum guarantee against missing even a setup.

The average hunter fancies himself quite a sharp number with a rifle, which, considering his complete incapacity to demonstrate, either to himself or to others, is an absolutely astounding conviction. As a boy, he knocked off an unlucky sparrow now and then with his BB-gun and did a little .22 plinking when he grew somewhat older. In his teens, he forsook the rifle in favor of the scatter gun and has regularly hunted water fowl, upland birds, or rabbits ever since. Gone from his mind are the frequent misses of his early days, and now his memory is aglow with the occasion on which he perforated that distant sapsucker with a shot which seemed so hopeless that he hardly bothered to aim at all. Chances for helping this man are as hopeless as his shooting ability, because no one is so blind as the person who refuses to see. Just as long as the average man believes that a bad shot is a good shot because he fired it, and further believes that the natural ability to shoot well is part of his heritage, then so much the better for you and me. If every hunter strove diligently to improve himself there wouldn't be enough deer to go around.

The average man who has become fairly proficient with the .22 rifle but has done little high-power rifle shooting labors under three mistaken convictions: that practice with the small-bore arm will entirely substitute for practice with the larger weapon; that high-power rifles are not nearly as accurate as twenty-two's; and that he positively does not flinch with the more powerful deer rifle. He is wrong on all three counts. He flinches with the high-power rifle, which causes his shots to scatter, and this convinces him that the piece is inaccurate. And only by repeated firing of the large-bore rifle, plus the exercise of great will power and determination, can mastery of the heavy weapon be attained. Twenty-two pistol shooters experience some of this same difficulty when they graduate to the forty-five.

"Flinching" is the sudden involuntary contraction of the muscles during, or immediately prior to, the discharge of the weapon. It is a natural reflex which gets somewhat ahead of itself, so to speak. If allowed to persist, it may become such a conditioned reflex that it will be almost impossible to overcome. The sudden distant shriek of frantically-applied brakes will cause us to tense our muscles in anticipation of the horrifying crash. We deliberately spring a steel trap and flinch as the jaws snap together. The anticipated jump and roar of the big rifle has a tendency to cause us to tighten our muscles at just about the time we expect the arm to fire, and this is what we term flinching. The only big-rifle shooters who have never flinched a shot are those men with abnormal reflexes—and liars. It's as natural to flinch as it is to fight the water the first time you try to swim. A "fairly good" shooter cannot win a major small-bore match, but many a large-bore match has been won by a run-of-the-mill shooter who managed to fire the required number of shots without flinching even once.

The small-bore shooter must concentrate on hold, breath control, and trigger-squeeze, but the large-bore shooter, in addition to the three things just cited, must also concentrate on not flinching. No one should ever fire a shot carelessly or with little interest in its result. Every time you press the trigger it should be with the firm determination that the shot will be the best of which you are capable. The more intensely you desire to hit your mark, the less tendency you will have to flinch.

The recoil of a properly-stocked big-game rifle of reasonable weight, when properly held to the shoulder, *will not hurt you.* Neither will the barrel jump and muzzle blast. But *everybody* who shoots powerful rifles is subject to flinching, and most of us must struggle unceasingly against this enemy of good marksmanship. Flinching is the hunter's curse and the deer's best friend. If you do not walk regularly your feet will become tender, and if you do not practice regularly with your big-game rifle you will probably develop a tendency to flinch. Tender feet are corrected only by taking regular walks and flinching is overcome only by regular shooting sessions with Mr. Big. There is no other way. "Flinchitis" is like halitosis—the afflicted person seldom realizes that he has it. Don't ever kid yourself into believing that you are immune, for your only hope of keeping this malady arrested—there is no known specific cure—is to openly recognize the possibility of its existence. The disease is kept in check by taking "shots."

A few seasons back I was out at the club range, burning a little powder, when a near-by shooter began to complain about the accuracy of his rifle. I turned my spotting scope on his target and diagnosed his trouble as caused by flinching, but he promptly scouted such a possibility. I sneaked the cartridge from my chamber and persuaded the fellow to try a few shots with my rifle, assuring him that it was ready to fire. The violent jerk of the muzzle as the rifle snapped on the empty chamber instantly convinced my aquaintance that he did flinch unconsciously when shooting.

Flinching can be readily induced by firing a weapon whose

recoil actually hurts you. Old-fashioned rifles with deeply-curved butt plates of narrow width, and with their razor-edged excessively-dropped combs, will eat you up like a bitin' sow. Not only will such rifles hurt your shoulder but the point of the comb will upchuck and bang you on the cheekbone. One of my friends who shoots a modern 30-'06 with perfect enjoyment will blanch and start sweating at the very thought of shooting his dad's old 30-30 "long" gun. A stock that is too short can allow the nose to be whacked by the thumb of the trigger hand, and even a soft rubber recoil pad will not tame a heavy-caliber featherweight rifle to the point where it can be shot well by the average shooter.

Each year, many 308, 30-'06, and 358 featherweight rifles are advertised for sale by owners who describe the weapons as "once fired." The following season the same rifles will be advertised by different owners as "twice fired." Only in sales involving these types of rifles is the prospective purchaser fully justified in accepting without question the seller's claim of very low mileage. I have shot a standard weight 375 Magnum quite a bit, and, though is snaps my head around with each shot, it doesn't hurt me. I once owned an eight-pound-plus 45-70 which was quite pleasant to shoot, but I just won't be able to find time to sight-in your featherweight powerhouse.

Aside from a rifle which is murdering him with every shot, only a hard, creepy trigger will cause a veteran large-bore shooter to flinch-off a really bad shot. If your rifle has a trigger answering to this description you are whipped before you start, and no investment that you will ever make in your equipment will reward you as well as the few paltry pesos spent with a capable gunsmith on a trigger job. Most veteran shooters simply refuse to fire a rifle that has a hard or dragging trigger, because to do so will completely unnerve them.

Around the deer camps you will meet such a large army of hunters who are toting small-caliber "peashooters" that you may wonder if Hayes could be wrong in recommending adequate rifles. To your further confusion, these varmint-rifle toters will each swear that his mighty midget kills "better" than your "old-fashioned" pumpkin slinger. Before you burn this book and write me a nasty letter, just remember this: these hunters never used a man-size rifle enough to learn to hit well with it, because it kicked them and their shots were consequently either poorly placed or complete misses. These fellows are manly enough in all other ways, but they are still boys when it comes to shooting big-game rifles. Incidentally, the day you see sporting magazines flooded with offers by African white hunters to swap their heavy-caliber rifles for 220 Swifts, you will know that small, light bullets kill heavy game more reliably than do large, heavy bullets, and that I have had to go to work for a living.

The preponderance of bolt-action rifles encountered in the whitetail coverts is another manifestation of the average man's misguided effort to give himself an edge in the deer-slaying business. Fortunately, the type of action chosen by the whitetail hunter is probably the least influential of all factors affecting success; but analysis of the various action types will indicate that the average hunter will most often be better served by the lever action or the autoloader. This statement has been made many times before, but usually in a weak, unconvincing manner in a very short paragraph at the end of a very long eulogy on the outstanding virtues of some bolt-action arm. Bolt-action arms most certainly do have outstanding virtues, but the autoloaders and lever actions are also blessed with advantages, and, despite the fact that their outstanding accuracy is generally exceeded by the bolt-action rifle, their nature and design permit of greater intimacy, which promotes a feeling of partnership and camaraderie. Those who may be inclined to scoff at the idea of a feeling of rapport between a man and his rifle need to be reminded that all outstanding hunters know this feeling, and that no person completely dedicated to logic will ever make a good hunter. The quality that engenders this feeling of rapport is not lacking in the bolt-action rifle, and the man who is faithfully served will eventually develop this spiritual bond with his rifle, irrespective of its physical characteristics.

Long range, when the term is applied to big-game shooting, usually refers to ranges exceeding two hundred yards. Effective shooting at long range requires the congenital accuracy of the bolt-action rifle, assisted by the magnification provided by the telescope sight. No other type of modern sporting rifle will provide consistent long-range field accuracy, and this accuracy will be unavailable without a good scope sight. Except when employed by a timber hunter with defective eyesight, the big-game scope needs a good bolt-action rifle under it in order for it to earn its keep. Each is of little use without the other in big-game shooting at the longer ranges, and I personally will consider no other combination for my own long-range big-game shooting.

However, the whitetail deer's coloration, the nature of its habitat, and its physical size have pretty well established it as a very generous 200-yard maximum proposition, regardless of the rifleman, the rifle, or type of sight used. In the hands of a good shot with good eyesight, any modern center-fire rifle equipped with good apperture sights will reliably place its first two shots in an area roughly half the size of the vital area presented by the average whitetail deer at two hundred yards. This will leave quite a bit of margin for the shooter with less skill, and should reassure anyone concerned with the accuracy potential of his rifle. The third shot from autoloaders, trombones, and lever actions, generally lumped together under the term "woods" rifles, may, on rare occasions, exceed the permissable margin of error at this extreme range, but very few uninjured deer will hang around for a third shot.

Nine times out of ten, your whitetail will appear at less than one hundred yards range. Very seldom will you have an opportunity beyond one hundred fifty yards, and 200-yard offerings are once-in-a-blue-moon propositions. Any well experienced whitetail hunter would jump at the chance to make a compact with the Red Gods to pass up all attempts at ranges exceeding eighty yards if, in return, he were guaranteed invariable success at lesser ranges. You should bear in mind that I am speaking of standard English yards, not deer yards, which vary considerably but seem to average about eighteen inches.

The average hunter seldom becomes aware of the handling ease, snap-shooting adaptability, and repeat-shot speed typical of the average woods rifles. He continually hears the high accuracy of the bolt-action rifle touted, so he buys one for his whitetail hunting. Being unacquainted with all the facts, his choice seems a logical one; the bolt-action rifle is more accurate, so, *ipso facto,* it will improve his chances of hitting his deer.

Many of the early woods rifles gave very poor accuracy, and the same may be said for the majority of our current featherweight autoloaders and lever actions. However, all non-bolt-action rifles of recent manufacture, *weighing not less than seven pounds,* are quite accurate; the Remington Model 742 autoloader is amazingly so. My own Model 742/ 30-'06 will group consistently into 2 minutes of angle which is excellent accuracy for *any* hunting rifle of *any* type. Most arms writers judge a hunting rifle's accuracy by its grouping ability, just as they judge target rifles; the hunter is concerned only with the field accuracy of his weapon—a horse of entirely different color. The accuracy of all hunting arms should be evaluated chiefly on the result of the first shot fired from a clean, cold barrel. True practical field accuracy should be judged by the first shot's deviation from the normal center of impact under the great variety of extremes in temperature and weather as encountered in nature's great outdoors.

A favorite target of many gun writers, and one of the rifles most often pointed out as a horrible example of inaccuracy, is the now-discontinued Remington Model 81 autoloader. I doubt that many writers have ever given one of these rifles a fair test, most of them feeling perfectly justified in dismissing its accuracy potential just by examining the arm. The barrel can be moved perceptibly by the fingers, and the whole works slams back and forth with each firing cycle. Everything is wrong except the results it produces. Now it just so happens that there are two of these rifles in my own family, and day in and day out, year in and year out, hot or cold, wet or dry, they will put their first two shots within two inches of dead center at two hundred yards. The third shot, fired after a ten-minute pause, will form a three-shot group which can be covered by the palm of the hand. These rifles do *not* have telescope sights, and I might add that the third shot is of little concern to the whitetail hunter. These rifles are both of 35 Remington caliber, and their bullets seem to home-in on a deer like guided missiles.

It is patently unfair and misleading to condemn a hunting rifle on its multi-shot, rapid-fire grouping ability. Woods rifles seem to throw their first shot or two about as close to center as do the average over-the-counter bolt-action rifles; it's the succeeding shots that rapidly open up the group. I will go so far as to say that, with the care and use given it by the average hunter, the woods rifle may deliver better practical field accuracy than will the average bolt-action rifle. Except bolt-action rifles equipped with custom laminated stocks, the one-piece stock which stiffens the weapon into a chipmunk hitter can warp sufficiently over a damp period to make the rifle a cow misser. A slight change in the guard-screw tension can cause more than a twelve-inch shift in the 200-yard impact center, and if a guard screw works really loose it can cause the shots to scatter all over the pasture. Arms writers should be careful to state that the modern bolt-action hunting rifle, under conditions of reasonable use, care, and adjustment, will generally deliver better accuracy than other types. Woods rifles, it may be remembered, rarely shift their impact centers radically, and, unless you drop yours over a cliff or back a truck over it, it may never perforate a distant woodchuck but it will never miss a deer.

When a new rifle is acquired for hunting purposes it is necessary to sight it in before any attempt is made to use it, and periodic checks are required thereafter to determine if the point of impact has shifted, and if so, to make the necessary corrections. Only an innocent would take his new rifle out hunting without first having checked the sight setting by firing the rifle. It would be a minor miracle if the factory-set sights should exactly coincide with the purchaser's eyesight, choice of ammunition, and desired point-blank range. Secondhand and borrowed rifles are usually so mis-sighted as to cause you to miss a pregnant bull at twenty steps.

The old-time method of sighting-in was to select a small

white rock on a hillside or a knife blaze on a tree, as the aiming point. The shooter would then ease back to a distance he considered proper and proceed to blast away and tinker with the sights until the results were satisfactory. Believe it or not, this method is still used extensively. But there is a better way—the use of standard black-and-white targets on a regular shooting range. Almost every community in the country has at least one organized shooting club with a rifle range, and I advise you most earnestly to join your nearest club. For city dwellers, the club range offers the only feasible means of keeping in shooting practice. There are many other advantages, too numerous to list here, to be gained by membership in such a club, but the able and kindly assistance of experienced members and the thoroughness with which your rifles may be sighted-in are well worth the cost of membership. Proper sighting-in requires that the target be a known and measured distance from the shooter, and the rifle range will provide this requisite.

Choose a clear bright day for the sighting-in job and do your shooting at such times as there is no noticeable mirage, which is usually before nine o'clock on a summer morning. You are warned against the practice of sighting-in on neutral-colored objects at times of poor visibility, as recommended by some writers, who back up their position by explaining that most deer are shot under similar circumstances. This is about as reasonable as having a companion stand beside you to jiggle your arm while you are firing your sighting shots, on the theory that you will probably be seized by buck ague when your opportunity comes. A windless day is best for this shooting, and you will do better to postpone the sighting-in job if a fairly strong wind is blowing.

Before you begin firing, check the bore for obstructions and go over every guard, tang, and sight-mounting screw with a proper-fitting screwdriver, and make certain that all are tight. I cannot overstress the importance of this procedure. Telescope sights and bolt-action rifles are the most susceptible to loose screws and the most vulnerable to their effect, so should be doubly checked.

If your rifle is equipped with iron sights, the front blade should be blackened with the smoke from a wooden match or with shoe polish. It is also a good idea to screw in the auxiliary peep disc with its small target-size aperture, but under no circumstances must you fail to remove it when the sighting-in job is completed. If you have a hood for the front sight, it is not a bad idea to put it on for this firing; but don't fail to remove it for hunting. A sunlit target and a shaded firing point will give you the sharpest contrast possible.

In addition to elevation and windage adjustments, which are properties of all good rifle sights, the telescope has two other adjustments whose proper setting is of the utmost importance to the user—focus and parallax. These last named adjustments must be made before sighting-in, and they may be made at home before going to the range. If you wear glasses while hunting, be sure to have them on while making these settings; and you should have the manufacturer's sheet of instructions at hand. The particular means by which these adjustments are made will vary with the brand and model of the scope, but both can be made while using the same setup. On a clear day, brace the rifle firmly on a table, with the barrel pointed out the window at a small sign, such as an auto license plate. Loosen the locking ring and turn the focus adjustment— usually the rear lens—until the numerals on the target are as clear and sharp as you can make them; then tighten the locking ring. This is *your* focus adjustment and will seldom be exactly right for another person—a thought to remember in lending or borrowing telescope-sighted rifles. The sighted object used in making this adjustment should be approximately one hundred yards distant in the case of the whitetail rifle. Next, check for the presence of parallax by slowly moving the aiming eye in a small circle, which will cause the viewed object to appear to move to the edges of the field of view. The reticle should appear to be glued to the viewed object and move exactly with it. If the reticle seems to move, in relation to the point of aim, your scope has parallax which must be adjusted out. All scopes demonstrate parallax at close ranges, but in the case of big-game shooting the huge image of near-by game in relation to the amount of maximum aiming error reduces this effect to insignificance.

Since factory-loaded ammunition of differing bullet weighs will shoot to quite different points of impact, and even differing types and brands using the same weight of bullet will shoot to slightly different points of impact, the user should always sight-in with the exact brand, type, and bullet weight that he will use in his hunting. One of the most grievous mistakes a rifleman can make is to embrace the false premise that a cartridge is a cartridge so long as it was made to chamber in his gun. Some bullets are designed for target shooting and do not expand at all. There are other bullets designed to blow up on striking a small varmint. There are other bullets designed to expand on small antelope at long ranges where the striking energy is low, and such bullets will not hold together reliably at close ranges. Some bullets are designed with tough jackets and hard cores to give deep penetration on large animals such as elk, moose, and grizzly, and might easily slip through a deer's ribs without expanding at all. There are several bullets expressly designed for the deer hunter, and some are better than others; but all the best ones have two things in common—a blunt or much-rounded nose shape and a generous portion of *exposed* lead at the tip which can be easily scratched with the fingernail. The Remington and Peters *blunt* core-locked and inner-belted loads are the most reliable in performance of any we have used for brush and timber hunting of all large game, from whitetail to elk. Whatever cartridge you decide on, have a plentiful supply on hand when you begin the job of sighting-in. If everything is right, including the shooter, only a few shots may be required. Again, it could take thirty.

Sighting-in should always be done from the steadiest available position. You must always remember that you are testing the *rifle* and *not* your shooting ability. The best possible position is from a shooting bench, which is found on all modern high-power rifle ranges. Most bench-rest shooters support the rifle at forearm and toe of butt stock with small bags of sand, but I am inclined to favor something softer for the hunting rifle, such as a large sponge or boat cushion. Shooting from the prone position with forearm of rifle resting over a bedroll is the next best substitute for the bench rest.

Opinions differ as to the best dead-on distance to which whitetail rifles should be sighted, but one hundred yards is a distance which is commonly favored and is the distance which I recommend to the average hunter. Although many experienced hunters sight-in to the distance which will give a three-inch rise to the bullet at mid-range (my usual practice), I hesitate to recommend that you do likewise. This setting will extend the sure-hitting range of the rifle to at least two hundred yards but will shorten the sure-missing range to about one hundred yards, the point where the bullet is highest above the line of sight, if the let-off is not good and occurs when the sights have drifted near to the top of the target area. Overshooting a deer is so commonplace that anything that could possibly contribute to this soul-deadening occurence might well be avoided by the less-experienced hunter. I therefore suggest that you sight-in your whitetail rifle to be dead-on at one hundred yards. This setting will permit sure hits of deer and black bear to about one hundred and fifty yards with no need for the shooter to make allowance for bullet drop. Many expert riflemen sight-in for this shorter range, especially where turkeys or javelina use in the deer covert. In the case of turkeys, you must strive to take your bird with a head or neck shot, which requires the bullet to strike very closely to the point of aim. Nobody ever shoots more than one turkey in the body with a soft-nose high-power bullet.

Now you are all set up to commence firing the sighting-in shots and only one more thing is needed before you begin—a competent rifleman to do the shooting. This last-named requisite is often the stumper, because the average hunter is such a lousy shooter that he is simply incapable of properly sighting-in his rifle. Until you *know* you have developed the ability to hold closely and fire your deer rifle without flinching, I believe the best procedure is to have a competent high-power rifleman do the shooting for you, if you are so fortunate as to find such a person who is willing to go to this trouble to help you. The only readily-available supply of such men is around a shooting club, and they can save the tyro many dollars in the cost of wasted ammunition, as well as frustration and heartbreak.

There is one drawback to this arrangement—no one can sight-in a rifle to be exactly right for another shooter. Two expert riflemen may shoot the same aperture-sighted rifle, without changing the sight setting, to centers of impact which differ as much as two or three inches at one hundred yards. The groups may be equally good, but no two pairs of eyes will see the sight picture exactly the same. Open iron sights, good only on "stopping" rifles used for dangerous game, usually show such a great variation as to prohibit their use by another person, while telescope sights are seen almost identically alike by everyone. But even if the expert doing the sighting-in sees the sights two inches differently from the rifle's owner, this will be a great help to the man who can't hold three shots within six inches at the same range.

I once sighted-in a friend's pump-action rifle, a notorious buck misser, with only three shots. First, I tightened all the scope and mount screws, beginning with my thumbnail and finishing the last few turns with a screwdriver. After firing two shots at the 200-yard target, I peeked through the spotting scope and saw that the bullet holes were only an inch apart and four inches both high and left. Clicking the elevation knob two minutes down and the windage knob two minutes right, I waited ten minutes for the barrel to cool and then fired a third shot. This bullet centered the bull, and I handed his rifle back to my friend.

No more than three shots are necessary to establish the center of impact for a particular sight setting. In fact, no more than three shots is desirable and a lesser number may be unreliable. One reason for limiting the test group to three shots is the tendency of many rifles to shift their center of impact as the barrel heats up with repeated firing. It is a good practice to let the bolt-action hunting rifle cool five minutes between shots, and I suggest a ten-minute cooling period after each shot is fired from other types of rifles. The nearer we can duplicate the first-shot-from-a-cool-barrel condition for every shot that is fired, the more accurate will be our zero. Another important reason for limiting each group to three shots is the progressive difficulty encountered by the shooter in squeezing off perfect shots. There is a pronounced strain on the shooter and he is unlikely to produce longer strings as accurately fired. A shot known to be badly let off by the shooter should be marked but disregarded, and another shot fired in its place.

Any time you get three-shot groups larger than four inches at one hundred yards, something is wrong with you, yourself, the ammunition, the sights, or the rifle. If you are satisfied that your ammo is fresh, all screws are tight on both gun and sights, and there is nothing visibly wrong with either the rifle or the shooting conditions, then turn the job over to a more experienced shooter if you are not getting results. If this shooter also fails to get decent groups, the rifle should be taken to a gunsmith for correction of the trouble.

While sighting-in, always strive to rest the rifle on its padding in exactly the same way for each shot, and be sure to hold the arm in a uniform manner. Pressing the rifle butt firmly but lightly to the shoulder will produce the minimum effect from the recoil. Holding the rifle slightly away from the shoulder in an effort to lessen the recoil effect will produce the opposite result, and so will pulling the butt deeply into the shoulder. If the weather is warm and you are wearing only a thin summer shirt, you will not experience the softening effect on recoil provided by heavy winter clothing. Under these conditions, and if your rifle is not equipped with a soft-rubber recoil pad, I suggest that you place a folded towel or other similar padding under your shirt, between the butt plate and your shoulder. The position assumed for sighting-in produces *much* more recoil effect than normal game-shooting positions, and the paper target won't take your mind off a little pushing around as would a pair of gleaming antlers.

If you followed my suggestions regarding sights for your

new rifle there will have been changes made which may cause the shots to be completely off the paper at one hundred yards. If your first shot misses the paper and its striking point escapes detection, don't keep blindly shooting. Move up to within fifty feet or so of the target, where your bullets can hardly miss the paper, and roughly adjust the sights to reasonably center the bull. Now when you move back to the firing point your shots will be well on the paper. Once you get a shot on the paper, fire two more before changing sight adjustment. The three shots will outline a triangle and the center of this triangle will be the impact center for that particular sight setting. Let us now suppose that you have fired those three shots and we now walk down to the target for a close examination. We discover that your shots have formed an acceptably small triangle in the lower right-hand corner of the target, and the center of this triangle is seven inches to the right of the center line of the bull and five and one-half inches below the center line of the bull. Remembering that one minute of angle equals one inch at one hundred yards, we will now raise the impact point five and one-half minutes and shift it seven minutes to the left by adjusting the sights.

All first-quality sights—both aperture and telescopic—are provided with continuously variable (micrometer) adjustments which are usually turned by means of a coin-edge or screwdriver. A calibrated dial, or linear scale, operating in conjunction with a reference mark, is another feature of the quality sight, and some sights are further provided with an arrangement which produces an easily felt "click" at each small movement imparted to the adjustment knob or dial. Though not essential, the "click" feature is very helpful when making fine (or final) adjustments. You should know the minute-of-angle value of each graduation on your sight's dial, and the value of each "click," too, if this feature is present. If the instruction sheet is unavailable, you should be able to determine this figure by turning each knob twenty clicks, then firing a shot and measuring the shift in impact center.

All quality sights of modern design have the direction of impact change marked clearly on each knob by an arrow pointing to the words "up," "down," "right," or "left." If the arrows on both knobs point to the letter "L," this will stand for "left" on the windage adjustment and "lower" on the elevation adjustment. Should the letter "R" be encountered on each knob, this would indicate "right" and "raise," respectively. In the case of a sight having quarter-minute clicks, which is most usual, each click will shift the point of impact one-quarter inch—in the direction indicated by the arrow—for each one hundred yards of range. At one hundred yards, each click will shift the striking point one-quarter of an inch, and at four hundred yards each click will cause a one-inch shift.

Returning to the firing point, where we were preparing to adjust your sights for a seven-inch left horizontal correction and a five and one-half inch up vertical correction, we will assume your sights to be graduated in quarter-minute clicks. We now give the elevation knob a turn of twenty-two clicks in the direction indicated as "up" by the arrow, and we give twenty-eight clicks to the windage knob in the direction indicated as "left." Your next three shots will all be definitely in the bull, and probably sufficiently well-centered to call the sighting-in job completed.

Because of necessary manufacturing tolerances in the sight's mechanism, and, in the case of aperture sights, variations in sight radius caused by differences in barrel lengths, graduations of the adjusting mechanism do not always correspond exactly with the amount of movement induced in the center of impact. Therefore, the calculated number of clicks will not always produce exactly the desired amount of shift in group center on the target. Though usually fairly close to calculated results, your first correction—especially where it entails a drastic shift, as in the imaginary case we have discussed—may require a final further adjustment of a few clicks.

An expert rifleman who can outshoot his tack-driving rifle can refine his group center to a very high degree, but if you get a group that is reasonably close to the desired mark—and your rifle is outshooting *you*—you are well advised to quit while you are ahead.

Now that your rifle is zeroed-in, you will tighten any lock nuts with which your sight may be provided, and set all sliding scales to indicate zero as a permanent reference mark for any future changes. Receiver aperture sights having quickly-removable slides are provided with a slender perpendicular screw which must now be adjusted to just barely touch the sight frame. Proper setting of this screw is essential in returning the slide back to the correct zero after it has been removed. Now that you are all ready to go hunting, may I offer one last piece of advice regarding your sight adjustments? *Leave them alone.*

5 ——————————— GAME SHOOTING

Game shooting differs as much from target shooting as a wrestling match differs from a tavern brawl. Targets are generally shot under conditions which are conducive to hits, while game is shot under conditions which constantly conspire to produce misses. A target will reward you with a percentage figure indicative of your relative prowess, but you don't get 40 per cent—or even 99 per cent—of a deer; you either get all or nothing. Target shooting is conducted under definite rules; it's every man and every deer for himself in the game coverts, and the devil take the hindmost.

The three major differences between the two types of shooting are as follows: targets are clearly defined, sharply contrasted, and stationary, while game is seldom clearly visible or well contrasted with its background and is often moving; targets are fired at from conventional, orthodox positions, while game is shot at from every conceivable position from which a firearm can be effectively discharged; practically all target shooting fosters deliberation of aim and a high degree of sight-picture refinement, while he who hesitates in game shooting is lost.

The first thing we will discuss will be the shooting of

124

running game. To be quite specific, we will talk about boogered whitetails, in typical heavy brush, making an all-out effort to escape a bushwhacking. I will go along with the old saying that to hit a running whitetail *anywhere* is not a poor shot. I do not believe there is a man alive who will draw blood with more than half his bullets if he tries for every chance offered by running whitetails. We have hunted for many years, in many places, and with many other hunters. We have killed many running deer over the years and we have also had many misses. Except at near bayonet ranges, or on those rare occasions which catch the game out in the open, when a running whitetail falls the shooter will have no more idea where his bullet landed than will his representative in congress. Therefore, no sportsman worthy of the name will shoot at a running whitetail unless (a) the animal is already wounded and is attempting to escape, or (b) unless the shot offered appears to be a good one which promises to be well within the shooter's ability, and then only when (c) the rifle used has the power to kill the deer humanely with just about any solid body-hit. This is why the more astute gun writers urge deer hunters to use elk rifles and elk hunters to use moose rifles.

The last running whitetail I shot was quartering away toward my left at about a hundred yards. The 200-grain 35 Remington bullet struck center on the left haunch, which is about as poor a place to shoot a deer as I can think of but about what you can expect when you cut down on departing whitetails. To users of "pea shooters," this is rightly considered to be only a crippling shot which will result in a wounded deer that will hobble off to die a lingering death. This buck didn't drop his flag or miss a stride, but I knew instantly that he was hit because he swerved quickly to the left and noticeably slackened pace as he entered the brush. My bullet had smashed the thigh bone, exited from the ham and reentered the flank, crossed the body cavity, then exited about center of the rib cage on the right side. He took a bit of trailing but soon bled out. At the time I took this shot I had every reason to believe that the buck had been wounded by my companion, but this proved not to be the case.

The beginner who has yet to see a whitetail over his sights will be quite cocky and self-confident. He can hit a tin can at fifty yards, so how in the world could he miss a great big thing like a deer? I'm not yet wise enough to give a cut-and-dried answer to that question, but I can assure him that *only* beginners have never missed a deer. I was a competitive small-bore shooter before I ever hunted deer, but I have missed several setups, including one heartbreaker at twenty yards. I honestly believe that a whitetail deer is, relative to its size, the easiest creature to miss that God has yet created. Remember that, though many of our writers are poison on running whitetails, it's a damned sight easier to hit one with a typewriter than with a rifle.

Snapshooting is frequently discussed in hunting books and magazines, and there are just as many ideas on the subject as there are writers. I have never known any two authorities to be in substantial agreement on the definition of a snapshot, and most descriptions of it are so vague and ambiguous as to leave the reader even more confused. Most writers fail completely to distinguish clearly between a true snapshot and a hurriedly-aimed conventional shot. In fact, many writers define a snapshot as one taken at the instant the sights fall on the game. This being still a relatively free country, I hereby thrust my neck out to its fullest extent and declare that a snapshot is a purely instinctive shot in which the sights are neither needed nor employed, with the weapon pointed by the hands as it is being raised to the shoulder, and with the trigger released simultaneously with the butt's settling to the shoulder by the trigger hand yielding slightly back along the grip as it pulls the butt into the shoulder. In other words, the piece discharges *as* it settles into the shoulder by the *act* of settling into the shoulder. In my book, I'll string along with the dictionary description of a snapshot and flatly state that any use of the sights at all, or any delay whatsoever in discharging the weapon after the butt has reached the shoulder, definitely eliminates the word "snap" from any connection with the resultant shot. The snapshot is the counterpart of the "hip" shot employed by handgun shooters, wherein the piece, immediately after clearing leather, is discharged from a point well below the level of the eyes, thus precluding the use of the sights. Like the Colt Peacemaker revolver, the best snapshooting rifles seem to point instinctively.

A good snapshooting rifle has a clean crisp trigger, ample weight for the needed inertia, and fits the user like an old hunting cap. When a rifle of ample killing power possesses these qualities, it may go off hunting alone if not kept securely locked in the closet. If your rifle seems to leap to your shoulder with its barrel pointed right on the target, as confirmed by a quick glance down the sight, you will be amazed at your ability to hit deer-size targets to a distance of about forty yards providing you do a little practice. This is the only feasible shooting method known to me for taking fast-moving game at fairly close range in heavy cover, and I have no doubt that this method is often employed by professional white hunters when stopping a charge at point-blank range. Slings and telescope sights are a definite handicap to the snapshooter, and if there is the slightest delay in discharging the weapon after it has settled to the shoulder, you will have little chance of making a hit on moving game.

I discovered snapshooting many years ago down in Mexico, where there seems to be no law prohibiting the roost-shooting of ducks. I was standing out in knee-deep water in a flooded, lightly timbered flat, and the full moon was rising out of the east. The ducks didn't come in until night and they couldn't be detected until they were whistling almost directly over-head, black rockets briefly glimpsed in the moonlight. Having little to lose except my temper and my ammunition, I started snapshooting those low-flying meteors, and I started killing ducks! It was too dark to see the effect of my shots because the muzzle-flash would blind me, but nearly every shot would be quickly followed by a silvery splash which would guide me to my bird. I must have been centering those ducks with my pattern, because I didn't have to chase a single cripple. I once approached a wounded buck to within fifteen yards, and amazed myself by snapshooting a bullet into the exact spot that I had willed to hit, crumpling the deer in midair as it made a dash to escape.

There is quite a bit of psychology connected with snap-shooting, as it is the product of instinct, practice, habit, and the subconscious mind. If you employ the snapshot within the bounds of probable effectiveness—and have faith in its result—you will get a trophy now and then that could have been taken in no other way. And the ability to snapshoot well may save your life someday.

Every shooter must learn to hit stationary targets before graduating to moving ones, and he should begin with regula-tion black-and-white targets. He doesn't have to become a finished match shooter, but, with competent instruction and

Whitetail country

Skyline deer. The bucks are just "horsing around."

Heading for the brush

Courtesy Roy Swann, Corpus Christi Caller-Times

A good day's work for the author and Tom Junior

Right where he fell

If you can't see his horns—she hasn't got any!

Here you can clearly distinguish the scent glands: the light spot at bend of hind leg directly beneath tip of tail and the small white spot just above the hoof on the near hind leg.

Typical buck rub

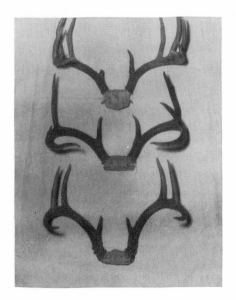

Good examples of mature whitetail antlers

Skinning out the cape

Skinning out a small forkhorn

Hill country bucks and gobblers

A mesquite grove, a proud hunter, and a nice five-pointer
Courtesy Roy Swann, Corpus
Christi Caller-Times

A typical forkhorn, a young gobbler, and a Javelina sow

The author with an exceptional trophy buck taken in 1943

Trophy of a lifetime

Swivels? Who needs 'em if they have a Gunslinger sling? Tom Jr. points the way to camp.

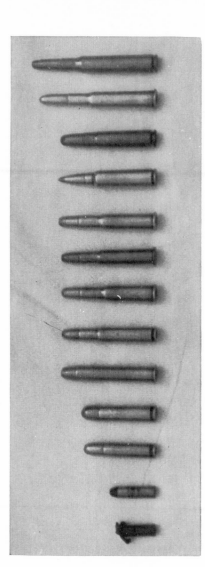

Representative deer bullets and cartridges. LEFT TO RIGHT: Expanded 30 caliber 180-grain bullet recovered from deer; similar bullet unfred; 351 WSL; 401 WSL; 38-55; 30 Remington; 303 Savage; 30-30; 32 Winchester Special; 300 Savage; 35 Remington; 30-40; 30-'06.

Author's rattling antlers, binoculars, and hunting belt. Note the short neck strap on the Bushnell 7x35 "Custom" binoculars. Gunslinger gun sling is shown on belt, just above the Marble 4-1/2" sheath knife. Next, spare clip for the 742 autoloader in a special holster to which is attached the removable staff from the Redfield receiver sight. Below knife is a small hank of leather lacing and a small flashlight in a special holster. Two Avey cartridge holders and a coil of rope (in a Hayes Rope-Holster) complete the belt-carried items.

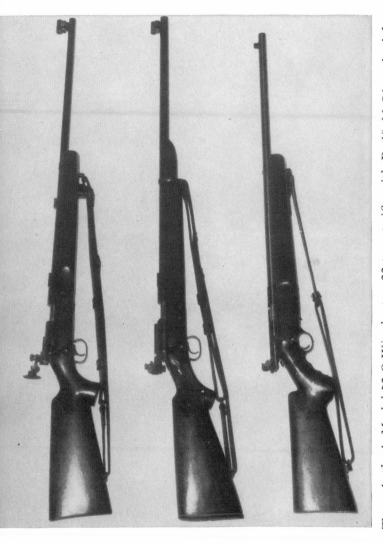

Top: *Author's Model 52-C Winchester .22 target rifle with Redfield Olympic sights and military type sling.* Center: *Tom Jr.'s heavy-barreled Model 52 with Marble-Goss sights and military type sling.* Bottom: *Tom Jr.'s seven and one-half pound squirrel rifle—modified Mossberg Model 144-LS .22 target rifle with Lyman #57 rear sight, Sourdough front sight, and Guntoter sling.*

Three of the author's rifles. TOP: *Dual-sighted 30-30 Savage.* CENTER: *30-'06 Enfield.* BOTTOM: *35 Remington autoloader.*

TOP: Tom Jr.'s plinking rifle—Remington Model 511 .22 caliber with receiver aperture sight. CENTER: Author's long-range magnum rifle (with scope removed) equipped with Hayesling—Schultz & Larsen Model 60 chambered for the 7 x 61 Sharpe & Hart cartridge. BOTTOM: Tom Jr.'s favorite deer medicine—caliber 30-40 Jaeger barrel, Springfield Krag action, stock made by author—front sight is Redfield Sourdough, rear sight Lyman #57.

Three of Charles Hayes' favorite rifles. Top: *Model 8 Remington autoloader in caliber 35 Remington with Redfield sights—aperture rear and Sourdough front.* Center: *Customized Remington Model 721 in caliber 30-'06. Royal Arms' walnut stock with maple fore-end tip and grip cap; Hayesling on 7/8" Jaeger Q.D. swivels. The scope is a Lyman All-American 4x in the fine, streamlined Conetrol mount.* Bottom: *Model 62 Winchester in caliber .22 LR. Lyman 2-A aperture sight on tang.*

Top: *Author's squirrel rifle, Winchester Model 74 with lace-on Monte Carlo cheek rest; Redfield 2-3/4x Bear Cub scope in Weaver Q.D. side mount.* CENTER: *Charles' long-range rig; Savage Model 110 Magnum in caliber 7mm Remington Magnum. 4x Realist scope in Weaver Q.D. top mount.* BOTTOM: *Author's combination plinking, varmint, and turkey hunting rig. Remington Model 700ADL in caliber 222 Remington Magnum. Redfield 2x-7x Variable in Lyman Q.D. top mount.*

Charles Hayes proudly poses with his magnificent trophy, one of the best whitetail bucks ever to come out of the Hill Country.

A fine 10-point buck taken by author in December, 1963, and the rig that "done him in." Remington Model 742 with Weaver K-4 scope attached.

Author glasses distant deer through the K-4 Weaver mounted on his Remington Model 742 Autoloader. Photograph taken in the Nueces River valley below Campwood, Texas.

In this typical whitetail cover, the autoloader is king.

Arkansas deer hunter Robert L. Jones waits hopefully for the drivers to push something his way.

This set of rattling "horns" consists of two "left" antlers from different deer. The picture shows how antlers are held preparatory to crashing them together.

Correct position of hands and antlers at moment of impact. The gloves help in case of a miscue.

Typical Arkansas buck and typical Arkansas deer woods.

This prime javelina fell victim to a Corelokt bullet from the 30-40 Krag.

regular practice, he will firmly establish good shooting habits and will develop muscular coordination as he masters both breath and trigger control. Plinking with a good .22 sporter, along with small game and varmint hunting, will sharpen the shooter's eye and prevent him from fixing the habit of dillydallying over a shot. The whitetail hunter must develop the habit of squeezing-off a shot at the instant his sights hesitate on the spot he desires to hit.

The best practice in the world for the whitetail hunter is the still hunting of squirrels with his .22 rifle. Both fox and gray squirrels will soon bring out the best in a hunter, especially the gray—called "cat squirrel" in the South—which is faster, more wary, more active, and presents a smaller target than his rusty cousin. Rabbits of all varieties are probably the best targets on which to practice the shooting of running game, while the western hunter should cash in on the opportunities offered by rock squirrels and coyotes. The deer rifle should be used on coyotes and can also be used on running jacks. The shooting of stationary targets is a science, but the shooting of moving targets is an art.

Overshooting a deer is such a common occurrence that it is repeatedly discussed in print. Many theories have been advanced in an effort to explain and prevent this tendency, but I have heretofore never seen correctly identified what seems to me to be the primary cause. Open iron sights, whose multiple faults are so legion that I refuse to discuss them, are definitely conducive to overshooting and have long been held to be the prime cause of this frequent fiasco. But some of our more astute writers began to soft-pedal the theory that open sights were the prime villains when hunters equipped their rifles with aperture and telescope sights and still continued to overshoot deer. However, some of our writers keep mistakenly insisting that the problem is purely an optical one, which will be eliminated by the installation of a telescope sight. Experienced hunters have long been aware of the contribution to overshooting provided by a hard creepy trigger and by over-excitement on the part of the hunter, but exactly how these factors correlate is generally unknown. Actually, the primary cause of overshooting deer is the involuntary rising of the arm which supports the rifle, which in turn is the product of intense excitement. This phenomenon can be artificially induced and easily demonstrated by simply standing slightly away from a wall with your arm pendant and supporting your weight for one minute by leaning on the back of the hand. Upon stepping back and relaxing the arm, you will notice the arm rise involuntarily in a most mysterious manner.

A featherweight rifle will accelerate this rise, open sights will often be unconsciously aimed high to begin with, a creepy trigger puts on the clincher, and, if you are a sight dawdler or flincher, some dozing squirrel high in a tree is in much more jeopardy than your intended victim. However, it is quite interesting to scare hell out of a huge trophy buck which you could have easily hit with a brickbat. David Crockett or next year's Wimbledon winner can go right out in the woods and over-shoot a deer under the right circumstances. However, since I don't want any smart aleck reader to ask me how I have come to know so much about overshooting deer, we will consider the subject closed. Incidentally, though, if I ever draw a bead on a fine buck and experience no more emotion than if I were preparing to shoot a tin can, I'll lower the safety, go directly home, and hang up my guns forever.

One of my favorite rifles is a remodeled and restocked En-field 30-'06 military weapon, which I used for many years with the original two-stage trigger reworked to remove the first staₑe of pull and much of the slack. This trigger was nearly on a par with that of the average over-the-counter sporting rifle, but was a long way from being clean and crisp. I grew more and more dissatisfied with it over the years because of a mounting suspicion that it was the primary cause of several bad showings. That trigger finally wrote its own death warrant high on a Colorado mountain one fine October morning when two hunter-altered muley bucks came slipping fast through a stand of quakies, about a hundred and fifty yards from the spruce log on which I sat. I began to gloat over this abundance of venison and decided to give both deer a good sample of the Hayes treatment. The smaller trailing buck was pretty much in the clear but the larger muley was a little farther back in the timber and I knew that I must take him first or not at all. Big Boy would take a few nervous steps followed by a very short pause, but finally he hesitated where his shoulder was well exposed, and I began the trigger squeeze. During the short interval in which the trigger crawled and crept, the buck wheeled his front end sharply to starboard and took off in a new direction. Too late I saw my target remove itself from the crosshairs and I knew my chance was gone even as the rifle recoiled from the wasted shot. I had to content myself with the lesser buck, which paused for a brief moment to re-appraise the situation. I had to lose a fine trophy worth many times the small cost involved before I was sufficiently spurred to have a good trigger installed.

At least half of all the whitetail bucks you will ever kill will be obscured to varying degrees by vines, rank grass, tree trunks, bushes, stumps, limbs, leaves, down timber, or a combination of these things, which goes under the general heading of "brush." Bucks and brush seem to be as inseparable as poker chips and cigar smoke. Many a buck has walked away unscathed because his would-be slayer did not know how to bring him to an instant halt in a brief opening that would have provided a clear shot or else turned down a reasonably good opportunity in the vain hope that the deer would eventually present him with a lead-pipe-cinch shot. There is an optimum time to shoot when man meets game, and only experience will develop that certain something which suddenly tells you, "Now!"

If you live to kill a thousand deer, each will be taken under somewhat different circumstances from all the others. The only circumstance under which I feel reasonably safe in giving blanket advice is where the deer is still quite a distance away but is advancing steadily toward the hunter. If the hunter is well concealed and there seems no possibility of the wind betraying him, he should feel justified in holding his fire until the range becomes certain. However, even in such cases as these, there always remains the possibility of a tattletale squirrel, or another deer crossing the hunter's scent stream, which could spoil everything in a trice. Any time a deer you may want shows the slightest sign that he is in any way aware of you, then you are well advised to shoot quickly, because if he steps behind a bush you will be unlikely to lay eyes on him again. Generally speaking, suspicious whitetails seldom "depart" from your vicinity—they just disappear. If possible, never let a deer get too close to you, and, if you see that he will offer a shot only at very close range, be sure that he is looking directly down your barrel when he steps into the clear. Don't give him a very long look, either.

Unless a deer is already aware of you, smells you, discovers you right under his nose, or you charge at him waving your arms and screaming, it will take two separate sounds or movements—or one of each—to stampede him. The proper knowledge and application of this fact is the key to successful deer shooting. Remember, the first sound or movement detected by the deer will alert him and the second will trigger him into rapid departure. As I have said earlier, you can fail at the very moment that complete victory is within your grasp. Here is a factual illustration.

One of our party, armed with an exposed-hammer, lever-action rifle, took a pre-dawn stand in the edge of a field, near a trail which skirted the fence. As the darkness dissolved into daylight the hunter became aware of a deer feeding slowly toward him, which, at thirty steps, resolved into a huge, heavy-antlered buck. As it was now light enough to use his sights, our hero slowly cocked his rifle and the deer cleared the fence in a bound. The hunter wrongly ascribed this spirit-withering development to plain hard luck, but his own detailed account of the incident provided proof that his failure was the result of ignorance regarding the proper operation of his weapon. The hammer had been resting against the firing pin instead of being retracted to the safety position, and when the act of cocking brought the sear in line with the safety notch there was an audible click which alerted the deer. The next audible click, as the hammer came to full cock, triggered the deer right over the fence. Had this hunter known how to cock his rifle silently, which can be done with ridiculous ease, the game would almost surely have been his.

The successful shooting of deer hinges almost invariably on your becoming aware of the game before it discovers *you*. I will go so far as to say that this is the cardinal rule of whitetail hunting. Unless you scorn all but running shots, never lay your rifle down beside you or drape it over your shoulder by a sling. Always keep the rifle ready, with both hands, whenever practicable, in their proper shooting positions. The first thing you should then do, when you become aware of game, is to cock—or slip the safety on—your gun. Unless you see that the deer will emerge from the brush practically on top of you, or you find yourself in a posture that makes a change of position mandatory, make no movement or sound unless and until the deer reaches a position where he can be taken. Right here is where the men and the boys begin to separate.

If you are a normal person, your eyes will begin watering, your mouth will be wide open and powder dry, your lungs will be fighting for air, and your heart will be pounding so thunderously that it will seem impossible for the deer not to hear it. If you are a man, you will cuss yourself roundly for being in this condition, and by a supreme effort of sheer will power you will keep your wits about you while you proceed with the work at hand. You must always remember that the first sound or movement detected by the deer will bring him to an abrupt halt. If that halt occurs while the deer is protected by brush, you have lost the game then and there.

First, let us suppose that your deer is approaching an opening which will take him several steps to cross. As he steps into this opening you will bring your rifle to bear in one smooth motion. In all probability the deer will detect the movement and freeze, your rifle will buck and roar, and your deer will be down and thrashing. In variation number two, the deer does not notice the movement of bringing your rifle to bear and continues walking. In such a case you speak the word "whoa" sharply, the deer freezes, the rifle roars, and so on.

Now, let us suppose that you must take the deer as it steps across a very narrow opening. You will sweep the rifle to your shoulder and say "whoa" as the comb settles against your cheek, and you will be mighty glad if your rifle fits you properly and is centered on the deer's shoulder as it comes to rest. In this case you can't afford to risk the deer's not seeing your movement and stepping on out of sight, so you must take a lesser risk and be quite certain of halting him. When he is stopped in this way, you must shoot immediately. Any time you deliberately stop a deer be absolutely certain that you have picked the right place, because you'll get no second chance. Never fear a deer's overrunning your stop signal—an unalerted deer stops instantaneously with the sound of your voice.

Whenever you realize that an approaching deer will not offer a shot until he is practically on top of you, you must take a calculated risk and very slowly re-position yourself, if necessary, and slowly bring your rifle to bear. Keep your movements very deliberate, avoid making any sound, and move only when the deer himself is moving and his head is obscured by brush. There is always the chance that the deer will detect your movement, but you will have a better chance than if you should meet him face to face with your weapon reposing in your lap. The same procedure is recommended when a deer approaches you from a direction which will not allow a shot from the position in which you find yourself sitting.

Most authorities recommend that you whistle to halt a walking deer. This is an unreliable method, because you are often unable to whistle due to the extreme dryness of your mouth, and often a deer will fail to be alerted by a whistle because of mistaking it for the call of some new kind of bird. Again, if the deer is the least bit uneasy he will not stop to a whistle until he has gained the protection of the next piece of brush. An unalerted deer will obey the command "whoa" better than will any horse.

The bow hunter should now be able to draw several vital conclusions from the preceding disclosures of a deer's reaction to the hunter. Obviously the bowman, even much more than the rifleman, must beat the deer to the discovery of the other's presence in order for the drawing of the bow to become the alerting movement instead of the triggering movement. The archer should either stand on both feet or kneel on one knee, and keep an arrow ever nocked and ready.

Many authorities will disagree with my recommended shoulder shot, correctly maintaining that it will destroy considerable edible meat. Most writers recommend the high lung shot which calls for a bullet placement just to the rear of the shoulder, on a broadside shot, and from one-third to one-half the way up the chest from the bottom body line. This, too, is a very certain shot, the animal generally running anywhere from fifty to two hundred yards. When—and provided—you find your animal, it will always be completely bled out and there will be no wasted meat. We ourselves invariably attempt the center shoulder shot when the game is positioned broadside and when the range and shooting conditions are such as to rule out the absolute certainty of exact bullet placement. Where a powerful rifle is employed, the center of the shoulder is also the center of the largest vital area on the animal's anatomy—a one-foot circle in the case of a small buck deer. We recommend the center shoulder shot to the beginner in all cases where the game is positioned broadside to the shooter. As you gain in experience, marksmanship, and trailing ability, you may feel inclined toward other bullet placements; but, except for a couple of pounds of wasted meat, a six-inch error in your shooting should lose you no game with the center shoulder hold, and few animals will move out of their tracks if your hold is near perfect. Personally, in our family we hunt for sport and not for meat. We like to see our game go down to the shot and dislike trailing wounded game, and we find the remaining edible meat sufficient for our needs.

A deer quartering even slightly toward you should receive your bullet directly on the near shoulder. Should it be almost facing you, drive your bullet just ahead of the near shoulder into the hollow formed where the neck and shoulder join. There seems to be little difference of opinion regarding these types of shots, and most hunters agree that a shot into the rib cage—directed so as to break the off-shoulder at point of bullet exit—is the best choice for the animal which is quartering away. Where the animal is quartering steeply away, the pea-shooter boys should exchange their weapons for cameras and try for a good photo. The bullet from an elk rifle directed into the deer's flank so as to break the off-shoulder will seldom fail to anchor a steeply quartering-away deer, but deep, reliable penetration is a must for the bullet employed. The powerful-rifle users can try for the withers or root of tail on straight going-away shots, but the peashooter must try for the neck or keep its mouth shut.

Many writers recommend that the bullet be placed, in the case of head-on shots, low in the chest at the base of the neck in what is called the "sticking place." Using heavy rifles, we attempt to center the oval presented by the deer's front end and have never failed to have the animal either pitch forward on its nose, if the shot was at all well centered, or collapse in a heap, if the spine was struck.

Leave the heart shot, taken near the bottom edge of the chest, on or just behind the elbow knuckle, to the "experts." The same is to be said for the neck shot. A deer's heart, roughly the size of a man's clenched fist, lies at the very bottom of the chest cavity almost directly between the forelegs. Though death is certain to the animal shot through the heart, this organ is a very small target, and, if undershot, the only result can be a clean miss or a broken leg, and neither is to be desired. A shot forward of the forelegs will result in either a clean miss or merely a flesh wound in the brisket. A wound to the rear of the heart will result in a very low lung shot, which usually allows the stricken animal to travel a considerable distance. Only when the bullet is placed either high or dead-on will desirable results be obtained when the heart shot is attempted. Regardless of a hunter's fame, his experience has been wasted and his judgment is highly suspect if he recommends the heart shot in preference to the high lung or shoulder shot.

Contrary to common belief, the animal shot in the heart seldom falls to the shot. This is especially true when the forelegs are not broken. The alerted animal, on receiving this shot, normally wheels and dashes madly away, usually in the direction of his back trail and often running blindly. On the other hand, the heart shot usually causes an unalerted deer to jump forward and race away in the direction it was already facing. Deer thus shot will pile up in midstride after running somewhere between twenty and two hundred yards, and, like lung or liver shot animals, will be completely bled out by the time the hunter comes up to them. About as many deer run away, even after receiving a fatal hit, as those that drop to the shot; so the shooter is well advised to keep firing at the obstinate victim as long as it remains on its feet and within sight. You can afford to lay your rifle aside and nonchalantly watch your once-hit quarry depart the scene only when you are *certain* of your bullet placement and are using a powerful rifle.

An animal will usually drop instantly to a solid neck hit, but may suddenly regain its feet and be away in a flash if the spinal column is missed. In this case, unless a large artery has been severed, you will seldom lay eyes on such a deer again. This shot is just too uncertain, and there is the added difficulty of striking such a small target as the neck.

The head shot is one that should also be avoided. A deer's brain is a very small target, and the probability of shattering the jaw or blasting the snout will discourage all but the most brutally thoughtless hunters from attempting the head shot. Aside from humane considerations, a cranial shot will separate the antlers of a trophy head and a near miss can shatter and spoil the antlers themselves.

The hunter should always remember that, with the exception of the liver, all the internal organs immediately essential to life are located in the forward portion of the body, ahead of the diaphragm. The liver lies immediately to the rear of the diaphragm and just forward and above the exact center of the body when the animal is viewed from the side. This organ seems to be almost as immediately essential to life as the heart, and, with the possible exception of causing the animal to hump up and depart more sluggishly, the liver shot will ordinarily produce about the same expiration time and animal reaction—when the organ is badly smashed—as will similar injury to the heart or lungs. The liver lies adjacent to, and is partly shielded by the paunch, and a deliberately-aimed shot for the liver is not recommended. Several deer which we have killed with unintentional liver shots succumbed so quickly that I once decided to make a deliberate attempt to strike the liver of a partially hidden deer with my 35 Remington. The shot didn't come off well and resulted in a gut-shot deer, and only the great killing power of my rifle saved the day.

Except when a ridiculously over-powered rifle—in relation to the game—is employed, such as when a fox, turkey, or javelina shoat is blasted by a heavy deer rifle, the only shots which can be depended upon to kill instantly are those which strike or cause injury to the brain or spinal column of the neck, from the withers forward. Any severe injury to the spine back of the withers will cause paralysis of all members rearward of the point of injury. Any shot which strikes the spine aft of the withers will put the animal down, but a finishing shot will be required. The great arteries leading from the heart, as well as a major nerve center, lie between the shoulder bones, and even a shot which misses bone will be very deadly in this area. When the bullet smashes the shoulder bone on entry to this area, it immediately expands to maximum diameter, which means maximum tissue destruction. Bullet fragments and splinters of bone are scattered throughout the chest area, adding to the debacle and often causing injury to heart and spine as well as to the lungs. A completely unsuspecting animal injured in this way will almost invariably go down and will seldom be able to rise again. Should the opposite shoulder be broken also, the crashing fall and inability to rise will be made certain. When both shoulders are smashed or the spine broken, the animal will go down never to rise again, regardless of its mental state at the time.

We often employ the shoulder shot on a deer which offers us the opportunity for another reason—to fix the habit of subconsciously seeking this bullet placement under the blank-mindedness produced by intense excitement. We often hunt game larger than deer, and occasionally go out for animals which, under some circumstances, could be termed dangerous. In such cases as these the relative power of our rifles—and yours—is greatly lessened, thereby lessening the importance of saving meat as compared to the importance of extracting the full killing potential of the bullet. The broadside shoulder shot we have been discussing is the universally-recommended bullet placement for all dangerous game except elephant and possibly rhinos. When shooting conditions and the hunter's ability permit, the high shoulder shot—taken just above the center line of the body—is the absolute champion game flattener. When placed with accuracy by a rifle of sufficient power, both shoulders and the spine will be shattered, and the animal, for all practical purposes, will be stone dead before it can even begin to fall. This point on the shoulder where the spine crosses is generally referred to as the "T."

Under normal circumstances the hunter should be able to "call" his shot and know at once almost exactly where his bullet has landed. This ability, aquired only through shooting practice, will help to guide his actions in trailing, following, or approaching the animal after the shot is fired. However, the hunter should never closely approach down game in a careless manner or find himself unprepared to take proper and immediate action in case the animal springs suddenly to its feet and dashes away. All deer, and especially whitetails, can move with such lightning speed that a radical shift in their position can occur during the instant of trigger pull. Once, at thirty yards, I slowly brought my rifle to bear on a suspicious buck's shoulder and fired instantly. The deer sprang forward so nearly coincidentally with the discharge that I wasn't sure whether the movement was made with, after, or before the shot. The deer had moved more than half the length of his own body, as I later learned, and received the shot far back in the flank. The 30-'06 slug brought this deer down within five hundred yards, but if a light rifle had been used I would never have known why he ran away. Recall this incident the next time you hear some rocking chair expert belittle the killing power of some highly reputable caliber, claiming that he blasted a deer "right through the chest" and it escaped over the next mountain.

On another occasion, I had a huge buck swap ends so fast I was astonished to learn that my bullet had raked him from flank to shoulder—rather than from fore to aft—because he was almost directly facing me when the trigger squeeze was begun. My son Charley once had a buck jump at the shot, and the high shoulder shot turned into a high hip shot. The 35 Remington slug smashed both hips and the pelvis, and kept going. And that, gentle reader, demonstrates *power*. Regardless of ballistic figures to the contrary, the 35 Remington cartridge has repeatedly demonstrated knock-down and killing power nearly equal to the 30-'06 up to at least one hundred yards, and that's saying plenty.

The four orthodox shooting positions are, in order of their accuracy potential, prone, sitting, kneeling, and offhand. Opportunities for using the prone position will be very rare in whitetail shooting, or any other shooting that is done in brush and timber. The still hunter and those who participate in deer drives will have to take most of their shooting opportunities from the offhand position. The hunter who watches extended openings and feeding areas, which offer less restricted visibility, will get a higher percentage of sitting shots, and all hunters will find use now and then for the kneeling position. Every hunter should strive to take his game from the steadiest position that circumstances will permit him to assume.

The prone position is recommended on those exceedingly rare occasions when the game is rather distant and unalerted and there happens to be no high grass, rocks, logs, or bushes to obstruct your aim. The sitting position is the next most accurate, is much faster and more flexible, and can usually be employed anywhere and anytime except when game is suddenly encountered by the standing hunter at close ranges. Except when speed is of the essence or the game is too close to permit of any nonessential movement, your best bet is to plunk your bo-hind on the ground, place the elbow of the supporting arm over—not on—the kneecap, and rest the arm firmly against the shank *below* the knee. This position will resist much of the tremor induced by buck ague, as well as the chest heaving produced by exertion, and is practically proof against overshooting your game. Under no circumstances should the hunter place his weapon on or against a tree, rock, log, or any other hard object in an effort to steady his aim.

Many writers urge the shooter to make use of any convenient rest, although they correctly warn against placing any portion of the rifle, and especially the barrel, directly in contact with the hard surface of the object used to support the weapon. The hunter is well advised to place his hand, hat, jacket, or other shock absorbing object between the forearm of the weapon and the object used for the rest. Any direct contact between the rifle and some hard object will cause the shot to fly wild, and, if the barrel itself is the point of contact, the ensuing shot may be so far from the point of aim as to escape detection. My own opinion is that, if the shooter's body position is in any way strained, the use of a rest will worsen rather than better the resultant shot. It's a good idea to brace your *body* against a handy tree or rock, but your rifle should remain completely supported by your arms unless a rest for the rifle presents itself that will allow of use without disturbing the rock-steady position of your body. You may easily demonstrate the worth of these statements by standing in your doorway, aiming your rifle at some object in the back yard, purposely swaying your body about an inch, and noting the approximate deviation of the sight relative to the target. Now, rest the supporting hand against the jamb while continuing the one-inch sway and note the greatly exaggerated deviation from point of aim. This demonstration should quickly convince you.

The shooting position most often used by those who hunt

whitetails properly is the sitting-offhand. This position is not listed among the standard ones and is very seldom mentioned, but probably more whitetails are taken from the sitting-off-hand than any other position. This position is more easily illustrated than described. You are sitting with back to tree watching a fresh scrape, and presently you detect a movement from the corner of your eye which slowly resolves itself into a fine buck. You don't move a muscle until the deer pauses with his chest and shoulder well exposed, then you raise your rifle and it suddenly goes off with a roar. How did you do it? Why, from the sitting-offhand position, sometimes called the off-hand-sit.

6 ——————— AFTER THE SHOT

Unless our deer falls to the shot, staggers, flounders, flinches noticeably, hunches its back and departs sluggishly, departs limping or with a flopping leg, it is not always possible to know that our bullet has connected. Often a deer will give little indication of a well-placed hit, and this fact needs to be regularly brought to the attention of the reader. Much that has been written is somewhat misleading, especially in regard to an animal taking off instantly with the shot, veering sharply, or dropping its tail, all such behavior often being expounded as positive proof that the animal was hit. None of these reactions, though they are by no means to be disregarded, are necessarily indications of our deer having received a bullet, and will often cause the shooter a lot of hard work and wasted time in vainly tracking an unwounded deer.

The power of the rifle used and the deer's mental state at the moment of receiving the bullet have tremendous influence on the deer's reaction, and must be taken into consideration when evaluating the probability of one's having scored a hit. The faster a deer is moving and the greater its fright, the less reaction it will display upon receiving your bullet. Also, after receiving one bullet, the deer's nervous system will have reg-

145

istered all the shock of which it is capable, and, until it collapses from loss of blood, the animal will seldom react at all to subsequent and repeated hits from even the most powerful rifles unless the bone structure is broken down—a fact which has caused many inexperienced hunters to condemn a good caliber for supposed lack of killing power.

A deer that is already aware of you will break instantly into a run with the crack of the gun, no matter if you shoot straight up. An unalerted deer will not depart so instantaneously unless he is hit; but sometimes deer *are* aware of you without your knowledge, as they occasionally disguise this fact in order to place themselves in a better strategic position before making their bid to elude you. It is true that an escaping deer will often change course immediately upon receiving your bullet, but he will often do the same thing if your bullet kicks dirt or bark immediately in front of his face. It is true that a bounding whitetail will sometimes drop his flag on receiving your bullet, but a bullet that whistles close to a deer will often spur him into a dead run, if the deer was already aware of you, and the tail will come down automatically whenever this gait is employed. Mule deer will sometimes wring their tails when hard hit but I have never known a whitetail to do this. Though stricken whitetails will occasionally bleat, I personally know of but two instances when this occurred, and both deer were down in the hindquarters and unable to travel at the time.

Slight and instantaneous reactions of the game are often obscured by the muzzle of the rifle rising during recoil and momentarily blotting out the scene, a possibility which must be taken into account by the shooter. One evening at dusk I was returning to camp after joining two other members of our party, and as we stepped around a bend in the soft dirt road we came upon a young forkhorn buck at close range. One of my companions elected to take the shot, and the deer took off rather leisurely, but *after* the crack of the gun. The shooter had no explanation for the result of his shot, and the recoil of his rifle had prevented close and immediate observation. The other hunter instantly pronounced a miss but then decided that the deer was favoring a leg as it made off. I observed a very quick but pronounced flinch on the impact of the bullet, noted that the deer started sluggishly but gradually gained in speed, detected nothing wrong with the deer's legs, and pronounced the animal to have been shot near the heart. I was so certain the deer was fatally hit that I insisted on more than a perfunctory search next morning, which finally resulted in finding the deer dead, shot low and just behind the heart.

The hunter should strive to note and recognize a deer's reaction to receiving a bullet, but rifles lacking in penetration and shocking power may cause such slight reaction as to escape the shooter's notice, or may even fail to produce a visible reaction at all. A thoroughly-frightened deer making an all-out effort to escape will often give no indication of a hit which would have caused a violent reaction from an unsuspecting animal. Unless the striking point of your bullet is positively known to be quickly lethal, a deer that drops immediately at the shot should always be suspect of being able to jump up instantly and depart, as many men have learned to their sorrow when their bullet struck an antler or grazed the skull or backbone. The neck-shot animal is the one most often responsible for this disheartening development. An animal which stands a moment, walks or staggers a few steps, or makes a jump or two before falling, will seldom be able to rise again; but you should not relax your vigilance, as there are notable exceptions to this behavior. Any deer that regains its feet twice after falling will almost certainly have only a broken leg.

The unalarmed deer that freezes momentarily at your shot, and throws its head up alertly before scampering away, was not hit. The deer which has not located the source of the gun-fire may not move until you work the action, but that is equally conclusive proof that your bullet went astray. Your second shot, whether a hit or a miss, will almost invariably trigger your deer into rapid departure. This makes the result of the second shot less likely to be identified by the shooter, and, in common with all shots taken at thoroughly frightened game, marks the only probable situation where a shot from a power-ful rifle could leave the shooter in any doubt as to its result. In our own experience, we have never had an animal fail to give conclusive evidence when hit *anywhere* by the powerful rifles which we employ.

Considering the fact that the average hunter is incapable of trailing an unwounded deer over most types of terrain, the often-heard advice to trail every deer shot at for at least one hundred yards, on the off-chance that the deer could have been fatally hit in such a manner that blood would not appear on the trail before this distance was covered, is not directed toward any type of hunter with which I am familiar. Except over snow or bare wet ground, the average hunter couldn't trail a herd of buffalo through a green cornfield without a heavy blood trail to follow, and a veteran hunter will be using a heavy rifle, prop-erly loaded, which he knows will prevent a well-hit deer from traveling half this distance before leaving blood on the trail. We have hunted country so impervious to an animal's passage that a deer moving two hundred yards could stop and die of old age before a good tracker could come up to it, and I don't believe that Sitting Bull and Hiawatha could collaborate and track a bulldozer through that country unless it were leaking oil.

All the advice I have to offer is based on the use of an adequate rifle, and will not necessarily apply to deer hit by a small-caliber arm. Users of peashooters will be forever plagued with lost and crippled deer, and, if they insist on making their own beds they will, perforce, have to lie on them. If they have gagged at my arms recommendations they may as well be consistent and refuse to swallow any other of my advice.

Only once in my experience have I known of a fatally-wounded deer failing to leave an easily-followed blood trail after being shot by a powerful rifle. This was the buck shot low behind the heart, just mentioned. This failure to leave an obvious blood trail can be squarely laid to the bullet, a sharp-pointed affair designed for long-range shooting and known as the *pointed* soft-point Corelokt. Though one of the best bullets available to the open-country hunter, the sharp point of this bullet left such a tiny entrance hole that practically no blood could come out, and the pointed construction caused the bullet to turn sharply after entry and follow the skin on around to the off-side hip, where it made a noticeable bulge under the hide. This deer was found through a combination of good luck and dead reckoning, as he had traveled more than three hundred yards over hard, dry ground that virtually precluded our following his tracks. We found only one drop of blood, no larger than a pinhead. The bullet performance in this instance, though unique with the 30-'06 caliber, is typical of high-velocity, small-caliber arms.

The hunter's nose and ears can often assist in determining whether he hit or missed his deer. Any time there is a probability that you have scored a hit, you should continue shooting as long as the animal remains in sight. As soon as it has disappeared from sight, you should remain absolutely still for at least ten seconds and listen intently for sound of the departing quarry. If the deer is known to be hit, a sudden silence as it disappears from sight could indicate that it was hard hit and had stopped behind the first cover, or that it had dropped just beyond your sight and that its fall was muffled by soft ground or the sound of your rifle action as you reloaded. A badly wounded deer will often stop just out of your sight, but will usually leave a large pool of blood even if he later summons enough strength to move on. Long-continued sounds of crashing brush will almost certainly indicate a hard-hit deer, and the last such sound heard should be noted well both as to direction and distance, as this clue may prove of great help if trailing should prove difficult. Very often it marks the place where the deer has fallen. The rhythmic drumming of fading hoofbeats may mean that the wound is superficial, but estimating approximately where the sounds faded from hearing may be of help when you begin to trail. The ordinarily-recommended procedure when you know a deer to be hit is to go directly to the spot where it disappeared from view and begin tracking from that point.

Should there be any doubt whether the deer has been hit, your nose will often give the answer. Instead of going straight to the place where the deer disappeared, go quickly to the nearest point which will intercept any breeze blowing from the spot where the deer, if hit, intercepted your bullet, and approach this spot directly up-wind. Should your bullet have passed completely through the animal, you will almost certainly detect the odor of venison.

When a high-power bullet exits from a deer it blows a fine spray of blood and pulverized tissue into the air. This spray, or mist, has a powerful and penetrating odor which can often be detected after fifteen or twenty minutes, if the air is calm. Practically all deer are shot more or less up-wind from the hunter and, unless a very strong wind is blowing or the deer is shot at from a great distance—both rather unlikely—the shooter will almost certainly be able to smell venison if the deer has been transfixed by a bullet from a powerful rifle. I have never yet had this test fail me, and if the shooter makes this test under favorable conditions with negative results he should feel justified in abandoning the search after following the deer's tracks for fifty yards without finding either blood or bits of tissue.

Whenever it is determined that the deer was hit, it becomes incumbent on the shooter to make every possible effort to recover it. If it received your bullet in the boiler-room, you should have no trouble at all in recovering it—just follow the blood trail until you come up to your deer. If the bullet entered from a raking angle and failed to exit, the blood trail should still persist, though normally less copiously, because the relatively-small entrance hole will not allow the blood to escape freely. Look for blood on both sides of the trail, as well as in the trail itself, because the blood may be spurting out under pressure of the heartbeat. Blood on both sides of the trail indicates that the bullet exited. If a very heavy and regular blood trail ends suddenly, your deer will most likely have bled out completely while running, and you will probably find it dead within twenty-five yards straight ahead. It will have run this last distance blindly and will not have turned. A fatally-hit deer which is not bleeding copiously will seldom quit bleeding until it falls, though it may travel an amazing distance. Anytime a light blood trail peters out, the hunter should feel perfectly justified in calling it quits, unless he knows definitely that the animal was solidly hit, or the tracks, if discernible, indicate a hard-hit deer.

In the case of a deer fatally hit by a proper bullet fired from an adequate rifle, I have never experienced a diminishing blood trail. I have seen light blood trails increase to heavy ones and moderate blood trails hold relatively constant; but I personally know of no instance where a deer was recovered when a light to moderate blood trail played out. (This statement does not apply to cases where peashooters were employed.) Also, I have never seen an instance where a deer hit *anywhere* with a powerful rifle didn't give instant and visible proof that it had been hit.

Although this chapter is chiefly intended to benefit the average urban hunter, the reader must not imply that knowledge of woodcraft and sign reading is unnecessary. Every tiny bit of trail knowledge and woodlore will be of great help to you in every phase of outdoor activity and will make your hunting more profitable, as well as more enjoyable. At the same time, good shooting and a powerful, properly-loaded rifle, will help make up for a hell of a lot of ignorance about tracks and signs.

As you track a wounded deer, always keep a sharp lookout ahead and be ready for instant action should you detect your quarry attempting to escape. Sometimes the wounded animal will be standing or lying in plain sight while the hunter struggles slowly along a difficult track. When you come upon a deer lying with its body pointed away from you, there is no need to start shooting hastily, because the deer will be unable to rise no matter how alertly it holds up its head. Wounded deer lying thus have fallen while trying to put more distance between themselves and their pursuer, and are finished. The deer that lies down deliberately will first turn and face his back trail, and, though he may later be unable to rise, such was not the case when he first lay down.

A deer that looked as big as a moose when you cut down on

him will look mighty small stretched out on the ground, and is often difficult to see. It is amazing what a small gray ball a dead deer makes when he pitches and rolls under a low cedar tree.

Unless a deer is badly wounded, it will place its feet just slightly to right and left of the direct line of travel. A staggering deer will leave a zigzag trail like that of a drunken man trying to walk a chalk line. The track of a deer walking normally will show only the hind hoofprints, because the animal places his hind hooves almost exactly in the prints of his forefeet. Trotting or walking very rapidly, the deer will place the hind feet slightly ahead of the forefeet and all four hooves will print. A bounding deer will print all four hooves in a tight group little larger than the crown of your hat and these groups will be quite a distance apart. A hard-running deer will usually hit the ground at intervals of twenty feet, the toes will be widely separated, and the individual prints will be strung along, somewhat apart. One forefoot hits the ground first and the other is placed somewhat ahead of it, then the hind feet pass around the forelegs and print well ahead of the forefeet. The faster a deer is traveling, the wider will be the spacing between the toes.

A broken foreleg will hamper a running deer very little, and, unless it is flopping, will seldom be noticed by the unskilled observer. A broken hind leg is a different matter, and definitely hinders a deer's progress. Even so, a deer can run from now on with a broken hind leg—and much faster than you can. You will have little chance of recovering a leg-shot deer unless it bleeds to exhaustion; but this does very often happen. Anytime the blood trail plays out on a leg-shot deer you will be very unlikely to see him again, unless a dog is used to trail him down. Muscle wounds, including the heart, will leave bright blood on the trail. Dark blood indicates a gut-shot deer and the flow is seldom copious, although splashes of stomach content often appear in the trail of an animal so shot. Light, frothy blood indicates that the animal is lung-shot, and this discovery should bring rejoicing to the hunter's heart, because there is almost the certainty of a dead deer await-ing him at the end of the trail.

A deer will favor an injured leg, and soft ground will reveal a lighter print made by the injured member. The print of a foot that is definitely out of position, or a drag mark in the trail, will confirm the diagnosis of a broken leg, and blood will frequently appear in the print made by this member. Sometimes the point and extent of a wound can be roughly estimated by the appearance of blood smears on brush along-side narrow passages in the trail. The color of this blood, as well as the height of the smears above ground, will help in estimating the type, point, and severity of the wound. Gut-shot deer seldom bleed freely and a deer shot high in the lungs may show little or no blood for the first few jumps. Frothy blood from an animal's nose is often the first substantial sign from a lung-shot deer.

The average hunter, unskilled at reading sign, will have very little chance of recovering any deer that is able to travel any considerable distance. Unless you are a skilled tracker, the only deer that you will have a good chance of recovering will be one that has received a quickly-killing jolt from a powerful rifle. When the blood trail is through, so is the aver-age hunter. A wounded deer with plenty of vitality left will double back on its trail and do everything possible to elude you, and it will finally head for the thickest and roughest cover in the area. As the hunter gains experience he will also gain the desire to do all his hunting *before* he shoots and will learn to avoid broken legs and gut shots as he would avoid two mothers-in-law.

The whitetail hunter should normally operate separately from his hunting partner but keep within summoning distance. When faced with a difficult trailing job, he should call his partner to him by some such prearranged signal as a blast upon an empty cartridge case. Your partner can probably help you to find your deer and certainly can help in the event you do find it. Where two men are engaged in trailing, one should do the actual trailing while the other stands at the last-known position and keeps his eyes peeled and his rifle ready in the event the deer tries to move out ahead. As the trailer uncovers a new bit of evidence, the watcher can move up and mark it.

Unless a deer is well past you when he receives your bullet, he will most often, if still able to travel intelligently, circle sharply and endeavor to go back over the trail by which he has just approached. As a general rule, he will radically change direction the moment he is out of your sight, especially if he is hard hit. If he is by then in a dying condition, he will seldom change course again—a very good thing to remember if you become confused while trying to unravel his trail. If darkness is near at hand you should press the trailing job to the limit of your ability, and never fail to plainly mark the last place that sign was found. This mark will be of help when you return to resume the trailing job next morning, especially if rain, snow, or heavy dew should partially or completely obliterate the trail in the meantime.

A gut-shot deer will almost invariably hump his back upon receiving the bullet, and a deer that humps his back on being hit is almost invariably gut-shot. A shot in the liver may also result in a pronounced humping of the deer's back, and often the animal will jump a few steps forward and then stand in a hunched-up position, with drooping head. If you don't bust him again, and in a better spot, you will have the devil to pay if the deer once gets out of your sight and a trailing job is to be done. A gut-shot deer that dies and lies unfound all night will almost certainly be spoiled by next morning. This also applies to a deer killed with any bullet placement when the weather is warm. A deer that dies from a shot forward of the diaphragm may possibly be edible if the night is a very cold one, but as a rule the antlers will be all that can be salvaged. However, a small deer has a much better chance of remaining sweet than has a large fat one that requires a much longer time to cool out.

I have received several valuable tracking lessons from a friend who has spent fifty seasons in the deer coverts and who is the most highly-skilled woodsman I have ever known. This man has killed so many deer that, were his total bag divided by his fifty seasons, his average annual kill might give the impression that he started each season in Alaska and worked down through every state permitting a two-deer limit, winding up in Guatemala. He has very sensitive ears and frequently hunts with a very light rifle, out of consideration for others in the vicinity who might be similarly afflicted. Aside from a frequent confusion as to direction, which often leads him quite innocently into areas where deer are zealously husbanded and extremely plentiful, this man is a peerless woodsman. He played a part in the little incident I am about to relate.

I have previously mentioned the buck which jumped forward at my shot and received the bullet far back and very low in the flank. This shooting occurred at twilight, and the deer, after being hit, quickly came to a brief halt behind screening brush and stood a moment with his back humped up and his head drooping. Then he started off sluggishly, but gaining speed with every bound, and my second shot went right over his back. He was running noisily until he put a thick cedar between us, then all sound suddenly ceased. I was very quickly around the tree and surveying the area where the sound had stopped, quite naturally expecting to find my deer lying at this spot. There was no deer anywhere to be found, and I was at a complete loss to explain how the deer could possibly have gotten out of my sight in one brief moment in this almost completely-open spot. Though it had now grown too dark to see the ground clearly, I could tell that there were at least no large blood splotches in the vicinity, and I went dragging into camp feeling discouraged and not a little foolish. I realized that I had a long and probably difficult trailing job ahead of me, with only a spoiled deer to reward my efforts.

During the night, the friend of whom I have spoken arrived in camp to join our hunting party, and, after hearing my sad story, kindly offered to help recover my deer. The next morning, as we approached the scene of the previous evening's fiasco, I was busily giving a run-down of the happenings, while my companion's eyes were sweeping the ground. Suddenly he interrupted me to point out the place where the deer had cut sharply to the right the moment he had placed the tree between us. Following the almost invisible tracks at a fast walk, my friend showed me how the buck had gained the shelter of a tiny cedar seedling and had then taken off down the same trail by which he had approached me, but in the opposite direction. When we came on the first spot of blood in the trail, my friend immediately and correctly stated that the deer was gut-shot, confirming a suspicion which had been gradually growing in my own mind. We soon came upon the dead animal about five hundred yards from the spot of the shooting, but the night had been warm and all that I recovered were the antlers.

I was still a relative beginner at deer hunting in those days, this buck being only my sixth kill; but I learned several important lessons that day, both from the buck and from my helpful friend. Both you and I learn something from every deer we kill, and if I should happen to know more of deer hunting than you it is only because I have killed more deer than you have. But both of us, unless you happen to be most expert, will have to bag a lot more deer before we can read sign like my woodsman friend. Even today I believe he could work out any trail in half the time it would take me to do it.

I've tracked down many wounded deer since that day, but most of them have been shot by other hunters. I sometimes toy with the idea that the better the deer hunter, the less proficient at trailing he is going to be. But this thought gives me a rather uncomfortable feeling, so I just switch to some other line of conjecture. I don't believe I have ever failed to find a recoverable deer, but there is always a lot of luck connected with this kind of record. Sign reading requires close observation, great perseverence, and lots of practice, and you should frequent the nearest patch of woodland cover to practice the trailing of rabbits, coons, squirrels, and birds, if you have no ready access to big-game coverts. And never pass up an opportunity to receive tutelage under an experienced woodsman.

The hunter is often advised as to the circumstances under which he should either press the trailing of wounded game or sit down and wait for it to stiffen up. A very experienced hunter *may* be able to determine which course of action to pursue, but the less experienced is well advised to get on the trail at once. Many veteran hunters, myself included, are quite skeptical as to the advisability of ever relaxing pressure on your wounded quarry, except in the case of potentially-dangerous game. There is plenty of evidence that blood will flow more copiously and with less tendency to coagulate if a wounded animal is stimulated by fear and exertion. If the average hunter feels inclined to continue the pursuit after the blood trail has petered out, he will give the pursued animal plenty of time to stiffen up while he labors slowly along unraveling the trail.

The native moose hunter is often cited as an example for the whitetail hunter to follow. His reported action of sitting down, after a bullet has been planted in his moose, and smoking a cigarette or brewing himself a pot of tea, may be applicable to the more bovine-like moose, but not necessarily to a deer. The fact that these hunters employ fairly light rifles, relative peashooters when turned on such large animals, and the fact that the stricken moose usually goes but a short distance before lying down, are factors which should be absent in the case of the deer hunter. Also, the normal receptivity of the ground to an animal's footprints is quite high in moose country, and the size and weight of the animal makes its trailing a relative picnic to the skilled tracker.

It is a revelation to watch a skilled tracker operate. On soft ground, he will measure and study the hoofprints for individualized splits, chips, and other identifying characteristics, so that he can follow the trail through a maze of other deer tracks. Over hard, dry ground, he will note pebbles that have been disturbed, even grains of sand. He will circle the area of the suspected trail and endeavor to get the light on it from some angle that might reveal a trace of evidence that an animal has passed over it. Over forest litter, the expert tracker will detect the slightest disturbance to leaves and twigs. A moist leaf observed among dry ones will indicate that it has recently been turned bottom-side-up, and even in very dry country the freshly overturned leaf may have a slightly different shading from those long undisturbed. The expert tracker will probe with his fingers under pine needles for the imprint of a hoof where there is no visible surface evidence of the animal's passage. A suspected dark spot on a rock may be rubbed with a moistened finger, to see if it will dissolve into blood.

Every deer you trail will increase your ability to trail the next one, but few people will ever get as many opportunities to practice as my woodsman friend, and few of my readers will ever be so fortunate as to receive tutelage under such a man. But spare no effort to learn as much about sign reading as you can, and overlook no opportunity to practice this art every time you step into woodland cover.

Though the art of woodscraft embraces all there is to know about every living thing in nature, and volumes could be devoted to the subject and but barely scratch the surface, every serious hunter is urged to add a good book on this subject to his outdoor library. No hunter can hope to learn more than a small fraction of the available knowledge, but everything learned will be of tremendous value. Still-hunting success, especially, is so closely related to the hunter's woodsmanship that the average nimrod can seldom make this form of hunting profitable. The better the woodsman, the better the hunter.

7 ——————— WHEN THE DEER IS DOWN

The average whitetail buck is as heavy as you are, and probably has five times your strength. He also has five times your speed, and, when hurt and frightened, has five times your determination to win the desperate game which is being played at his expense. To closely and carelessly approach such an animal, unless it is positively known to be beyond physical activity, is the height of folly—a fact that can be confirmed by numerous thoughtless hunters who have known the desperate sense of helplessness caused by the slashing hooves and goring antlers of a fear-crazed buck. Although the animal devotes every act of its life to escaping its enemies, as long as there is hope, the buck which senses the end may devote the last act of his life to the destruction of his nemesis.

A hunter is very rarely deliberately injured by a deer, but such cases are not entirely unknown. Most such instances are the direct result of the deer's attempt to escape. I personally know of a hunter who took a wild, backward ride on a buck's back, and the episode almost ended tragically. This man carelessly straddled the fallen buck, which he though was dead, and prepared to start the gutting operation. Without warning, the buck came to its feet, inadvertantly catching the tine of an ant-

161

ler in the hunter's groin, then headed for a fence about thirty steps away. The hunter very nearly lost more than his overalls and some hide when the tough barbed wire strands separated him from the wildly-plunging buck.

Like this buck, very few deer ever entertain any idea toward their enemies other than escaping them, but the larger any animal is in relation to its persecutor, the more potentially dangerous it becomes. If rabbits grew to weigh several hundred pounds, there would likely be reports of some hunters getting a good kicking around. A hunter once told of taking hold of a yearling buck's horns, and being literally undressed when the deer whipped both hind feet up past his ears and then swept them backward, ripping the man's clothing to shreds. Then there is the oft-told story of the hunter who draped the sling of his new rifle over the downed buck's antlers, and watched in dismay as his rifle was dashed against every tree the deer passed until both disappeared forever from his sight.

Should you find your deer still alive and alert when you approach it, I suggest that you circle to one side and shoot it through the lungs from a broadside position which will not allow the bullet to enter back of the diaphragm and result in the dreaded gut shot. Our object is to definitely anchor the animal, but also to keep the heart beating as long as possible, so that a minimum of blood will be left in the tissues. In other words, the meat is best when the animal bleeds to death. "Sticking" the deer or cutting its throat will not be necessary if the deer is shot in the forward section of the body cavity, because a shot in this area with a high-power rifle bullet will incur such destruction to so many blood vessels that the total blood flow will equal that produced by either sticking or throat cutting.

Sticking is much to be preferred to throat cutting, if the

reader chooses to disregard my advice to employ the much safer course of lung shooting. A throat-cut deer certainly doesn't photograph to advantage, and this huge rip in the hide will surely be regretted if you should decide to have the head mounted. The sticking place is located low in the very center of the chest, at the base of the neck—a soft and somewhat sunken spot found directly above the apex of the vee formed by the collarbone. The heart lies lower than this spot, but the huge artery that carries blood from the heart rises directly behind, and very close to, the sticking place. With the animal lying flat on its side, the knife should be held with blade straight up and down but with the back up. The knife should be thrust into the center of the sticking place but the point should angle upward, and when the blade is fully entered the handle should be lifted sharply, thus sweeping the blade across the artery and thereby completely severing it with one quick motion.

A deer dies as it lives, with both eyes open, and immediately following death its eyes will begin to glaze. You should never approach your deer more closely than is necessary to clearly observe the eyes, unless you know positively that it is dead. Stand facing the animal, but somewhat off to the backside, so that the eyes will be plainly visible but you will not be in the animal's direct line of departure should it suddenly rise and run away. Should the air be so full of moisture as to leave the eye-glaze test in doubt, you may finally approach the animal's backside, and, leaning over as little as necessary, rap a hind shin sharply with your rifle barrel or with the back of your hunting knife. A poke in the eye with a very long stick is a good test for a grizzly, but such a drastic measure shouldn't be required to determine whether a deer is still alive. Ordinarily, the eyes will glaze very quickly, and this will be positive proof that the animal is quite dead. However, don't be too hasty in getting at the deer with your knife, because one of the most frequent types of hunter accidents is caused by a convulsive kick from a dying animal which strikes the knife or knife-arm and causes a serious gash. Also, for a short time following death, certain nerves can trigger violent muscular reactions when stimulated by the knife.

The first thing that you should do, upon determining your deer to be good and dead, is to drag it to an open spot—if necessary—where you will have plenty of room for the dressing operation and to turn the animal in such a position that escaping blood will drain away from the carcass. Your second task will be to remove from the hind legs the four scent glands which are imbedded in the skin and which will come off with the hide. It is most important that you do not touch these glands or their surrounding areas with either knife or fingers, because to do so will impart a most unpleasant flavor to the meat—the primary cause of the "I don't like venison" brotherhood. Pinch up the skin a couple of inches *above* each gland; then cut through the skin and remove each gland, along with a generous slab of hide large enough to include the whole tainted area. Discard these patches at a distance from the scene of operation which will preclude their contact with the meat while the carcass is being rolled and turned during the gutting operation.

The reader should be aquainted with the objectives desired in handling any animal which is to be used as food. These include removal of all blood possible from the tissues, the quick cooling of the carcass by rapid elimination of the body heat, and avoidance of contacting the meat with any contaminating substance, such as hair from the animal, wastes from colon or bladder, content of stomach or intestines, and the scent glands, if any. Furthermore, the carcass should be protected from sun, rain, and from blowflies, and should be hung as soon as possible in such a manner as to prevent contact with the ground. Hanging permits the necessary free circulation of air and also allows the juices which ooze from the meat to drain away.

When the animal is bleeding externally, the carcass should be turned, if the ground is sloping, in such a manner that the blood will drain away. As soon as the bleeding has greatly diminished, the gutting operation can be begun. Supposing the animal to be a male, your first operation after removing the scent glands should be to cut off the testes and slice the penis away from the belly to the point where it emerges at the rear of the pelvic girdle. Now tie a hard knot in the penis, so that no bladder fluid will seep out to taint the meat. After this operation, the male and female animal will be treated the same. Make an incision at the root of the tail and circumscribe the entire area closely surrounding both the anal opening and the sexual organ so that these members are completely free of the exterior body and remain connected only to the tubes and ducts which emerge through the pelvic opening. Include the small wedge of muscle tissue which lies between the penis and the anus of the male. Now turn the animal on its back.

Starting about three inches forward of the pelvis, and holding the knife with blade edge up, rip the body open along the entire belly line, clear to the throat at the base of the head. The bladder lies near the front edge of the pelvic plate, so be *very* careful to cut only through the abdominal wall as the opening incision is made. You had better have your sleeves well rolled up before starting a gutting job, because the old saying, "bloody as the hunter," is a perfectly apt description. When you have carefully split the belly a couple of inches, push the first two fingers of the left hand into the opening with the palm turned down. Your knife is inserted at the fork between the fingers, with edge up, and the fingers will travel ahead of the blade and keep the guts pressed away from the blade so they will not be cut or punctured. When you reach the breastbone, or sternum, which is really cartilage, you can dispense with the guiding fingers, and, taking hold of the knife handle with both hands, you can easily rip right up through the chest. The breastbone of even a large animal is easily cut, unless you are unwise enough to be using a dull knife or a miniature imitation of a hunting knife which some "expert" has advised you is "plenty big enough." The deer can be held on its back by propping a foreleg with your knee.

After the rib cage has been opened its entire length, keep splitting the carcass right on up the neck clear to the jaws. Along the gullet, or "goozel," cut just to one side, so that the gullet will not be cut, but you will sever this large tube at the voice box between the lower jaws. Now split straight down through the muscle between the hind legs, thus exposing the pelvic plate, then carefully extend the opening incision to join this pelvic split. You now have only one major problem remaining—the splitting of the pelvis itself. Expert meat dressers have a knack for unjoining this pelvic bone which requires no hacking or pounding, but you will probably find it necessary to cut a short club, or amputate a foreleg, to be used for driving the knife through this bone. A stone can be used, but this is generally hard on the knife and even harder on the hand used in holding it. Place the knife edge nearly parallel to the bone and never strike so hard that the blade penetrates deeply enough to cut into the colon, which lies directly beneath the bone. When the pelvic plate has been cut across its entire length, the pelvic arch can be broken by grasping each hind leg by the shank and pressing the legs apart with your weight. Sometimes you may have to place a log or rock directly under the rump before the pelvis can be broken.

Now the way is completely cleared for the removal of the entrails, and the animal should be turned crosswise to the slope of the terrain, so that the entrails will roll down and away as they are loosened. The entrails will be removed as one unit from throat to rectum and you will begin by ripping out the gullet. Next, the heart and lungs are cut loose from their moorings, then the diaphragm, a thin fleshy membrane which separates the body cavity into a forward and rear compartment, is cut loose completely around the rib cage where it is fastened. As you work down the animal from head to tail, you will cut, snip, and pull loose all organs from their points of attachment, which will be generally along the back. Finally, the last of the "innards" will have been ripped and cut loose from the pelvis, and the gutting job is finished. If there is clean, dry grass or moss handy, you should wipe out the inside of the carcass and also wipe your hands, arms, and knife to the best of your ability. If the animal is exposed to the sun, your next move will be to drag the carcass into the shade. If you have spent over twenty minutes on the entire job, you were fumbling around.

If your deer was shot in the body cavity forward of center, you will have found a great deal of blood floating around in the chest cavity, possibly in the form of huge, liver-like clots. This demonstrates the futility of sticking a chest-shot deer, as it will always be found to have completely bled out internally. And, in any event, all blood flow ceases immediately when the heart stops beating. Some hunters are rather fussy about getting all blood possible from the meat, and these men will turn the gutted carcass over on its belly, pump the legs up and down, and massage the limbs with their hands, in order to wring additional blood from the tissues.

The heart and liver should now be trimmed from the unwanted viscera and placed in a small plastic bag, which you should have carried in your pocket for this purpose. If no bag is available, cut a two-foot willow limb of small diameter, or one of some other sweet-flavored wood, just below a fork. Trim the forking branch to about three inches and spit the heart and liver on the main limb, which allows them to be easily carried.

If you wish to have the head mounted, you should make a few variations in the gutting process just outlined. In this case, you should not split the belly past the forelegs and the gullet should be severed at the point where it enters the chest. After the gutting operation is completed, you should make a cut in the hide which completely encircles the frontal chest area. This circumscribing cut will begin at the base of the brisket, immediately in front of the forelegs, and will be made at right angles to the belly cut, crossing the top of the body at the withers, which is the slight hump at the top of the shoulders directly above the forelegs. Now, starting at the withers, split the hide down the center of the back of the neck to the back of the skull, and then skin out this forward section of hide, which is called the cape. Work the hide loose from the flesh at the shoulders and continue peeling the neck down to the skull; then turn the cape back over the head and remove the head by cutting all the way around the neck to the bone and then twisting the head off. The remaining length of gullet should then be removed.

It will be assumed that you will take this head and its attached cape immediately to the taxidermist, or at least to cold storage. The head and cape must be kept as free of blood as possible, and I suggest that you wipe off all blood stains with a damp cloth before they set permanently and cannot ever be entirely removed. Heads and capes will deteriorate so rapidly that the wilderness hunter will be put to an unbelievable amount of work and trouble in preserving them. This includes the complete skinning-out of the skull, including ears, eyelids, lips, tear ducts, and nostrils, as well as the removal of the brains and all flesh from the skull and inside the mouth. A vee cut from the back of the skull to each antler will be made so that the cape can be removed over the antlers, and the cape will have to be completely fleshed, salted, aired, and partially dried. The proper preservation of trophies is one of the many duties of a professional guide, and is just one reason why a guide is needed when sportsmen hunters attempt serious trophy hunting in wilderness areas.

If your deer was gut-shot, stomach content and waste matter will probably be well smeared around in the body cavity. Under these circumstances, you are advised to wash out the inside of the carcass, if water is available. Water promotes the deterioration of meat, and washing is therefore not recommended in cases where the deer has been cleanly killed and handled. A gut-shot deer, or one that has lain ungutted for a considerable length of time, will never have as good a flavor as a cleanly-killed animal that has been well bled out and gutted within a reasonable time after its death.

Now that you have your deer gutted and pulled into the shade, you must decide whether it will be carried out of the covert within a short time or will have to remain for several hours, possibly over night. In the latter case, the deer should be hung, and about the best you will be able to do in that direction is to swing the rump clear of the ground, unless there is someone to help you. The deer will have to be dragged under a stout limb that is at least head high, and your rope passed over this limb and tied to the head or antlers. Pass the end of the rope two more times around the limb, so that you will be able to hold all upward gains, then start lifting the deer by the head with one-arm surges, while instantly snatching out the slack in the rope with the other hand. Unless the deer is very large and heavy you should be able to swing the rump clear of the ground by this method.

If the animal is very heavy, leave trailing from the antlers as long a tail of rope can be spared. After maximum height has been attained by the direct lift method, possibly the tail of rope can be passed over a limb off to one side, and then pulling on this rope will provide considerable leverage, which should raise the carcass a little higher off the ground. Even getting the front end of the animal clear of the ground will help, and often the deer can then be turned belly down and the hind legs be braced outwardly, so that no edible portion of the carcass is touching the ground. Be sure to cut several sticks about seven inches long, for bracing open the hams and chest cavity, so that air can freely circulate. Where there are no nearby trees suitable for hanging a deer, about all you will be able to do is make a large pile of brush and roll your deer up on it. Always insert sticks crosswise in the chest and pelvic openings, so that air will get to all inside areas. Tie a hankerchief to the carcass, if it is to be left overnight, in order to discourage predators.

I have read of a number of schemes for raising a deer, but I doubt that all of them are practical. Having hunted and traveled over most of this country without ever having seen any of them put into practice, I am inclined to believe that some exist chiefly in the authors' imaginations. One of the most publicized methods entails a tripod of timbers with the deer tied to the apex. The idea is to raise the deer by alternately moving the legs of the tripod inwardly. There is no doubt but that this setup could be made to work, but all deer coverts do not provide an adequate supply of such timbers, and their preparation would require an ax and considerable expenditure of time and energy. If the hunter is willing to go to the trouble of toting an ax, he might do much better to carry a very light block-and-tackle, which is extensively advertised and made expressly for raising carcasses as large as elk. I once killed a mule deer so large and heavy that the best I could do was to roll it atop a pile of sagebrush; but the carcass survived the night in good condition.

The best advice I can give a man who is faced with the problem of toting out a deer unaided is to go get some help. Despite innumerable accounts in which the hunter nonchalantly hoists a buck to back or shoulders and blithely hikes over a few mountains to camp, only very exceptional men and powerful, trained athletes are capable of such prodigious feats of strength and endurance. Such physical accomplishments, like boudoir experiences, are never minimized in their telling, and most of these long-distance, one-man, big-deer carries are pure malarkey. I am probably the first author to risk disgrace and flatly state that the average city-bred man is incapable of such feats. I am as strong and tough as the average man, and I will never again risk rupture or a heart attack in attempting, unaided, the grueling task of toting out any large deer—or even a small one that has to be carried any appreciable distance. About one-quarter mile over good terrain, using the back-to-back drag-carry, is about all I want, and I will go to great lengths to avoid even this much terrific exertion. In this carry, the buck's neck is pulled over your shoulder with the throat up, and the hind feet will drag with any but the smallest deer. The antlers are grasped firmly by both hands and held at chest height, but the deer will still roll from side to side and you will get plenty of blood on your back. You should walk leaning well forward, and the weight will be very evenly distributed along your back.

Many authors suggest that the deer be dragged out by means of a short length of rope tied to the head or antlers, but unless the animal is to be moved only a short distance, or is to be dragged over snow, deep pine needles, or a thick carpet of grass, the flesh will be badly bruised and the hide severely damaged. Personally, unless conditions were quite favorable, I would prefer to hang my deer or place it atop a brush pile, protecting it from blowflies by encasing it in a cheesecloth bag, which I carry with me for this purpose, and spend the next twenty-four hours, if need be, scrounging up a man to help me, rather than drag the deer out alone. Incidentally, this cheesecloth bag, which comes folded into a light, neat package which fits easily into a pocket, completely encases a deer and costs only about a dollar. It will give a deer more than a dollar's worth of protection wherever blowflies are present. Most men who make a practice of hunting alone carry a packsack; they quarter their deer and make from two to four trips in getting it out of the woods.

Few men should, or do, hunt completely alone. The sportsman hunter should remain sufficiently near his partner to plainly hear the latter's shots. You should have a prearrangement with your partner to join him at a certain place, so that you may always leave the covert together, and each should know approximately where the other intends to hunt. Neither man should ever fail the appointment without leaving an unmistakable sign at the meeting place, such as a large limb in the trail pointing in the direction of camp. You and your partner should agree on a system of cartridge-whistle signals, and each of you should have an explicit understanding of their meaning. I suggest that a single blast on an empty cartridge case, immediately following some shooting, indicate success to the partner. Two whistles could mean that you are in need of immediate help, such as assistance in tracking down a wounded animal or in the possible event that you have become ill or have injured yourself. Such a double whistle should always be immediately acknowledged by the partner, so that the summoner is left in no doubt that the needed aid is forthcoming. Hunters should go to great lengths to avoid spoiling their partner's hunting, but when a deer must be carried to camp on the same evening it is shot, the partner must be summoned in time to help get the carcass out.

If you are faced with the problem of a lengthy carry, you should start scouting around for a suitable pole as soon as the gutting is finished. A sound, seasoned pole ten feet long and one and one-half inches in diameter at the smaller end is ideal, but in some areas you may have to settle for something less desirable. Green cedar is amazingly strong, and unless the deer is a very heavy one you might possibly get by with a pole as short as eight feet and no larger around than one inch at the smaller end. With a pole of this shorter length, the lead man may have to endure an antler tine gouging his back and the rear man may have his face shoved into a place where something else used to be; but that's the way the ball sometimes bounces.

Hunters who have not had your advantage of learning how to carry out a deer will usually tie the four feet to the center of the pole. The deer hangs like a huge bag and swings from side to side as the bearers walk, and this not only makes walking extremely difficult, slow, and tiring, but the deer is close to the ground and subject to catching on every obstruction in the path. The entire weight of the animal is concentrated at a single point, which necessitates a very strong pole, and I've seen small logs used for this purpose which appeared to weigh as much as the deer.

The experienced big-game hunter is as likely to leave his rifle at camp as the length of small-diameter rope which he carries neatly hanked and looped to his belt. Quarter-inch sash cord will hold an average-size elk, and the deer hunter could use rope of even smaller diameter. Nylon cord of amazing strength can be had in diameters not exceeding one-sixth inch, and will serve our purpose admirably. You should carry at least twenty feet of rope, and even more of the light nylon-type just mentioned would be a pious idea, as a longer rope will often come in very handy when a very large deer must be brought in. There are countless ways to skin cats and bring in deer, but where two men are faced with the task of bringing out a whole deer, here is the best method I have found to date.

The pole is laid right into the opening of the carcass and locked into the pelvis by pressing the hams together. The pole is first adjusted so that about the same lengh will protrude from each end of the deer. Tie the root of the tail to the pole with one end of the rope, then fold the hind legs into a couchant position and throw a hitch tightly around the rump. Throw another hitch around the loin just ahead of the rump, and then another around the chest. Now fold the forelegs up against the body and throw a hitch around the shoulders. The next hitch should be just ahead of the shoulders at the base of the neck, the next one at the back of the head, and then finally the antlers are tied to the pole and the lashing job is finished. The deer is lashed in much the same manner as a trunk is lashed, and when the job is finished the deer will appear as though spitted and ready for roasting whole. Each man must wrap his end of the pole with his sweater or jacket, and the burden can be shifted at intervals from shoulder to shoulder without a pause in stride. On a long carry, the front and rear bearers should change positions periodically, and when either man needs to rest he should have the good sense to call a halt. One of my friends suffered a heart attack while wrestling-in a heavy deer on a warm day.

Unless the hunter is skimped for rope, a good lashing job should be completed easily in five minutes, especially if two men engage in the work. Twenty feet of rope is just sufficient to do a perfect job on a medium-size deer or a passable job on a large one; but when you and your partner pool your supply of rope you should have plenty for any requirement ever likely to arise. Where there are other hunters in the area, be sure to tie a red bandana to the deer's antlers or head and another to the center of the back. A third bandanna tied to the tail won't be too many, and you should keep up a loud and continous conversation with your partner as you progress through the no man's land of the usual public whitetail covert. Though hunters as a class are among the most conscientious and emotionally-stable members of society, it takes only a single less-dependable one to give our fine sport a dangerous reputation through shooting at a target not clearly defined and positively identified.

Back at camp the deer should immediately be unlashed from the pole and properly hung so that it is protected from both sun and rain, and be sure to prop the body cavity open with several short sticks. It must also be protected from blowflies, whenever they are present, by a liberal coating of pepper, a cheesecloth bag, or both, and the carcass must be hung where the breeze can circulate air around it. If the weather is unseasonably warm and damp, you are well advised to start home at once with your deer, if the journey is a short one; or, better yet, the deer should be taken to the nearest responsible icehouse, for cold storage until the hunt is over. As long as the weather remains cool and dry, with near-freezing temperatures at night, your deer will remain sweet almost indefinitely if it is properly hung. I have kept venison in camp up to a week, under favorable conditions, but all bone splinters were first removed and all bloodshot tissue trimmed away. A gut-shot deer or a warm weather kill would probably not have lasted so long. If given halfway decent treatment, venison is the most durable meat known, and it will be your own fault if you allow your deer to go bad on you. Properly dressed and hung, venison will definitely improve with a certain amount of cool-weather hanging, and about ten days of proper hanging will usually bring the meat to maximum tenderness and flavor.

Virtually every sizable town now has a food-processing plant, which will skin and cut up your deer, wrap the meat in conveniently-labeled packages, freeze it, and hand it back to you in a cardboard box, ready to be taken home and placed in the freezer. Most hunters who are far from home have their deer so processed, and the meat, packed in the trunk compartment of the car, safely survives a lengthy journey home. A whole frozen carcass will survive a twelve-hour journey, even in warm weather, if it has been well wrapped in blankets or newspapers to help keep the heat out. The common practice of tying the carcass to the fender of the car is not recommended, although a short haul in very cold weather should result in very little damage to the meat. If your deer is killed during a warm spell of weather, I again suggest that it be taken immediately to an icehouse for freezing.

Butchering your own deer is not recommended if you are an urban hunter. The local rural hunter will probably know how to butcher meat, but unless the amateur is given the benefit of personal instruction his efforts will probably result in reducing the carcass to crude chunks of meat. Butchering is a highly developed art which calls for practiced skill, and it cannot be learned satisfactorily from printed instructions or from charts and diagrams. For instance, there are certain glands, called kernels, located in the groin and shoulder areas. These must be carefully and completely removed or the meat will be ill flavored. Not only are a sizable array of special tools and instruments necessary for a good butchering job but you will likely spend a full day in fumbling around with a job which a skilled butcher can complete properly in two hours. A day's time is more valuable to the man who can afford the luxury of a deer hunt than the amount a professional butcher will charge to do a much better job. Your butcher, who benefits from your regular trade, will probably butcher and package your deer for a ridiculously small fee. My own butcher charges me nothing, and that's what I call a bargain. I have all the less choice cuts ground into chili meat, sausage, and burger—and if you don't like venison patties encircled by a thick strip of bacon, you are mighty hard to please. The sausage should be mixed half and half with pork, which makes it an epicurean's delight.

Throw away every "venison" recipe about the place and cook venison exactly as you do beef. Venison which requires special soaking, treating, or saucing is inferior meat which has been improperly killed, dressed, or handled, and if you keep a dog you will know exactly what to do with such meat. Good venison is tender and delicately flavored, and is superior to all but the very finest premium beef obtainable.

Unless you pack into wilderness areas, you are unlikely ever to be faced with the necessity for skinning or cutting up your deer on the spot. The western hunter will have a jeep or pack animal to bring out his deer, and rarely will one be so heavy as to require cutting up for transporting. Proper quartering of an animal requires the use of a saw or hand ax, but the largest deer will seldom need to be divided into more than two sections. This can be easily done by separating the backbone just ahead of the last rib with your hunting knife. An animal could be crudely chopped into four quarters while lying on the ground, but a decent job of quartering requires that the animal be hung and that the splitting be done by hatchet, saw, or hand ax. The animal is cut centrally down the spine when a saw is employed, but immediately to one side of the backbone when the cutting is done by hatchet or ax.

If the animal is being reduced to smaller pieces because of difficult transportation, you might as well jettison all unnecessary weight, including the head, unless the latter is wanted as a trophy or unless the local game law makes its separation from the carcass illegal. The front legs should be cut off at the knees and even the tail may be amputated. Unless you have a saw or hand ax, you will probably do better to leave the hind shanks alone, although they may also be removed if every ounce of weight is important. The shank should be cut just below the knee joint, and it *can* be done by scoring the bone completely around and hitting it very sharply with the back of a heavy hunting knife. There is a knack to this, and some men can do it quite easily.

Field skinning of deer should not be attempted unless the weather is unseasonably warm and you are in a remote area from which it will be impractical to move the carcass for several days. Game that is skinned immediately after gutting will lose body heat more quickly, which, when the weather is unseasonably warm, will definitely improve the meat's flavor and its ability to withstand deterioration. I have skinned both deer and elk on the ground and this is a real job, especially with elk. Skinning will take the edge off a knife faster than an inexperienced person will believe possible; so if any field skinning is contemplated, the hunter should include a small pocket stone in his belongings and use it repeatedly during the skinning operation. Any animal will skin more easily while still warm than after being chilled, as will be the case with your deer after you reach home with it.

Supposing your deer to be lying on the ground, to skin it you first completely ring the hide around the neck at the base of the head and around each leg just above the knee joint. Split the hide down the inside of each leg from the knee to the central belly cut. Now skin out each leg and then the belly, making the last severance of the hide along the animal's back. When finished, the carcass will be lying in the center of its own deerskin rug. A satisfactory skinning knife must have a well-rounded point and must be extremely sharp.

Some men hang their deer by its head; others hang theirs by one hind leg only; still others use a gambrel stick, which also leaves the head hanging downward. On large game such as elk this latter method of hanging seems to be advantageous, but I much prefer my deer to hang by its head. A gambrel stick is a heavy stick about a yard long, with both ends sharpened. The sharpened ends are shoved through the hide between the bone and the large tendon at the gambrels, or hocks, of the hind legs and thus hold the legs spread well apart. About a four-foot length of rope, with each end tied to an end of the stick, prevents the legs from slipping off the stick and also serves as a harness for the lifting rope to be tied to the center. Personally, I seldom use the gambrel stick because I much prefer to gut a deer-size animal on the ground, and I believe that head-hung game will both drain and keep better. I also find that the head-hung animal skins better, as no leg splits are necessary. The skin comes right off the legs "cased," and "knuckling" seems to be more effective when working from the head back toward the rump. "Knuckling" is the term used for separating the hide from the carcass by the use of the kuckles. Done properly, only the last two joints of the fingers are clenched, each lower joint being held stiffly straight with the hand. The loosened hide is held by one hand while the other hand knuckles more skin loose, the knuckler often working up to his armpit. An expert knuckler will loosen the larger portion of the hide without the use of a knife, reducing the time and effort enormously. The belly, flanks, and lower leg regions always give me the most trouble as a certain amount of flesh seems determined to come off with the hide.

A deer hide poses so many problems to the hunter that he usually winds up discarding it with as little regret as he does the intestines. I definitely warn the amateur tanner against attempting to tan his own deer hide. Though thousands of deer hides are imported annually into this country, there is no sale for them one at a time. It takes three average-size deer hides to make a jacket, and, unless you hunt in several states or scrounge a hide or two from your buddies, it will be difficult to get as many as three hides together at one time. One hide will usually make three pairs of gloves, and though deerskin garments will not come cheaply, no finer material can be had for outdoor clothing.

If you intend to have gloves or jackets made from your deerskins, write for prices and instructions from a firm which specializes in this work. The early fall issues of all popular sporting magazines carry advertisements by firms who solicit this type of business. Deer hair is so brittle that deerskin rugs are not considered practicable, but they may be used for wall decorations in the den. Any hide which you intend to keep must be removed from the carcass with great care, in order to avoid holes, nicks, splits, and excessive thinning. Every bit of flesh and fat must be removed and some five pounds of table salt must be worked into every inch of surface and every crack and crevice. Keep the hide tightly rolled, with the hair side in, and unroll periodically for inspection and for resalting, whenever necessary.

8 ——— STILL-HUNTING WHITETAILS

Before Tom Junior came back from Korea with three Purple Hearts and a permanent disability owing to his having stepped on a mine, we did quite a bit of still-hunting—in fact, that had been our favorite method of hunting whitetails. But his subsequent inability to walk either quietly or for long distances resulted in our developing the "scrape and buck-run watching technique," which is much easier on the foot—or feet, if you are fortunate enough to have two of them. However, we now achieve much better average results than when we still-hunted almost exclusively.

Stalking and still-hunting are often confused even by persons who should know better. "Stalking" is the art of stealing closer to game which has already been sighted at a too great distance. Any form or method of hunting may produce a situation which calls for a stalk, and in many open hunting areas, such as the Scottish moors and our own rolling plains and high mountain country, the stalking of game which has been located at a great distance is the anticipated climax to any hunt.

In "still-hunting," the hunter moves slowly and quietly through the covert in an attempt to discover game within the killing range of his weapon. The term "still" as applied to this type of hunting is used in its ancient meaning of "quiet," and "still-hunting" is a very old description that has come down to us through many generations. Still-hunting is a most highly-developed art and, except when applied to whitetail deer, it is the most effective method for taking herbivorous game in heavy cover that is known to me. It is just as effective on squirrels as on moose, and a competent still-hunter will take any species of game which is amenable to this method of hunting wherever the terrain is suitable. While whitetails, too, can be taken by still-hunting, as thousands of hunters beside ourselves have often proved, it is not the most productive method for taking them, especially when practiced by the average unskilled hunter.

To still-hunt whitetails with any degree of consistent effectiveness, the hunter is required to be poison with his rifle on running shots and to possess an excellent pair of game-trained eyes. It is the method of the master, which can never be fully imparted to the tyro by means of the printed word. Still-hunting is definitely an art, while scrape and buck-run hunting can very nearly be reduced to a science.

In the case of big game, still-hunting is a wilderness proposition, and is not recommended for areas containing appreciable numbers of other hunters. Where the covert abounds with hunters, the man who slips along through the woods may get a chance to demonstrate that he has lots of guts. Also, still-hunting requires a large area in which to operate, so that the hunter is not continually pursuing the same smartened-up deer. Aside from the whitetail's acute faculties of hearing, movement detection, and smell, which are equalled by no other deer except the elk, the hard-hunted animal moves so little during the daylight hours and ordinarily travels such a short distance between his feed and bed ground that he can often give the most able still-hunter a frustration complex.

However, when the weather is pleasant and the terrain is not difficult to negotiate, still-hunting is a most enjoyable way to hunt—so much so that we often indulge in it when game is so plentiful that scrape hunting promises to fill our licenses too quickly. No genuine whitetailer wants to shoot himself out of business in one or two days and thereby remove any excuse for remaining longer in God's magnificent outdoors. When the hunting is good in two-deer areas, we usually get our first buck very quickly at a scrape and then try to take our second by still-hunting. If this latter method hasn't yielded results as our alloted time nears its end, we then go back to watching scrapes and buck-runs in an attempt to take our second deer. Though still-hunting is seldom the most logical way to hunt whitetails, the reader may recall a statement made earlier in this book, to the effect that persons completely dedicated to logic will never make deer hunters.

There is a great satisfaction in taking a buck by this method, and some of our most cherished recollections are of success-fully-executed still-hunts. I would like to recall one here that will illustrate several of the truths presented earlier.

The moon was low in the western sky and the first faint streaks of dawn were evident over the eastern hills as I began to pick my way up the slope of a good-sized hill that formed a ridge extending back into our choicest hunting territory. It was the opening day of the season, the weather was fine, and prospects were rosy. By the time shooting-light arrived I was atop the ridge and easing along it, expecting to contact game at any moment. When eight o'clock came, with little evidence of a deer having ever been in the area, I was completely baffled and not a little discouraged. Dropping down into the timbered flat, I proceeded along on old logging trail, which shared the valley floor with a dry, meandering creek bed having low, sloping banks with brush and oak trees growing about their edges. As I approached a place where the creek on my left turned sharply across the trail and curved on around to the right, I remember glancing at my watch, which showed nine o'clock, and I had not yet seen a single whitetail. Then, just forty yards ahead and off to the right of the trail, I saw a deer.

There was a growth of light brush between me and the deer—a small buck which soon stepped slowly past a tree and stopped with only his head and shoulders exposed, directly broadside. I had cheeked my rifle as the deer's head passed behind the trunk, and I was looking through the scope directly at the shoulder when it emerged from behind the tree. I most carefully and deliberately centered the crosshairs on the center of the shoulder, and squeezed the trigger. I had a feeling that the buck became aware of my identity at the instant he paused, but I was completely flabbergasted when, instead of crashing to the ground, he wheeled and dashed back out of sight into the brush. As I worked the bolt I assured myself that the deer would surely fall within a few strides, but I was not given long to cogitate. There was a tremendous crashing of brush to the left of the road, and a magnificent buck came charging over the creek bank and tore across the bare ground, intent upon following the tracks of his departing companion.

I could have hit that mossback with a rock, a bean bag, an air rifle, or a rotten egg, but I simply couldn't get on him with that damned scope. I made a loud, futile bang as he crossed the opening directly broadside to me, and then blasted a tree right in front of his face as he was about to dive into the thicket. By the greatest of good fortune, the deer had never located me exactly, and when the bark flew in front of his face he whipped around sharply and circled back my way. He saw me then as I worked the bolt, and veered suddenly toward the creek bank, which was only a couple of jumps away. He was in midair of the leap which would have landed him forever out of my sight when my snapshot, fired with head erect, sagged him visibly, though he recovered instantly and tore out of my sight. I followed the blood trail—which looked as though it had been made with a paint bucket and mop—about fifty yards to where it suddenly ended, and there, a few yards ahead and nestled at the foot of a cedar tree, lay my buck.

Several times, while I was gutting out this buck, I became aware of groups of does and fawns traveling along the trail. They would stand and gaze fixedly for several moments, but would be gone when I next looked their way. Presently a large deer caught my eye at thirty yards, and upon looking directly at him I discovered it was a young buck and that he was paying me no mind. I could have taken him so easily that there would have been little sport involved, but I still labored under the mistaken belief that I had another buck down in the brush behind me and I already regretted filling my license so quickly. After gutting and hanging my deer, I went back to where the first buck had stood but after following his tracks until it became foolish to continue I was reluctantly forced to accept the fact that the brush had deflected my 180-grain 30-'06 bullet.

My snapshot happened to pulp the big buck's heart, but I will always believe that, had I been using the 35 Remington, I would have dropped both deer within twenty feet of each other with one shot apiece. I have no regrets over my failure to kill the small buck, because I got another trophy animal a few days later, but there is little doubt in my mind that the heavier, more slowly-spinning 35 Remington bullet driven five hundred feet per second slower would have overcome the brush and the fine iron sights of my woods rifle would have allowed me to take the close-running buck with ridiculous ease. The fact that I moved in so closely to these deer is indisputable proof that my still-hunting technique was good despite the fact that the same cannot be said for my shooting.

These deer were intercepted on their way to the bedding ground at moonset, and their travel order, consisting of the mature bucks in advance, the does following by a later time, and a young buck bringing up the rear, is typical of whitetail behavior. Also, the facts that no more deer were seen again in that particular area and that no other bucks were taken so easily that season demonstrate the advantage of being in the deer coverts on opening day while the animals are relatively free-moving and unsuspecting.

All deer hunters should wear soft-soled shoes; the still-hunter *must* wear them. You're going to break a stick now and then—even deer break them. But a stick broken beneath a hard-soled shoe will make a sound different from one broken beneath a deer's foot, a moccasin, or a crepe-soled shoe. You must wear outer clothing of wool or wool-like material which will not swish as you walk or make a harsh scraping sound when dragged against brush or high weeds. You must have nothing in your pockets or on or about your person or your rifle that will rattle, jingle, creak, squeak, crackle, or flap. You must keep your cap or hat—preferably the latter—pulled well down over your eyes, and these new bright crimson and yellow "fire" colors are *out*. You should carry a pair of good-quality six-power binoculars suspended around your neck and held in place by an elastic band which completely encircles the chest. The suspension strap around your neck should be very short, just long enough for the glasses to clear your nose and chin when lifted.

The still-hunter should never creep or skulk, because such behavior would emulate the actions of a predator. He should take a few quiet and deliberate steps, then pause and take a good look around, as would a deer. Every main deer trail will have, topography permitting, a secondary trail which parallels it. The still-hunter should strive to move along the secondary trail, while keeping the main trail under observation, at a time when game would ordinarily be expected to be moving, and in the same direction. The main trails must be traveled when they cannot be observed from the secondary trails. Our knowledge of deer habit prompts us to advise you to move in a direction from the feeding areas toward the bedding grounds in the early morning and at moonset, and to reverse this direction in the late afternoon and at moonrise. Still-hunting whitetails is rarely successful except at feeding times and places. The wind direction usually controls your direction of hunting, or at least severely limits it, because hunting in any direction that is receiving your scent is utterly useless. It has been proven that a whitetail can scent a man a full mile away under the right wind condition.

Added to the still-hunter's difficulty of coordinating moon position, solar time, wind direction, and the direction in which the game may be traveling, is that of integrating the sun's position in order to place it at his back. With the sun shining directly on your game, you have a tremendous advantage. In the reverse situation, the game has the same relative advantage over you. It will seldom serve your purpose to move with absolute silence as the cougar does, and a *small* amount of noise, such as a deer would make, is probably helpful. However, coughing, sneezing, throat clearing, stumbling, bulldozing through thickets, clambering over obstacles, and falling over down-timber are not sounds that game would make, and they will ruin you. The first deer to blow at a still-hunter will sometimes blight his entire hunt, because all the deer will then be on the alert for him and his progress will often be relentlessly tracked and his position periodically broadcast by unseen blowers.

If you should arrive in a strange area after the season has already opened, I suggest that you give the place one good still-hunt, in order to learn the country, the trails, the bedding grounds, and to locate bands of deer. You will do well to skirt obvious or suspected bed grounds, but you should endeavor to locate all main trails connecting with these areas and especially be on the watch for scrapes and rubs. Be constantly on the lookout for good feeding areas, such as grain or alfalfa fields, acorn flats, fire scalds, berry patches, old orchards, or obvious browsing thickets, and make mental notes of all meadows, glades, and crossings, for future use.

The good still-hunter is an opportunist constantly on the alert to take advantage of any unusual situation. One morning Tom Junior fell in behind a small herd of cattle heading in the general direction which he intended to travel. Presently a huge buck jumped from behind a brush pile at thirty yards and, as he dashed clear of the cattle, Tom held for the chest and dropped him with a perfect neck shot. His rack is the largest and heaviest that we have ever taken. While hunting in an area where domestic goats were run, I once saved my still-hunt by bleating like a goat and instantly reassuring an alerted doe which had been quite interested in learning what I was. Since that time the boys have also employed this ruse on occasion, with helpful results.

Certain types of terrain lend themselves admirably to still-hunting, while other types are not at all suitable. Very level, semi-open areas allow the game to detect you from too great a distance, while very rugged and precipitous terrain prevents quiet walking. Unless snow is on the ground, the type of soil is also quite important. Sandy or rich loam soil makes silent walking very easy, while shale or gravel-covered ground can seldom be negotiated quietly enough to assure success. Ideal still-hunting country is a series of low hills quite close together and having soft loam soil. Where leaves and other forest litter lie thick upon the ground, they are apt to crackle under foot unless very damp. Many areas are so dry except following a rain, that quiet walking is possible only in the early morning when the dew is on the ground. However, we have hunted areas in Mexico, Texas, New Mexico, Arizona, Colorado, and California which were so dry that there wasn't even any dew. I'll politely tip my hat to any man who can still-hunt successfully over a thick carpet of powder-dry aspen leaves.

The cardinal rule of hunting—to become aware of your game before it becomes aware of you—applies just as much to still-hunting as it does to any other form. Though still-hunting usually allows you to put more game under observation it is the least likely to permit enforcement of the above rule. Of all American deer, the whitetail is universally accepted as being the most difficult to see, and when motionless he usually defies detection by even the best of human eyes. Expert hunters have estimated that they see no more than one of every twenty whitetails within their range of vision. The deer's eyesight renders you virtually invisible to him unless you are moving, and the deer's coloration renders him virtually invisible to you except under the same conditions. Therefore it becomes axiomatic that you must do as little walking and as much looking as possible while still-hunting. Move only sufficiently, from place to place, to gain a new view of the terrain, then meticulously scrutinize every object and patch of cover within the limit of your vision, even looking behind you occasionally. Strive continually to stay back in the shadows and pause only in the close proximity of a tree or other cover.

The good still-hunter must know the area like he knows his own back yard, must thoroughly know the habits of his quarry, and must be adept at reading sign. He must also be a good trailer of wounded game, because the high percentage of running shots which will be presented will result in many poorly-hit animals.

Since resting deer are motionless and motionless deer are almost impossible to detect, still-hunting whitetails is only practicable at such times as deer are moving. Should the reader, at this point, note that the above statement is becoming repetitious, it will indicate that he is getting the message I am trying to stress. The inveterate still-hunter can improve his future chances by removing his form and scent from the covert at about ten o'clock, when the moon is down, and putting in the next five or six hours at improving his mind by reading Shakespeare, Plato, or Hayes. The still-hunter can only operate with any degree of success in the mornings and evenings and at such other times as the moon is in the sky. The hunter is justified in moving in on the bedding grounds only when he is quitting the area, because by so doing he will shake up the deer so badly that they are likely to remove to another area for several days. The possibility of getting a decent shot is so remote as to virtually eliminate the bed ground as a possible area of operation. This leaves the feeding areas, and the game trails which connect them with the bedding areas, as the logical theaters for still-hunting. Since deer are usually more certain to be taken by waylaying them along the connecting trails or on the feeding grounds themselves, still-hunting whitetails is seldom the most productive method for hunting them.

Still-hunting is unreservedly recommended for those times when the wind continually shifts from one direction to another and takes in every direction of the compass so rapidly as to warn every deer in the vicinity of your presence. Though hunting at such times will be very tough, it's either that or stay in camp. By moving, you may sometimes get ahead of your scent.

Very seldom will a standing whitetail be seen clearly outlined and instantly unmistakable. You must learn to look for a patch of tan or white, an eye, an ear, or a muzzle. Most deer are first detected by a flash of white as they take a step or two, but even then it is often difficult to resolve the deer clearly the moment it stops. Binoculars come in mighty handy for a better look at any promising object, but never let a great distance lull you into a quick or careless movement as you prepare to focus your glass. A whitetail once spotted me instantly from five hundred yards when I carelessly raised my rifle for a better look through the scope.

Two competent still-hunters operating as a team can often more than double their individual chances for success. When two such men know the country well and each is thoroughly familiar with the other's hunting habits, they may often find opportunity to put a pincers movement on a particular piece of cover or to team up on working out a header or a draw. With each man taking a side of the draw or canyon and traveling abreast of his companion, deer put up by one hunter can sometimes be taken from the opposite slope by the other. Sometimes a draw can be worked out by having one man go around and cover the top while the other works up from the bottom. When two hunters are operating in flat country or on the same slope of a hill, they should walk parallel courses and keep from one to two hundred yards apart, depending on the visibility. When working cross-wind, the up-wind hunter should drop back about fifty yards, so that any deer put up by his partner will, in normally escaping into the wind, run in front of his gun. This also prevents the down-wind hunter from working cover which has received his partner's scent. Both hunters, and especially the down-wind one, should keep a sharp lookout behind them at all times. It is also imperative that each man know exactly where the other is at all times, in order to avoid an accident.

It is sometimes very difficult to remove from green hunters' heads the idea that still-hunting means hiking over a great deal of country and scouring it for game. Some men never abandon this method of "hunting" and come in late to camp each night completely tuckered out. No, they didn't get a shot, but Oh boy, did they see game! One of the poorest hunters I ever knew, a graying man who had hunted whitetails all his life, used to drag into camp each night telling of the thirteen— or thirty—deer he had seen that day. I never doubted his word for a moment, but I learned right then and there that poor hunters often see more game than good hunters do. Two to three miles in a whole day is about average for a good still-hunter in most types of terrain, when he is thoroughly working the cover.

Very accurate figures have recently been compiled which indicate that the average hunter requires fifteen whole days of hunting to bag one whitetail buck in good hunting territory. By hunting the scrapes and buck-runs, our average is less than three days for every buck bagged. Furthermore, we take a much higher percentage of mature trophy bucks than is taken by the average hunter. This type of hunting requires a lot of patience —just sitting, watching, and waiting—and many hunters do not have this patience. Some men will take their deer by still-hunting or not at all—and sometimes they do just that. Very few people could have less patience than myself, but my impatience is directed toward not having a deer hanging from the meat pole. Also, I can hardly refrain from remarking that it must require a peculiar type of patience to hunt for fifteen consecutive days without getting blood on your knife.

We often vary the monotony of sitting and watching by taking a pre-dawn stand in the vicinity of a feeding area, then, after the sun is well up, still-hunting back to the edge of the bed ground. We will direct our still-hunt to bring us to a scrape or buck-run at about nine o'clock, and we will survey this spot until at least noon before returning to camp for a bite of dinner. Immediately following the noon meal we will return to the covert and continue our watch until shooting-light fades, hitting the trail rapidly thereafter so as to be as close to camp as possible by the time all light has faded from the sky. When the hunting gets really tough, we usually carry our lunch and a canteen of water, so that we can take advantage of the two hours normally wasted by coming in to lunch.

One of the nicest ways of hunting, which combines still-hunting and watching, can be practiced in certain types of terrain. Where a series of low, easily-negotiated hills contains a good whitetail population, the hunter can work around near the tops of the hills and watch a given area for fifteen or twenty minutes. Then, by moving only a few yards around the hillside he will be able to put a completely new piece of ground under observation. By placing himself above his game and thereby taking advantage of the normally-rising thermal breezes, the hunter, under these circumstances, will be in excellent position to take deer. When executed correctly in the proper type of terrain, this is one of the most effective and pleasant methods of hunting that I know of, and it works equally well on most other species of game.

We once hunted an area like that just described and liked it better than any place we have ever hunted. It is one of the few places I have ever hunted where I would feel absolutely safe in saying, "I believe I will go out and kill a deer today." I took a bet on that one morning, around the breakfast fire. The weather had warmed up during the night, and a fog which reduced visibility to twenty feet lay over the hills, but just as I arrived on my selected hilltop the fog lifted. I had barely re-seated myself after making my second move when a feeding deer stepped into view near the foot of the hill. Visibility was still not good and it took me a moment to spot antlers, although I knew the deer to be a buck. The antlers were very small, and though they had the characteristic curve of a forkhorn I could not detect a single point which was needed to make the deer legal game. Carefully raising my rifle and peering intently through the scope I finally made out a tiny projection which dispelled all doubt; so, placing the crosshairs on the "T," I lowered the boom on the unsuspecting buck. That is the only deer I ever killed so emphatically that it fell on its back with all four feet sticking straight up in the air.

Many fairly successful hunters employ a method which normally combines still-hunting and watching. They will concentrate on scrapes, buck-runs, and crossings, but will move on to another location after from thirty minutes to one hour of fruitless watching. They will take several stands each day, moving only between stands. They occasionally take their deer while moving, but much more often while watching.

Once in a while, when a whitetail buck is not particularly frightened but decides to make a run for it on the theory that caution is the better part of valor, he will pause for a brief backward look at the very edge of safe cover. This happens only when he is not being chased and when some doubt remains as to exactly what boogered him. I once had still-hunted one entire morning with no results, and at eleven o'clock had decided to take a stand in a little oak mott, which I knew to be located in an excellent crossing. I had hardly seated myself and begun to search the area, when my eye was attracted to a spot of off-reddish color which was receiving the direct sunlight in the thick top of a recently-fallen oak tree. There was an abundance of vivid autumnal color everywhere, but that particular patch just didn't seem as if it belonged there. I put my low-power scope on the treetop and could resolve nothing, but for a full twenty minutes my eyes were continually redrawn to that spot of color. Finally my intense scrutiny was rewarded by the deliberate turning of an antlered head, immediately followed by a departing buck.

The limbs were so thick and low above my head that I could not rise, so I started crawling along on hands and knees in an effort to keep the brush-protected buck in sight. I was up on my knees and leaning precariously to peer around an intervening tree-trunk when the buck, deep back in the brush, stopped suddenly for a backward look. All I could see was the white throat-patch, and I attempted to strike it from a distance of over a hundred yards from the strained and awkward position in which I found myself. Weaving unsteadily, I called the shot four inches left; but I'll always wonder if that buck would have waited while I scooted my bo-hind around and assumed a good steady sitting position. I'll never know; but I doubt it, because bucks seldom pause more than a few seconds when they stop under such circumstances, and are off again in a flash if they detect the slightest movement.

9 ——————————— THE DEER STAND

As already stated, locating a likely place in which to kill a deer is only half the battle; approaching it without detection, choosing a suitable stand that will defy detection, and waiting there for long periods of time without arousing suspicion—all these take a bit of doing. The general procedure for watching scrapes is the same as that for watching trails, only much more highly refined. The difference is somewhat comparable to that between attempting to place a bullet at random anywhere in a straight vertical pole and trying to hit one particular spot on that pole. In the first instance, you can almost totally disregard the vertical movement of the sights while concentrating on the horizontal. But to strike the spot, you must concentrate equally on both.

Let us first consider the manner of approach. The trail watcher will ordinarily take his position before the hour when game may be expected to be on the move, and as the stand selected will usually be sufficiently far from the bedding ground to avoid alerting the game, the hunter may feel safe in approaching his selected stand quite casually. Though it is true that the scrape hunter should strive to give the illusion of strolling casually along, as he approaches his stand, he should actually be walking as quietly as possible and be alert to any development. The ever-present possibility that a buck—or a buck-interested doe—may be in the immediate vicinity or within watching distance of the scrape requires that the scrape hunter exercise the utmost caution. Remember, the chances of finding the buck at home are increased when the moon is down.

The trail watcher, except in such places as are severely limited by excessive brush or unfavorable terrain, will seldom find wind of fixed direction a serious problem. Normally, he will be able to find a position along some portion of the trail from which his scent will not reach an approaching deer or invade the area from which he expects deer to come. The buck's habit of lying up above his scrape, which also means that he will usually be above the main trail and all other usable avenues of approach, gives him the added advantage of the normally-rising thermal air currents during the daylight hours. To add further to the scrape hunter's problems, visibility in the vicinity of scrapes is usually so restricted as to seriously limit the choice of stands. Amorous does' habit of loitering and feeding around the scrape for upward of an hour, usually within about a seventy-five-yard radius, can put the watcher in a nervous sweat. Every passing moment increases his chances of being detected and also increases the chances of the buck's appearance.

The manner in which the vicinity of the scrape is approached can often be of vital importance. On several occasions we have had the buck appear within minutes of our arrival, and this was solely due to the fact that we convinced the buck that we were deer. Had we moved in faster or more slowly, made more noise or less noise, allowed him one breath of scent, or failed to position ourselves promptly and alertly, we not only would have failed to kill the buck but would have so boogered him that many days might have elapsed before that particular scrape could have been profitably hunted again. The countless days we have spent in the game fields have fixed in us the habit of moving through the covert at all times as though we expected to meet a buck around the next bend in the trail, even though we may be walking rapidly to reach a given objective. Except on those occasions when we are detected, we slip away quietly even upon leaving our stand; the less evidence that hunters are haunting the area the more chances that the buck will visit his scrape during the daylight hours.

Deer are quite intelligent and they reason very much as humans do in matters pertaining to their safety. Unlike a wolf or cougar, whose sight or scent spells unmistakable danger to the deer, man is a borderline enemy of quite unpredictable ways. Deer are therefore inclined to evaluate a man's presence in the covert. Our manner of walking up casually, though very quietly, will stand us in good stead should a sudden snort, a flash of white, or crashing brush tell us that our approach has been detected. Knowing that we are being watched from some well-screened position, we now hope to convince the deer that we are merely traveling through and have no interest in him at all. After a slight pause, such as any animal would make upon being startled by sudden sound or movement, we resume our progress in the general direction and in the same casual manner as before. From the corners of our eyes we will be searching for a shootable buck, but will pretend complete disinterest. The only change which we will make in our mode of progress is to begin placing our feet more noisily, in an effort to convince the deer that we were walking noisily all the time and that he failed to hear us sooner only because of the softness of the ground or freak wind conditions. Our whole purpose, upon being detected, is to mislead the deer into mis-judging our reason for being there and our ultimate intention toward him, and to cause him to underestimate our ability to approach his scrape quietly.

If the terrain permits, the area of the scrape should be carefully observed for several minutes from a distant vantage point before you closely approach it. This procedure calls for a definite knowledge of the scrape and the entire surrounding area and points up the necessity for having thoroughly scouted your hunting ground. On several occasions we have come upon previously-unknown scrapes while still-hunting or scouting, taken a stand close by, and killed a buck before leaving. This requires a lot of luck as to wind direction and timing, because we are as likely to locate the scrape *after* the buck has crashed away, in which case we then go over to investigate the area where the buck had been standing. If you should locate a scrape under the latter circumstances and have no other place in mind to hunt, you might return after several hours and take a stand. If you have not shaken the buck up too badly and the scrape has recently been visited by a doe, there is a good chance that the buck will return rather promptly.

Whenever a new scrape is located, we immediately evalu-ate all the nearby connecting trails in relation to the surround-ing cover, in an effort to establish the buck's bedding area—which will also determine his most probable line of approach. We determine and memorize the topographical features of the area and all possible avenues by which the scrape can be approached by the hunter. The exact lay of the land in rela-tion to north and south is established, so that we may later know, even before leaving camp, whether or not this particu-lar scrape might be profitably hunted under the prevailing wind direction.

Our next move is to locate three stands, if possible, from which the scrape can be observed within shooting range. One of these stands should be roughly opposite the direction of the buck's probable line of approach and the other two should flank the vicinity of the scrape. Never take a stand directly in a trail if there is any possible alternative. If we can find suitable stands on three sides of the scrape we will be able to hunt there under almost any wind direction, provided we are able to approach at least one of the stands without giving our scent to the scrape or to the bed ground adjacent to the area.

While scouting a scrape we never approach it more closely than is necessary to establish its exact location and its current activity level. Not wishing to leave man scent any nearer to this spot than necessity dictates, we widely circle the scrape while exploring every potential stand from which the area could be effectively covered. Right now is the time to prepare all likely stands for future use by quietly removing all stones, seedlings, and dead limbs from the bases of trees under which we will sit when we return later to hunt the place. We will often find it necessary to trim out an opening in the brush through which we can both see and shoot, and sometimes we find it necessary to trim off a limb stub or low branch from a tree that will support our backs should we return there to hunt. It is imperative that the hunter be seated comfortably when he takes a stand; if he is uncomfortable, he will be continually fidgeting and shifting position, with consequent ruinous sound and movement.

Many hunters are addicted to the practice of climbing trees when they wish to take a stand. In certain flatland areas covered with dense low brush this seems about the only practicable thing to do; but I never climb a tree except as a last resort and I urge you to follow this example. The perennial tyros, who constitute about 95 per cent of all hunters, devoutly believe that any living thing found in a tree is fair game. They labor under the mistaken belief that cougars, wildcats, bears, and turkeys spend the greater part of their waking moments in tree tops, and, since men, dogs, and livestock are terrestial animals, no serious consequences can possibly result from shooting an unidentified animal discovered in a tree. When a man climbs into a tree in hunting territory, he flaunts himself as a highly-visible target to those morally-innocent but potentially-murderous morons who occasionally stalk the game coverts disguised as sportsmen.

It is true that on a fair day the tree-hunter's scent will be wafted aloft by the thermal air currents and that, if he remains motionless, no hooved animal will detect him. In theory, this places the game at the hunter's mercy; but, though many otherwise unobtainable trophies are taken by the tree-hunter, this mode of hunting will lose him more heads of game than it will get him, over a long period of time. Most of the opportunities presented to the tree-hunter will be muffed because he soon becomes so uncomfortable that he can no longer remain still, and every time he squirms around he will shake the entire tree. He is helpless to shift his position to shoot in any direction other than the quadrant he is facing. He will also likely miss many easy shots because of his strained and awkward shooting position, and any breeze will sway the tree and cause misses at easy ranges.

Not only is there great danger of a fall while climbing a tree but there is the added risk of accidentally discharging your weapon while climbing with it or drawing it up after you by means of a cord or rope. Tom once fell about ten feet onto soft soil and escaped injury; but last season a hunter from a nearby camp went to sleep in a tree, and his resultant fall has left him totally and permanently paralyzed. The tree-hunter is often at a great disadvantage when a coup or follow-up shot is quickly needed, and the delay in getting down from the tree will frequently allow the game to escape. A hunter shot himself in the foot a few years ago while wildly scrambling down from a tree to dispatch the leg-shot buck, which, incidentally, got clean away. One of our hunters once downed a buck near the foot of the tree in which he was perched, and he finally reached the ground just in time to see the badly-injured deer disappearing into the brush. No, he never saw the deer again, but the animal's progress was so slow and labored that a hunter on the ground could have easily finished it off with another shot.

One of my friends once found a tree to his liking while scouting his hunting ground on the evening preceding the opening of the season. It was still dark when he arrived at the tree next morning, with only a glimmer of light in the eastern sky. The lowest limb was about eight feet above the ground, and when my friend leaped up and caught the limb, it broke away from the trunk with a great rending sound. The man hit flat on his back with an earth-shaking thud and the broken limb crashed down on top of him. Immediately, from a distance of about a hundred yards, came the throbbing of hoofbeats as a buck—which mistook the commotion for a buck fight—charged up to the scene. Lying there flat on his back, the hunter could hear the buck's heavy breathing and could see his dim outline, about ten feet away and silhouetted against the eastern sky. Still clutching his rifle, my friend fired at the deer, and missed. An orange flame stabbed the darkness when the gun discharged, but the buck didn't move a muscle until the action was levered.

The hunter is cautioned against trying to prop his back

against a tree which is leaning to any degree forward. A slightly backward-leaning tree will be of tremendous help in maintaining a motionless position in comfort over a long period. The legs, when you are seated flat on the ground must be extended straight forward; if the legs are folded back they will soon go to sleep and scream to be straightened. By all means attempt to sit some distance above the ground, on a log, stump, or even a large flat rock. A man can sit motionless all day if he can secure a chairlike seat with his back propped against a backward-leaning tree.

In addition to scent, sound, and movement, the three things that give the hunter away are the eyes, the face, and the hands. Your eyes, being moist, will glisten and attract the attention of passing game, and eyeglasses greatly increase your chances of being detected. The hunting cap or hat should have a large bill or brim, which is always worn very low over the eyes, particularly whenever the sun is shining. The hands, especially when not protected by gloves or mittens, should be held low in the lap, and that is also the best place for the seated hunter to hold his weapon. A good heavy set of whiskers is a wonderful face screen, and though it makes you look like a bum it will pay off more in the game fields than you will ever know.

When the stand has been properly prepared by the removal of all sticks and stones, twigs, crisp leaves, and any other noise-making litter, essential motions can normally be made without disturbing game, if the hunter exercises extreme caution. The head must be turned very frequently in order to spot any approaching game, and unless you are under intense and direct scrutiny this movement can be safely executed, if done very slowly. Since everyone has his own notion of what "slowly" means, let me suggest that you never consume less than ten seconds in turning your head from one extreme to the other.

All essential hand movements must be made in extreme slow motion, with arms and elbows held close to the body. If and when it becomes imperative to shift the legs or body, you should take a full minute or more in executing the movement. Be certain to make a full and careful sweep of the entire area before making any major body shifts, and always delay this action if there has been any recent sound or movement in the cover which could possibly indicate the presence of a deer.

You are advised against smoking on the stand. The smoke will not be scented unless you yourself are scented, because the smoke stream will coincide with your own scent stream— and, believe me, you smell worse to a deer than tobacco smoke does. Also, I don't believe the smoke itself is easily detected by the deer's eyes, because of its lack of substance in moving air and because it curls up so slowly in calm air. The sound and movement generated while lighting up and the hand movements connected with smoking are the things which are apt to disclose to the game the presence of the smoker. If you *must* smoke, I suggest that you choose a stand which offers concealment to the body below the level of your head; then sink down out of sight to light your cigarette and finish smoking it, before slowly straightening up and resuming the hunt. The pipe smoker may possibly get by with the smoking part because his hands are not used in the smoking. Always light your smoke with paper matches, which make less noise upon lighting than do wooden matches. Don't use a flint lighter, because the metallic click is a dead giveaway. For best results, I urge you to exercise manly self-control and refrain from smoking on the stand. And if you are able to master this senseless craving for tobacco, kindly write me at once and tell me how you managed to do it.

Always strive to seat yourself facing slightly away, in the

direction of your shooting arm, from the direction the game is most likely to appear. This should find you in perfect shooting position if the game appears where expected. Regardless of how you place your body, however, it seems that fate invariably presents you with a chance which requires you to shift your body before the rifle can be brought to bear effectively. Please do not ask me why this is so; I simply can't explain it.

After we have located a number of promising scrapes and buck-runs we are in position each day to plan a hunt tailored to the wind and weather conditions prevailing. We may know a good spot or two which can only be hunted when the wind is from the north, so that's where we head when a norther begins to blow in. By having a number of potential spots to hunt, we are in position to rest one of them if we are detected in its vicinity or if we make a kill there. We are so confident of making a kill at an active scrape that we will go to great lengths to keep from lousing it up. We will not hunt it under conditions which favor the buck's chances of discovering us, preferring to wait patiently for favorable conditions. By knowing the probable paths of the wind currents and correctly calculating the exact area in which the buck is lying, we can, as a last resort, sometimes operate successfully with a wind direction very close to ruinous. However, this ability to operate along the thin edge of permissible wind direction is one that has been many years in developing, and this risky business is not recommended to the tyro.

The buck that has made a fresh scrape will almost certainly, unless aware of enemies in the proximity, visit it several times during the day. He will fail to do this only at such times as he is actively occupied with a rutting doe, after which he will return and resume his visits immediately upon the end of the romance. Therefore, the odds are better than one to three that the buck will come to his scrape on any given day, provided the hunter slips in and remains undetected. Since two or more bucks frequently scrape in the same general area, and since virtually all scrapes are made on a much-used trail, the chances of the careful hunter seeing a buck are usually as good as even on any particular day. After one fruitless day, the chances are much better on the following day, and the third day will bring the odds to three to one in the hunter's favor. If the buck has not shown by the fourth day, you may safely conclude that he is either dead or has been aware of your presence.

The most terrible drought Texas has ever known began about 1948 and ended about 1957. The beautiful crystal-clear Frio River was completely dry for several years—the first time in history. So many deer drifted eastward that central and east Texas now have herds equalling those of a hundred years ago. The hardest buck I ever came by was taken during the 1954 season, in one of the worst drought years. There were very few deer about on opening day and there was virtually no browse, mast, or crops to hold them. To make matters worse, a cougar moved into our area and most of the meager herd bugged out. We began to spend whole days in the covert without seeing or hearing a deer, and the none-too-plentiful rubs began to weather badly; their makers had simply moved out. Finally, away back at the far edge of our hunting ground, I found a freshly-used chain of rubs. I determined to watch this buck run for three consecutive days before conceding defeat, and I saw no game bird or mammal throughout the first day. A small herd of javelina fed within twenty steps of my stand on the second evening, and though I was sorely tempted to take a couple of those little fifty-pound pigs, and thus avoid a complete skunking, I held my fire for fear of spooking a deer, determined to take home a buck or nothing. Just before shooting light faded on the evening of the third day, a fine buck eased into view like a shadow. If it hadn't been for a couple of successful hunts in Mexico and Colorado, I would have taken only this one deer that season.

Whitetails can bounce back amazingly from a low ebb, and the 1957 season was improved to the point where hunting wasn't really bad. The hunting in 1958 was almost the equal of the old days, and the 1959 whitetail season was fabulous. Actually, like a 43-to-nothing ballgame, the abundance of game became boring, and I soon exchanged my rifle for the camera, while Tom went to work on the turkeys. The ranch boasts two small cultivated fields, one sown to winter oats and the other to grain, and when the season opened most of the deer were concentrated within a quarter of a mile of one field or the other.

For the first few days of the season, anyone who could shoot a rifle might have sat at the edge of either field or gone back a short distance into the woods and taken a buck within a few hours. I had four legal bucks within shooting range the first day and a half of hunting, and Tom had six bucks under observation at once in the grain field on the first evening. The deer were temporarily camped in the vicinity of the fields and we found several scrapes where there were no rubs at all. But as the guns began to boom, the situation began to reverse itself rapidly.

There were five hunters in our party, and though each was allowed two bucks and three gobblers, we limited ourselves to one buck and one gobbler apiece on the first hunt, so that we could stay in business a little longer. Opening day followed a bad spell of weather, and another blue norther was expected in two days; so, despite the full moon, the game stuffed itself continually for those first two days. Then, as man scent and the scent of deer viscera began to taint the air, the deer began to feed much less during the daylight hours and many started returning to their regular home bedding ground. But of the five bucks taken by our party, only one was an old trophy mossback, which entered the field at deep dusk and would have been invulnerable to iron sights. This old buster had a badly-injured hind foot which was not completely healed, and we believe this to be his reason for lying close to the grain field, as did many of the spikes and forkhorns. An old buck that has dodged many bullets, and perhaps failed to dodge one or two, will seldom allow himself to be carried away by the mass hysteria of the does and younger bucks, no matter how compelling the reason.

You will hear the statement made that deer will return again and again to a favored feeding place, even under repeated gunfire. This is true only so long as the gunfire is ineffectual; there is a pronounced drop in daytime feeding activity as soon as deer blood taints the air, and after the second kill the deer will usually call it quits.

When the food is well distributed the deer herds will be found well scattered over the area, but there will be certain hot spots in every game covert. These places are known as game pockets, and the hunter should make it a point to seek out all such gamey areas in his hunting ground. A densely-covered south-facing hill, which breaks the force of the cold north wind, footed by a reasonably level semi-open flat that finally drops sharply away to a lower valley, will almost invariably be such a game pocket. The coldest air will drain down into the lower valley and the flat and hillside will be sunny and several degrees warmer than either the hilltop or the valley. During the warmer months of the year the game will usually repair to the cooler, shaded north-facing slopes, but we are not interested in finding game at these seasons of the

year. However, the hunter should bear in mind that an un-
usually warm spell of weather may temporarily drive the deer
back to such places even in the late autumn. Deep, steep-sided
canyons which seldom if ever receive the direct sunlight are
almost invariably devoid of game.

We once hunted a place which terminated in a wild and
beautiful blind valley, a paradise for deer. This valley lay almost due east and west and the upper hillsides were covered
with dense brush. A narrow, oak-lined dry creek wound
through the valley floor, and there were open grassy flats between the creek and the bases of the hills. Despite the large
numbers of deer in this valley, we took only six bucks from
this place in as many years—five from the near edges and only
one from deep in the interior. This was the most difficult place
for a hunter to enter undetected that I have ever known.

The prevailing winds are from the south and west, while the
dry cold winds come chiefly from the north and northwest
and the nastier weather from the east and northeast. Except at
such times as the weather was not suitable for hunting, both
north and south winds veered up this valley in an easterly direction. As we could enter it only from the west, our scent was
invariably funneled up the valley ahead of us. The rocky
creek bed, covered with dry brush and dead leaves, made
walking too noisy, and the brush on the hillsides was too dense
to allow of walking there. This left the open grassy flats as the
only practical avenues of approach, and these were plainly
visible to every deer on the slopes. As though our scent, which
always preceded us by a good half hour, were not enough to
give ample warning of our arrival, there were usually a couple
of "eager beavers," high up on the approaches, to blow long
and lustily as we cautiously thrust the first foot into the open
meadow.

Aside from the extreme difficulty of penetrating this valley without betraying our presence, hard luck, lousy shooting, or plain stupidity dogged nearly every expedition we made. On one occasion I succeeded in working a friend who needed a deer worse than I did into the heart of the valley—and he missed a standing shot of 125 yards at a magnificent sun-drenched buck. On another occasion I guided a companion into the same area, and cruel fate simply robbed us blind. Wishing to give my friend the better opportunity, I pointed out to him the choice stand as soon as it came into view, then remained behind, choosing a seat on the creek bank as my position. Before my friend had covered the hundred yards or so to his destination I heard several deer feeding toward me, and quite close, in the brush-screened creek bottom. Just as I was expecting the deer to step out into the clear a few yards below me, they unaccountably turned and I could hear them moving back in the direction of my companion's stand. As unalarmed deer never retrace their steps while feeding and as I knew these animals were unaware of me, I was at a loss to explain their action. A few minutes later there was a great deal of blowing, stamping, brush crashing, and all the commotion of deer in full flight—every kind of noise except shooting. As we plodded the long way back to camp through the gathering darkness, the details of our disaster began to unfold. My friend had reached the tree which I had pointed out to him and had just sat down, when he looked up squarely into the face of a near-by fawn, which was watching him with obvious fascination. For several long minutes the man and the deer gazed eye to eye; then the fawn raised a foreleg and stamped the ground. It had been this signal, unheard by me, which caused the deer to turn back to determine the cause of the fawn's alarm. My friend was only five yards from the creek bank and, though he heard the deer approaching, he dared not move a muscle, as he knew that his first movement would panic the fawn. Finally, at a sound immediately behind him, he turned his head and found himself looking into the eyes of a buck whose head was sticking up over the bank of the creek. That was when everything came suddenly unwound.

One season Tom made a couple of fruitless still-hunts in the valley, and on both occasions he jumped a big buck in a side canyon which topped out at the same place on the ridge. Figuring that he would follow the same route a third time, we cooked up a "sure-fire" scheme which entailed a drive. I made a lung-bursting climb over a couple of small mountains and stationed my brush-battered body in the agreed position at the appointed time. Tom made the drive—but this time the old buck went out a side canyon of the side canyon. I decided that I should get into the valley a couple of hours before shooting light, so that the deer would forget about me by dawn. I set the alarm for three o'clock and trekked deep into the valley by way of a wilderness cattle trail in the dark of a bitterly-cold morning. I was suffering badly from the cold when daylight finally arrived, and when the first spot of sunlight fell in a little flat below me, I rushed down, without a thought for anything but sitting in the sun and getting warm. About the time I was beginning to feel nice and cozy I discovered that I was sitting in the middle of a wide stretch of the main deer trail. The details surrounding this discovery will not be related, out of consideration for those readers with tender and sympathetic feelings.

Early one sunless morning, as I found myself at the mouth of the valley, I noticed that the wind was quartering over toward the north slope, which was almost completely shrouded by fog. I decided that a long and arduous sneak, first high up the slope and then down and across the densely-brushed and foggy hillside, would put me in a good position near the heart of the hunting area. A tough but masterly executed two-hour sneak brought me out exactly at the desired spot, on the high bank side of the creek, just as the fog lifted, and a wonderful view of choicest meadow land lay before me. I even found a small wash on the steep bank which made a natural chair; so I sat down to wait in comfort. And right there I made one of the greatest tactical blunders of my checkered hunting career.

The area was not well known to me and I was not thoroughly familiar with the major game trail, which lay at my back and closely skirted the high bank along this portion of the creek. Without considering the probability that this trail might bend slightly southward, to follow the contour of the creek, I mistakenly concluded that it would be a waste of time to watch behind me, in the direction of the hillside, which had been completely blanketed by, and was continuing to receive, my scent. I had been seated perhaps ten minutes, my eyes glued to the secluded meadow ahead, when a pressure tank exploded about five yards behind me. I could swear that I felt the blast on the back of my neck, and I expected my whole body—or my cap, at least—to be blown off the ledge to the rocks ten feet below. When I twisted around, I saw the grandfather of all bucks turning wrongside out, and I'll never forget those tremendous antlers if I should live a hundred years. The buck had traveled fifty yards before I could clamber out of the depression and gain my feet, and the telescope sight was not fast enough to catch him in the one brief opening which offered a quick shot.

On still another occasion I boldly entered the valley about noon, and followed the creek bed until I reached the area I wished to hunt. I walked as quietly as possible as I approached my selected position, which was well screened by high banks on both sides. I hid out there until late afternoon, counting on the watching deer to suppose that I had passed on down the hidden cut and on out of the area. In the late afternoon I crawled up the bank and lay down in a small clump of brush, which gave me complete command of the situation. Everything had come off as planned, and I was gloating over the certainty of my success as sundown neared. About an hour before sundown, and just as I was expecting game to show up at any minute, I had the misfortune to draw saliva into my windpipe and break out into a convulsion of strangling and coughing that was undoubtedly heard for miles around. When the spasm finally subsided I wiped my eyes, picked up my rifle, and headed back to camp, for I knew my hunt was over.

The ability to remain still for long periods of time requires much practice. The beginner seldom comprehends the real meaning of complete stillness, and is apt to resent any criticism directed at his constant squirming. The veteran will suppress a cough or sneeze with an exercise of will power unapproached by the novice, and will finally develop a stoic disregard for crawling ants, buzzing flies, and biting mosquitos. You will discover that a gouging limb or rock will cease to annoy you if you tough it out long enough. The fact that a cat napper very frequently sees game near-by immediately upon awakening is a very good indication that nearly everyone moves too much while on a stand. Charley once awoke from a nap to discover his stand almost surrounded by a band of feeding javelinas, and dropped two of them as they scrambled for the brush. These little wild pigs are as wary and furtive as deer and are as fast as greased lightning.

The buck-run or scrape watcher, especially the latter, should remain seated, but the trail and feed ground watcher may alternately sit and stand. These changes of position must, of course, be made slowly and quietly, and the standing position may only be employed where there is an immediate background of trees or brush higher than the hunter's head. The standing watcher is in the best possible position for taking game which suddenly appears from any direction, but few people can stand relatively motionless for periods longer than an hour. Unless I find myself in a situation where a movement would be imprudent, I usually rise to my feet about an hour before shooting-light fades and finish out the time standing. Should game appear at a distance which requires precise holding, the standing watcher can usually sink to a sitting position for the shot. While standing, the rifle muzzle should be held by the trigger hand while the butt of the rifle rests on the ground, or on the toe of the foot if the ground is muddy. From this position the rifle can be shouldered smoothly and rapidly while hand and arm movements are kept quite short and close to the body. The standing watcher has a tremendous advantage whenever game suddenly appears in a direction other than the one he is facing. Comfort, concealment, and coverage are the three requirements of a good stand.

Regardless of the care with which the stand is chosen, you will be continually plagued with the thought that another spot should have been selected. Until a man has spent many seasons in the deer woods, he will worry incessantly about those parts of the perimeter which are concealed from his view, always imagining that huge bucks with rocking-chair antlers are luxuriating in the areas hidden from his sight. Until the hunter gains enough experience to trust his judgment in the choice of stands and learns to resign himself to the fact that some deer will invariably escape detection, he may change stands so frequently as to spoil his chances completely. The hunter is advised to move only after careful and deliberate reflection has convinced him that a change of location will definitely improve his chances.

10 ——— OTHER HUNTING METHODS

The driving of deer, either by men or dogs, is a "hunting" method quite popular in certain areas of the country. Either form of driving depends on the skill and effort of others, and the deer are killed by shooters, not hunters. To the man who prefers to be a member of a large party operating as a team, cheerfully subordinating his will and effort to guidance by others, in order to produce a "community" deer, the individualistic conception of man versus buck will not appeal. Conversely, the man who likes to commune with nature in solitude, delights in a challenge to his skill and proficiency, and derives great pride and enjoyment from personal accomplishment will soon take a dislike for deer driving that matches my own.

Once in a great while a drive will really pile up the deer, but the average yield of deer drives in relation to the numbers of men and total expenditure of time, and effort is incomparably lower than that of an equal number of competent hunters working alone. There are men who claim that many deer coverts cannot be profitably hunted by the lone individual and can be "hunted" only by driving; but I choose to remain highly skeptical of this statement. Also, these men will often make the claim that only buckshot-loaded scatter-guns can be employed effectively in these areas, and again I say, "Phooey." Though many of these areas will defeat the most skillful still hunter, a man can go anywhere on earth a deer can go, and a good scrape hunter will take whitetail deer anywhere they may be found, and with a rifle.

To the man who became acquainted with deer shooting by joining a party of dedicated drivers and has had no other type of experience, but who longs to break away from mob hunting, this book will lead the way. To those incurably gregarious fellows who derive their chief pleasure from social contact with the group and who become immediately uncomfortable when separated from the sound or sight of other people, no other form of deer hunting would appeal.

I believe I may safely say that the hunting-accident rate among those who drive deer is greater than that among those who hunt deer by other methods. Some years ago we found ourselves members of a hunting party which consisted of several father-and-son teams, most of whom demonstrated less skill and familiarity with their weapons than we liked. One of the men became obsessed with the idea of a deer drive, although the terrain was quite unsuited and none of us was thoroughly familiar with the area. We stoutly objected to the idea, giving several pertinent reasons for our position, but we were voted down, and the master planner, a man with one whitetail kill to his credit, outlined the strategy. Just as soon as the others were out of sight I ducked up a side canyon, while the tumult and the shouting died away in the distance. I presently detected a movement on my back trail, which soon proved to have been made by Tom, who was trailing me after having discovered my footprints when he hit on the same idea as my own. We hid out until the drive was over, hearing only one shot, which we later learned was accidentally discharged as the hunters re-assembled.

I had my fill of driving one bitter cold autumn in the Ozark Mountains. This fruitless fiasco lasted a whole week and the driving was done by dogs. One of the chief participants, a very brave man confined to a wheel chair, made the only kill—a fox squirrel which ran by his chair and was dispatched with a pine knot. Each morning we assembled in bitter cold darkness and stumbled through the woods until assigned our stands. The drive master took the dogs deep into the woods and loosed them, and after an endless period of waiting we would hear the dogs give tongue. We followed the chase eagerly with our ears but invariably the sounds gradually faded away and died in the distance. Presently the drive master would come around and pick us up, explaining that the deer had run out by some unguarded route but that, if the dogs decided to come back before too late, we would try again that afternoon. About half the time the dogs didn't return until late in the night.

One of my friends, an avid deer hunter, was a hunting and fishing guide in Minnesota during his youth, and his father still follows that profession. Early in our aquaintance this man remarked that they always got their deer with no fuss or bother, so I was quite surprised when he asked me a few questions about whitetail hunting. When I reminded him of his former professional standing and suggested that he should be the one to give *me* advice, he confessed that the groups of drive-hunting sportsmen who invaded the woods each fall provided the venison for the local inhabitants. Knowing all the deer runs and crossings, the natives would learn where the drive was to take place and then station themselves at strategic points and kill deer that the amateurs drove their way.

No deer drive will turn out to be any better than its drive

master nor any better than the exactitude with which the drive master's orders and directions are carried out. Every drive is an entirely different undertaking, even in the same covert, because each differing wind and weather condition—as well as the differing numbers of hunters involved—will require a different strategy. No directions or instructions can be given for driving deer—the champion drive master of Podunk County would be as helpless as you or I if transplanted to an unfamiliar area, and, just as you and I, would be forced to place himself completely in the hands of the local drive master during the hunt.

The participant in a deer drive must resolutely curb an itchy trigger finger and he must follow the drive master's directions to the letter. Many drive groups demand a heavy forfeit from any stander who is found to have moved more than the length of his weapon from the exact spot on which he was placed. The unforgivable sin is for a stander to desert his post for even one brief moment, until directed to do so by the drive master. The drivers should move through the cover with no more noise than hikers would make and they should be certain to maintain their assigned position in the line-up. Shouting and stick beating will so pinpoint each driver's location that the deer will find it easy to slip back through the line, and excessive noise will also spoil the hunting of others in the vicinity.

"Horn rattling," which is the practice of striking two deer antlers together and thus simulating the sound of fighting bucks, is another method of whitetail hunting which is practiced extensively in certain rather localized areas. Like turkey calling, this method is practically impossible to impart through printed words, and it is generally considered to be ineffective in most whitetail ranges. The masters of this art are those who have actually listened to a buck fight, and their more apt pupils. Horn rattling is practiced in many parts of the South and is the accepted method for hunting bucks in that semi-arid portion of Texas which lies south of US Highway 90.

Some men claim this method can be employed with success in any whitetail covert, but many practitioners of this method have met with little or no success in distant areas. Few horn rattlers will even hazard a guess as to the reason for this drastic variation in results, but some believe the presence of sheep or goats on the whitetail range will render this method ineffectual; they hold that the frequent sparring and head butting of these animals, especially at certain seasons of the year, will condition the buck deer to disregard any similar sound. I am inclined to disagree with this belief, and will present my own views on this subject a little later on.

Each expert horn rattler has his own ideas regarding every phase of the art, even to the most effective size of antlers; but medium antlers are generally selected and they should be moderately curved and symmetrical. The two sections are split apart and the base of each antler is ground to form a rounded knob. All brow tines and rough projections are smoothed away, to form a comfortable hand grip, and occasionally an out-of-line main tine will be removed also. The pair of antlers are joined by a two-foot length of stout cord, which allows them to be carried slung about the neck. Very old or weathered antlers will give a "dead" sound; so the antlers are usually taken from a freshly-killed buck and are carefully stored out of the sun and weather. A few exacting rattlers use a set of antlers but one season, although the majority will use a set for several years, and many soak their antlers in water or bury them in damp soil for several weeks immediately preceding the deer season.

There are many reports of successful "rattlers" who scorn the use of horns, calling up bucks by striking their gun stocks with their hunting knives or by whacking a small tree with a limb or stick, but the reader is warned that these reports originate in Texas.

Once in a great while a curious doe may slip up for a peek at the source of disturbance, but the horn rattler will normally attract only bucks. There are three cardinal rules for successful horn rattling: the rattler must be operating in a remote and undisturbed area and within the hearing of a buck; he must be *well* hidden in a patch of thick cover such as that in which bucks normally fight and which will obscure the vision of a potential third participant; and he must be able to closely imitate the desired sound in a convincing manner.

Master buck rattlers operate within a hundred or two hundred yards of a thicket which they have reason to believe harbors a resting buck, and these men will take bucks any time during the day, although more often when the moon is down. The absolute masters of this art will locate a fresh scrape, if possible, and select a suitable calling place about a hundred and fifty yards away. After selecting their stand they will sit quietly for thirty minutes or more before rattling their horns, so that the buck, should he have seen them pass, will believe that they are well out of the area. Those men who have never delved deeply into buck behavior most often get better results in the early morning and late evening, when deer are apt to be moving about.

As in turkey calling, a little horn rattling goes a long way, and the most successful rattlers usually use their rattles very sparingly. Contrary to popular belief, the antlers are not held with points opposing, in the manner of a living buck, but one antler is reversed, so that all the points face the same way and one antler fits into the curve of the other. Whacking the antlers together can be very hard on the hands and fingers, especially in the case of a beginner, and many rattlers wear gloves to lessen the chance of injury. As stated before, each buck rattler has his own technique, but basically the method requires the antlers to be crashed together, twisted violently a couple of times while firmly pressed together, then snatched apart violently under side pressure. The rounded butt of each antler is then banged against the ground in a quick one-two cadence, after which the antlers are quickly laid aside and the rifle taken up, ready for action. When this method works, bucks often appear right on top of the hunter, out of nowhere and so quickly as to catch the operator with his figurative pants down. Two hunters sometimes work together, one doing the rattling while the other does the shooting.

No buck, of course, will approach the hunter if he receives his scent or has become aware of his presence in any way, and the older bucks, with less libido and more wariness, most often keep well back in the brush and circle the scene of the "battle" until they have the wind on it. The horn rattler must therefore keep sharp lookout for the slightest movement which could indicate a sneaking old mossback. Many of the younger bucks are quite impetuous, however, and will stalk right up to the rattler with their hair turned forward and their eyes dimmed by battle lust. Many will charge up like cavalry horses and their ears may seem deafened to gunfire. There are reports that as many as four bucks have converged simultaneously on a horn rattler.

When bucks fight, they lunge at each other with lowered horns, and meet head on. If the shock of collision fails to upset one of the contestants, they twist their heads violently in an effort to throw their adversary, each striving meanwhile to push the other into a back-pedaling loss of ground which could be accelerated into disaster. If one stumbles and goes down, the other will instantly disengage and then try to drive home a body thrust. However, like boxers, the stronger buck may be out-maneuvered repeatedly by the smaller one who takes advantage of his speed to extricate himself from unfavorable positions. Some whitetail battles last two hours or longer, but most of these prolonged affairs are inconclusive, ending by mutual consent of the weary contestants because they no longer have a *causus belli;* the prize for which they risked their lives is, by this time, gaily cavorting through distant glades with some enterprizing spike or forkhorn.

Like turkey calling, there is an element of danger connected with horn rattling. A trigger-happy hunter, unacquainted with the practice, might conceivably investigate the source of the sound, stalk the spot, and put a bullet into the rattler's dimly outlined body upon detecting a slight movement. I know a police officer who very nearly shot a poacher by mistake while hunting, putting a 30-'06 bullet through his coat. The officer was on private, posted property and had no reason to suspect another man's presence in the area. The poacher was an old man dressed in neutral-colored clothing and sporting a huge, full gray beard. He also had a large pair of rattling antlers suspended about his neck and was crouched under shaded brush at the edge of a clearing, about a hundred yards from the hunter's stand. The latter caught a slight movement and glassed the poacher with his low-power scope, but could resolve nothing. Then another slight movement caught a sunbeam full on a big antler, and the hunter fired. The police officer was so shaken by the close call that he allowed the old poacher to berate him unmercifully and stalk away unapprehended. Another man once told me of sneaking up to a spot from which he had heard a turkey call, to get a better outline of the bird through a bush, and was actually squeezing the trigger when the "turkey" stood up, placed his call in his pocket, shouldered his weapon, and walked away. The would-be turkey shooter sat down and vomited.

The rattling-up of bucks in not considered to be highly effective until very late in the season, December being the most rewarding month and late December being the best time of all. In the South Texas area, it is generally believed that the whitetails do not rut until December and the peak of success with antler rattling coincides with the rutting peak. Although experience has verified December as being the most productive rattling season, I am at variance with the other opinions in regard both to the time of rutting and the coincidence of the rutting peak with the greatest rattling success. I believe that the peak of the rutting season is past in South Texas by the first of December, as it is in other whitetail ranges, and that rattling is most effective for a period of time following the highly-active period of the rut. The doe's sex urge subsides as suddenly as it surges, but the whitetail buck, like most other male animals, is sexually stimulated by erotic thoughts and memories for a longer period of time. The abrupt disappearance of willing does from the covert leaves the bucks at the height of their sexual frenzy, and, after a few doe-hungry days, they will recklessly exploit any situation or development that promises even the slightest chance of producing a rutting doe. The skilled horn rattler, under such circumstances, should hardly fail of success in any secluded whitetail covert, because nothing but a doe in heat will induce two bucks to fight each other.

Whitetail deer cannot be lured by the use of a so-called "deer-call," intended to simulate a vocal call or bleat. There is evidence to support the belief that members of the mule deer family occasionally employ a vocal sound, or mating call, to supplement the faculty of scent in seeking out the opposite sex. The Columbian blacktail deer, and especially the Sitka variety, seem to employ a low, humming call quite frequently. But any whitetail that appears in answer to one of these calls does so only out of curiosity, and probably would have responded in the same way to a phonograph recording of orchestral music.

We have now outlined all the generally-practiced and accredited methods of hunting whitetail deer, although the hunter will be continually bombarded with other sure-fire schemes, gimmicks, lures, and methods. There is, of course, a remote possibility that a new and effective method for taking whitetail deer will appear on the scene, but you are advised to weigh the key points of any new method against the known habits and character of the quarry before embracing it.

Where the covert teems with hunters, you will have less chance to use various methods against the deer or even to verify a great deal of the whitetail lore imparted here or elsewhere. The deer, under such conditions, may be so constantly harried and so thoroughly disturbed that they will temporarily abandon their regular habits and suppress every instinct except that of self-preservation. The nation's best whitetail areas support a deer population of about thirty head to the square mile, which cooks down to possibly six bucks. When there are fifteen hunters to the square mile, as in Pennsylvania, you won't need a slide rule to figure out your mathematical chances. However, to demonstrate the worth of superior skill and hunting knowledge, even under this condition there are men who invariably produce venison. How can *you* win against these disheartening odds?

In the first place, the true odds against you are a great deal less than the statistics would indicate, mainly because less than one of every fifteen gun toters combing the woods is a competent hunter, the majority being perennial amateurs who add much to the confusion but little to the home freezer. Ignorance regarding the whitetail deer and its proper hunting technique is so widespread that, should you faithfully master the meager facts contained in this imperfect book and follow its instructions and advice, you will become one hunter in a thousand. In the second place, you will not likely miss your chance when it does come, as do the majority of hunters who, in addition to being poor shots, have not your knowledge of how, when, and where to shoot their deer when they are presented with the opportunity. You will have a properly-sighted, fitted, and adjusted weapon of good ballistic properties loaded with proper bullets—a combination enjoyed by less than one hunter out of twenty.

Hunting for sport should rightly be a contest only between man and his quarry—never a contest between men. However, as distasteful as these words may sound, where fifteen men are each seeking one of six bucks, the problem becomes how to "get there firstest with the mostest." Only half of all the bucks will be taken in any given hunting season, so the average hunter success ratio will be one out of five. Now for a review of the specific details that will increase your chances of getting your own deer.

If you are seriously determined to succeed you will make a real effort to discover a good hunting area as remote as possible, and you will devote a day or two just before opening day to scouting the area thoroughly. You will penetrate the brush edges and locate the major trails where they wend through well-screened cover, because you have learned that the seeker of bucks must get right in the brush with them. You will travel these secluded trails and make mental notes of all places where signs of buck are heavy. You will note all places where concentrations of deer are observed and will determine heavily-used feeding places, especially grain fields. If you locate such a feeding area, and, weather permitting, are well stationed there at daylight on opening morning, you will be in an excellent position to make the statistics look silly.

As soon as hunting pressure halts the daytime feeding activity or in the event no concentrated feeding ground is located, you will go immediately to the most likely spot you have discovered along a brush-protected major trail, take a good, comfortable stand, and wait for the horde of brush-beaters to drive a buck in front of your gun. Since you must put up with a woods full of other hunters, you will let them unwittingly work for you. If your stand is well chosen you may find yourself practically alone with all the deer, as the vast majority of "hunters" will confine their operation to the more open areas where they can "see." You, understanding a buck's nature and habits, will be delighted with a small hole through the brush which permits an unrestricted view of even ten feet of a major game trail containing a fresh scrape or rub, if the spot is fairly well isolated from other hunters. When you are thus positioned, and with the wind or breeze in your face, a buck will come by sooner or later just as surely as day follows night, and you will have only yourself to blame if you allow it to pass by unscathed. We attribute our well-above-average deer-hunting success to the fact that we have muffed very few opportunities rather than to any special gifts or qualificaions.

There are many men who have built enviable records as consistent deer slayers who are virtually ignorant of deer and their habits. They know only three things—how to take a stand on a well-used trail located back in the brush, how to sit still, and how to kill a deer when it walks by. Many of these men never heard of a scrape and some wouldn't recognize a rub if they saw it. They may even believe that the stork brings baby deer, but they have sense enough to keep watch over the kind of trail that deer use when fleeing from one part of their range to another, and they sit there quietly and let the other hunters move deer in front of their guns.

If you can locate places along such trails where there are fresh rubs, and possibly fresh scrapes to boot, your chances of taking a buck will be excellent, regardless of the hunting pressure in the immediate area. If there are but few other hunters around, the buck may come to your stand of his own volition; if many other hunters are in the area, they may booger deer along the trail in front of your stand. If you are located where two or more prime trails cross, your chances may be nearly doubled. About the only thing that might spoil your chances would be to have one or more like-minded hunters take up position on either or both sides of you. Should you find yourself in such a situation, you would probably do well to seek another location.

You should take every advantage of the weather during the hunting season, putting your knowledge of deer-weather relations to its best use. Unless the weather is fit for neither man nor beast, you should make a determined effort to be out on opening day. You will get a real break if there is no snow on the ground, because many hunters will then stay at home and await a "tracking" snow. Keep yourself well posted on predicted weather conditions for several days ahead, timing yourself to arrive on the hunting ground just before a storm is expected to be *over*. Though many observers will shake their heads when you depart in such foul weather, you will often be johnny-on-the-spot for one or two grand hunting days while most of the other hunters are assembling their gear.

Often a predicted storm will be delayed a day or two— or even fail to arrive at all—and the hunter who chooses to gamble and remain in the covert when most of the other hunters are bugging out will be rewarded with a day of wonderful hunting. You could, of course, guess wrong. We out-guessed the weather man twice during the fall of fifty-nine, which was a record breaker for foul weather, and enjoyed two fabulous hunts in perfect hunting weather. The weather forecast for opening day was so discouraging that only a person who was mentally suspect would have considered an outdoor expedition, but we felt impelled to go. If we had been sensible people we would have stayed at home and missed out on some wonderful hunting.

It is an ill wind which blows nobody good, and there are times when the scent of another hunter in the covert will help you to get a deer. I recall a late-season hunt a number of years back, in which my companion's scent presented me with a grand old buck. I had already taken a trophy buck earlier in the season, but my good friend had drawn a blank and I was striving to give him every break. On the evening of our last hunting day we decided to try our most promising area, although the wind was wrong for this place. Given his choice of stands, my friend selected what was probably the best crossing in the area, and I then positioned myself about three hundred yards away and directly in his scent stream. I had little or no expectation of getting a shot but felt that by keeping our scent streams merged, we would taint a minimum area and thereby promote my friend's chances. Just before sundown I detected several deer feeding about a large clump of laurel bushes in a gently up-sloping meadow about a quarter of a mile away. I carelessly raised my rifle in order to scope the deer for antlers—of which there were none; the deer noticed my movement and became instantly aware of my presence, as I was sitting in a poorly-concealed position. Very quickly a yearling doe detached herself from the group and started angling in my direction, on a slightly-curving path in order to take advantage of intervening cover. I groaned audibly at what fate had in store for me, for I knew beyond a shadow of a doubt that the young doe was coming to find out what I was and that she would unfailingly accomplish her mission.

By watching the distant deer, who were, in turn, watching the deploying doe, I kept track of her progress as she approached my left front, and then watched her cross slowly in front of me. After crossing to my right without making positive identification, she turned to circle me in order to get my scent. I was watching her from the corner of my eye as she drew nearly abreast. Then, just as I was thinking that my discovery was but seconds away, I caught a glimpse of a huge, heavy-antlered buck plodding steadily in my general direction from the direction of my companion's stand. The longest hour of my hunting career consisted of the next twenty seconds or so, as I watched the progress of both deer from the corner of my eye. The buck broke into the clear of a tiny opening about the time the doe was one step from my scent stream, and my sharp whistle, which stopped the doe dead in her tracks, was completely ignored by the buck. The doe remained motionless but the buck plodded steadily on and disregarded my second whistle, which I sounded as he entered the next small opening. He stopped only after he had crossed this opening and gained the protection of a large bush; he then turned slightly, to face me at a somewhat quartering angle.

Holding just behind the shoulder, to give myself maximum margin in case of bullet deflection, I touched off the old cannon and watched the buck turn wrongside out and race madly down his back trail. The startled doe quartered out directly in front of me, but I scarcely remember seeing her, as I was vainly attempting to keep the buck in sight and get off another shot at him as he flashed through the brush. But he suddenly turned away from the brush, dashed blindly out into the open meadow, circled tightly, and then piled up dead. My bullet had entered the exact point of aim, destroyed the rear of one lung, ploughed through the liver and completely separated it into two almost equal parts, then exited from the off flank. Although the heart area was untouched, this liver shot produced a reaction identical to that of the usual heart shot. This buck had approached the crossing, smelled my partner, and then attempted to circle the large meadow to reach his objective. He simply had the misfortune to walk in front of my gun a couple of seconds before the doe had a chance to warn him.

11 ——— RIFLE HANDLING AND CARE

The only men who have never discharged a firearm unintentionally are those who have not used or handled guns very much. Regardless of the caution exercised and the commitment to memory of the ten commandments of gun safety, sooner or later, if you use and handle guns a great deal, you will accidentally discharge one. Among veteran hunters, however, this type of "accident" is the least dreaded of all, because they have formed the unbreakable habit of *never allowing the muzzle to become pointed in the direction of any human being.* This habit is your *only* guarantee against a serious accident some day. There are numerous other rules of gun safety that should be everlastingly obeyed, but the constant exercise of this one rule will make all the others secondary in importance.

With that warning, we can eliminate from further discussion cases of adults being killed or maimed by their own weapons. It is in this connection that you will often hear the term "fool killer" applied to sporting weapons. This appellation is particularly appropriate when the the victim's death occurs while he is cleaning his weapon.

I have enjoyed the brief aquaintance of hunters who pushed

their safety to "off" position immediately upon entering the hunting field and carried their weapons in this dangerous position throughout the hunt. Companions who continue to hunt with such men are simply asking for trouble. You must form the habit of keeping the action in "safe" position at all times until you are actually preparing to shoot. You must also develop the habit of checking the position of the safety at frequent intervals, especially after you have shot the gun, or even contemplated firing it. Cocking of the arm or releasing the safety soon becomes automatic when the weapon is shouldered, but returning the gun to the safety position is easily overlooked and must be done by conscious direction.

A hunter who would fire at a noise in the brush or at an unidentified movement is beyond the help or influence of this treatise. Such a person should immediately seek the services of a competent psychiatrist. His case is only slightly less advanced than that of a person who would deliberately leave a live grenade lying on a public playground. I definitely resent the inclusion of such incidents, which result in mayhem or murder, in the statistics of hunting accidents.

Any person who would fire at a target only *partially* identified is but slightly better off mentally than the man who would fire into a shaking bush. Where the hunter has detected enough evidence to establish the *probable* nature of his target, the resulting murder perhaps should merely be termed manslaughter and the sentence reduced to life imprisonment. Oddly enough, many of these killers who blasted away "because that patch of color looked just like deer hide" are solid, substantial citizens who would foam at the mouth at the very thought of a hot-rod drag-race down a busy thoroughfare. Regardless of such a man's position in life, his firing at a target which has not been *positively* identified is a ruthless and callous act worthy of the most primitive savage.

No one of the hunters in my family would consider himself to be in great jeopardy should he unwittingly happen to sneak on hands and knees through a patch of cover being watched by one of the others. How many hunters do *you* know of whom the same could be said? How many of your hunting companions could say the same about you?

Readers are constantly admonished not to "monkey" with guns around camp, especially other people's guns. I heartily subscribe to this advice but can't go along with one author's statement that every hunting camp seems to have at least one "gun monkeyer." Such a person will be found in no camp of mine—or at least not for long.

It is incumbent upon every gun user to *know* that his weapon is in safe operating condition. Periodically, you should give your weapon a "shake down" test in which the cocked but unloaded arm is shaken, jarred, and jolted as hard as is possible without damaging it, to see if the firing-pin will fall. The safety should be movable only under deliberate pressure, and the safety-locked trigger must withstand *hard* pulls and yanks. If there is or has been even the slightest evidence to cause suspicion of the arm's safeness, it should be taken immediately to a competent gunsmith for dismantling and inspection. Should you ever knowingly take a defective arm into the field in the company of others, you place yourself in a class with the motorist who will drive his car when he knows the brakes to be defective.

The majority of guns which are traded in on new ones have mechanical defects, and sometimes these defects reduce the safety factor of the arm. Reputable dealers will give every trade-in a thorough test and satisfy themselves of the weapon's proper functioning before offering it for sale. However, an occasional obscure or intermittent trouble may not be detected; so the purchaser must treat any newly-acquired arm as suspect until a reasonable amount of time and usage has established its reliability. No properly-functioning modern arm, when placed in the correct "safety" position, will be discharged by falling over, even on solid rock; nor can it be discharged by "catching on brush" except possibly in the case of a weapon carried with the finger pressing on the trigger. Except in the case of double-barreled shotguns, I'm always skeptical of accidents for which the above-mentioned circumstances are cited as the cause. Remember, there are very few hunting accidents—the vast majority of deaths and injuries which occur in the hunting field are attributable to criminal negligence.

As in all situations in which groups of people live and work together in safety, peace, and harmony, every hunting camp must have a chosen leader to direct the activities. The first official action of the camp leader should be to outline the safety rules that will govern the conduct of all members. A sensible safety program would include these stipulations:

No weapon may be brought into camp with a loaded chamber.
No weapon may be placed in a vehicle with a loaded chamber.
No weapon will be handled or operated in camp except for the normal purposes of cleaning, care, or necessary adjustment.
No person will handle another's weapon without first asking and receiving the owner's permission.
No member will carry his gun loaded while in the company of another member, unless actively engaged in hunting.

When all members implicitly obey the above rules and all demonstrate sensible gun-handling technique in the field, no firearm injuries will occur. Members of a party in which these rules are flagrantly violated are in grave risk of mortal injury.

Any person who gets himself killed or maimed while engaging in horse play with a firearm or while drawing his gun toward him by the muzzle will get no sympathy from me.

About the only condition under which a properly-handled firearm in good working order can injure the shooter is when there is an obstruction in the bore. A hunter must exercise the greatest care to prevent the muzzle from becoming clogged with mud or snow, and a careful inspection must be made immediately following any slip or fall. Snow falling from tree limbs under which the hunter passes is probably the greatest single contributor to this condition. It is imperative that all bore obstructions be completely removed before the arm is fired or a burst barrel will almost invariably result.

The shoulder-supported weapon, while being carried in the presence of others, must be kept pointed sharply upward. In theory, a weapon pointed sharply downward should be quite safe, but this doesn't work out in practice. You will note that I make no distinction between loaded and unloaded arms in this statement. All safe gun-handling is predicated upon subconscious habit, which explains the oft-repeated admonition to treat all guns as though they were always cocked and loaded. Although this advice will sound childishly silly to the novice, his respect for its wisdom will grow with his experience. Never follow a man who carries his weapon over his shoulder in the manner of a soldier on parade, or you will place yourself in the uncomfortable position of frequently looking down his barrel. And never subject a following companion to that kind of treatment. A weapon slung over the shoulder in the conventional manner as provided by a gun sling will meet all safety requirements. Unless a sling is used, the proper transportation of a hunting weapon in the presence of others normally requires the use of both hands, unless one hand is otherwise occupied.

The lone hunter has considerable freedom of choice in his mode of weapon carry, as far as safety is concerned, but only a few of these methods will enable him to go into action quickly and effectively. The one oft-employed method of carry to be definitely avoided while actively engaged in hunting is the shoulder carry, already mentioned. Beside being an awkward position from which to go into action, the projection of the barrel above the hunter's head will add much to his visibility.

To the veteran hunter, his weapon has long ceased to be a separate instrument or piece of equipment, and has become an integral part of himself—an extension of his physical being. From any position of either his weapon or himself, and even in pitch darkness, the first contact of the veteran's hand with any portion of his rifle will permit him to bring it quickly to bear without conscious effort. The practiced gun handler accomplishes this action as easily and unthinkingly as one gropes for an unseen pencil, unconsciously manipulates it in his fingers, and brings it up, correctly positioned for writing. But some gun carries are superior to others and lend themselves more readily to fast efficient gun mounting.

The beginner should first familiarize himself with the cross-chest carry, which finds both hands in their proper shooting positions and the gun held in a slanting position across the chest. This is an excellent carry for the still-hunter likely to contact fast-moving game at any moment, and is the second-fastest carry known for getting into action. Its only objections are a tendency to tire the hunter over a long period of time and the need for using both hands almost constantly. However, where walking is easy and thick brush is not continually encountered, this is an excellent carry for anyone. I employ this carry extensively while still-hunting, switching occasionally to the Indian carry, which is slower, and to the hip carry, which is the fastest known to me.

To go into the Indian carry from the cross-chest carry, merely lift the fore end out of the supporting hand and drop it into the crook of the arm. Now fold the supporting hand over and grasp the wrist of the trigger hand. This carry is definitely slower than the cross-chest carry but is much less tiring. The hip-rest carry is simply accomplished by lowering the weapon from the shooting position without moving the hands, and resting the grip-encircling trigger hand on the hip. This carry is tops when the hunter stands still a great deal and when walking is slow and deliberate, as in still-hunting.

Where thick cover and narrow trails require the frequent use of one hand to fend off brush and, in addition, demand a more streamlined passage, the trail carry—also known as the woodsman's carry—is the one to be employed. In this one-hand carry, the weapon is grasped at the point of balance by the supporting hand and the arm is dropped to the side. The weapon is thus carried low and parallel to the ground with the muzzle pointing straight ahead. To go into action, sweep the weapon up and place the butt to your shoulder. The trigger hand grasps the small of the stock in the normal shooting position and releases the safety, while the supporting hand is slid forward along the fore end to the correct point for holding. When I first started my hunting career as a young boy, I fell into the habit of carrying my weapon in the trail-carry manner except that the gun was held in my trigger hand. I have never been able to completely break myself of this habit and still find myself employing this unorthodox carry at times. By pitching the weapon slightly upward into my supporting hand, and catching the grip with my trigger hand, I get into shooting position about as quickly as can be done from the correct carry, but the beginner should avoid such a practice.

The serious hunter will soon learn to avoid frivolous and irresponsible camp companions—the fellows who usually go along just for "kicks" or perhaps only to be with the "gang." Many top camp-fellows are sensible nippers, but the man who would rather forget to bring his rifle than his bottle will invariably ruin your pleasure, even if he fails to ruin your health. As you gain experience you will also learn to avoid hunting companions who are excessively quick-tempered or who otherwise demonstrate emotional instability. Many men who make the most genial hosts at a social gathering and can put life into any party will demonstrate a complete reversal of character when subjected to the imperfections of normally-rigorous camp life. Anyone who walks into game coverts with a firearm is a hunter, but you should strive to be a hunter's hunter and seek companions who are cut from the same cloth.

I know of nothing that will bring out a person's true nature more quickly than a wilderness hunting trip. Many years ago I sought and received acceptance into a party embarking on a hunt in a Western wilderness. Most of the men, including the owner of the vehicle in which we traveled, were unknown to me at the beginning of the trip, but none were strangers upon our return. During the long ride to our destination, the driver dropped the remark that high places made him quite uncomfortable. Under further questioning he admitted to an extreme phobia, and, as we began the final climb up a winding, unpaved mountain road bordered by a sheer drop, the man became almost insanely hysterical. Finally he cut the switch, yanked up the hand brake, snatched the door open, scrambled and fought his way a distance up the steep slope, embraced a jutting rock, and sat there a long while with teeth chattering and sweat pouring down his forehead. We finally coaxed him back into the car, and I drove the remainder of the way in the unfamiliar vehicle. That night around the campfire he described the circumstances surrounding his one and only deer kill. After downing the animal, he said, he threw his weapon down and ran the entire distance of two miles back to camp—an action he had never been able to explain or account for. Next morning when the camp leader asked me where I intended to hunt, I declined to commit myself until our hysterical friend had made his decision. When he pointed north and declared that direction to be his choice, I instantly chose to hunt toward the south. I followed this identical procedure every morning of our stay.

One final word on firearm and hunting safety—only in defense of his life would a sensible man ever employ his weapon as a club to subdue or dispatch his wounded quarry. Countless fine weapons are mutilated or destroyed each season from such abuse, and this practice has probably been responsible for more self-inflicted gun "accidents" than all other malpractices combined.

The proper care of your weapon in the field should commence before leaving home. You should begin by thoroughly rubbing a few drops of linseed oil over the entire stock surface about a week before hunting season, so that the oil will be completely dried before the arm is put to use. This thin, tough coating will help to protect against scratches, and I always repeat the operation at the end of the season, to help cover up the scratches acquired during the hunt. The chief value of an oiled stock, however, is its resistance to moisture. All working parts of the mechanism should be thoroughly but lightly oiled several days in advance of the season, and the weapon placed muzzle down on a pad of paper, so that all excess oil will drain off before usage. Unless some mishap should require complete dismantling and cleaning of the working parts, this one oiling should suffice for the entire hunting season. The weapon is placed muzzle down for several days so that excess oil does not drain back into the stock; gun oil is injurious to wood.

After several days of draining in a muzzle-down position, the weapon should be cocked and snapped a couple of times on an empty chamber, immediately preceding the first hunt. This is for the purpose of spraying excess oil from the bolt, as it is quite disconcerting to cut down on a buck and receive a squirt of oil in the eye as the firing pin falls, and equally as bad if you are wearing glasses. Your gun oil should be of the highest quality and should be specially treated to prevent gumming and stiffening in very cold weather. Anderol and Fiendoil are two oils I can recommend. Many oils stiffen so badly that they can render an autoloader inoperative in barely freezing weather, and render other types of actions so stiff that they can be manipulated only with the greatest difficulty. It often requires only a slight stiffening of the oil to hinder the fall of the firing pin sufficiently to cause misfires.

The exposed metal parts of your rifle should be wiped down with an oily rag at the end of each hunting day. This should require only a minute's time and will repay you well in the long run. You should have a supply of cleaning patches of the proper size for your particular bore, and a dry patch followed by an oiled one should be run through your barrel each evening in wet weather and days on which the weapon has been fired. Your weapon should always be cleaned from the breech end if its construction permits, and it is considered good practice to keep the rifle's chamber free of excess oil or grease.

A thoroughly-wet gun should be field stripped, vigorously shaken to drain out as much water as possible, wiped with a dry cloth, then placed overnight by the fire to dry. But never place the weapon any nearer the fire than you can comfortably hold the back of your hand; this same rule applies to clothing and especially to leather articles. Should your weapon have been dunked in fine sand, salt water, or any gritty muck, a quick and complete dismantling is called for. This should be followed by a complete flushing with clean hot water, a thorough drying, then a complete cleaning in gasoline or other solvent, if it is available. The metal parts should be well oiled before reassembling, and don't forget to check the center of impact before using the rifle again.

Your knife should be thoroughly washed and dried as soon as practicable after its use on game. Blood contains much salt, and sometimes causes rust almost as rapidly as sea water does. Your knife should also be resharpened on a fine whetstone after every gutting job, and a drop or two of cooking oil rubbed on the blade will help to protect it without affecting the taste of the meat of any animal on which it is later used. Butter, bacon, and margarine contain too much salt for them to be used on your knife blade.

Every hunter should keep a can of neat's-foot oil in his closet or gun cabinet, and every piece of his leather gear should be given a liberal application once a year. His all-leather footgear will be equally benefitted. Rubber equipment, on the other hand, is quickly and permanently damaged by any kind of oil. Leather gun cases, slings, belts, saddlebags, saddleboots, and knife and pistol scabbards should receive a liberal application of neat's-foot before each hunting season. Not only will your leather accouterments be softened, preserved, and made water-resistant, but you will be spared the accursed squeaking that flexing leather so often produces.

A flexible, felt-lined gun case is very useful for transporting a weapon, and a stiff fleece-lined case is even better. But never, never leave your gun stored in such a case for any extended period of time. Any conventional gun case will absorb moisture and a weapon left inside will "sweat" beads of moisture which will cause rapid oxidation. The fleece-lined case is the worse offender in this respect.

12 ——————— PERSONAL EQUIPMENT

The two basic necessities of the whitetail hunter, beside his weapon and ammunition, are his knife and his rope. The wilderness hunter must also carry a good compass, and matches in a waterproof container, but wilderness hunting is beyond the scope of this book as it is not frequently encountered in whitetail hunting. The man who hunts alone, even in thoroughly familiar territory, should carry waterproofed matches against the possibility of an accident or any other circumstance that might force him to spend a night in the woods, as he might easily find himself in need of a fire. Dry matches can mean the difference between life and death in the event of a thorough wetting, even in temperatures slightly above freezing. A small cylindrical seltzer bottle, packed tightly with kitchen matches to prevent rattle, makes a good substitute for a water-proof match case, but it should be wrapped in heavy paper, to contain the fragments in case of breakage. In addition to the regular supply of safety matches, smokers should carry a freshly-filled lighter, for emergency use. It takes a complete dunking to put a lighter out of working order.

Since the hunter's rope, a most important accessory, has already been discussed, we now pass on to the hunting knife. You will do well to avoid the tiny, slender sheath knives which are becoming quite popular. If a need is felt for a small-bladed knife, it can be better met by a very sharp jackknife carried in the pocket. When there is a pelvis or brisket to be cut, or a heavy pole, you will quickly discover the advantages of a real hunting knife. You need not go overboard, as a friend of mine did, and purchase one of those huge, massive-bladed imports which appear to be a cross between a Roman sword and a Philippine bolo. But the deer hunter needs a knife of ample proportions. The elk hunter who scorns to carry a light belt ax might possibly get by with a surplus Marine Corps knife with a 5-inch handle and a 7-inch blade. These big bear-stabbers are of excellent quality and their proportions would make old Colonel Bowie proud. Though too long and heavy for the whitetail hunter, these knives will go through a six-inch tree like a gay divorcee through an alimony check.

Probably the best knife for the whitetail hunter is a good-quality sheath knife of medium-heavy weight, with a broad well-rounded five-inch blade. My own favorite knife is of the Marbles pattern, and the blade, though only four and a half inches long, is thick and heavy along the back. I believe that the deer hunter's knife blade should be limited to five and a half inches unless his own experience has indicated the need for a longer one. I could not be induced to use a knife of the Finnish pattern which has no hand guard, and I have found little or no need for back-ground points, although most hunting knives have them. Although the straight-sided, wedge-shaped blade is more difficult to sharpen, I believe its added strength makes it more suitable to hard usage than the hollow-ground blade. The three-layer laminated blade, made of two differing steels, is probably the finest type of blade available.

Until the Avey belt-supported cartridge holder came along,

I always experienced difficulty in carrying my ammunition. Conventional cartridge belts are quite expensive and their excessive weight, bulk, and cartridge capacity have limited their use almost exclusively to greenhorns and dudes. The small leather belt box which holds an entire box of twenty cartridges is very useful to the wilderness hunter, especially in the West; but that many cartridges, in addition to those in the rifle's magazine, is excessive for the whitetail hunter. The Avey holder will take six rounds, has little weight and bulk, and costs only about a dollar. Two of them may be strung on the belt, if more cartridges are thought to be needed.

Many hunters, especially in the West, carry a belt gun in addition to their rifle. This practice is not encountered in some of our states, because of foolish legislation, but much can be said both pro and con in regard to the advantages of an auxiliary weapon. For many years I carried a .22 autoloading pistol in a belt holster when hunting big game, but now confine my pistol toting to wilderness hunts. Hunters sometimes spend the first half of their lives seeking knowledge of all the equipment they could conceivably need for an outdoor expedition, then devote the remaining years to the ever-delightful discovery of the infinite variety of gear they can quite comfortably do *without*. The longer I hunt, the less gear—especially that to be carried on my person—is taken along. Not only do I take less and less gear into camp but I find fewer and fewer uses for many of the items taken. A lifetime of pistol toting by the whitetailer will seldom provide a single incident to prove the positive need for this practice.

I definitely like the *idea* of having a dependable pistol on my person for emergency use, but the added bulk and weight, plus the time and trouble necessary to properly care for the weapon, have made the price of this pleasure higher than I am willing to pay. An auxiliary side arm of .22 caliber is strictly an optional item, and its possession will stamp the wearer neither a greenhorn nor a veteran. However, in the case of heavy center-fire hand guns, only two classes of hunters will wear them—the master shooters who could hit you with every shot at a hundred yards and the gourd-green tenderfeet. Unless you wish to make a fool of yourself, never strap on a heavy pistol or revolver unless you can demonstrate a proficiency sufficient to justify its possession. There is an old saying down in Texas: "Just because a man smells like horse manure, that's no proof he is a big ranch owner." In the event you have decided to carry a side arm while hunting, choose a lightweight, short-barreled .22 rim-fire autoloader. The flatness of this type weapon promotes ease and comfort of carrying, but if the barrel is longer than four and a half inches the weapon will become a complete nuisance, requiring shifting, twisting, and adjusting every time you sit flat on the ground.

By all means use a separate belt on which to carry your equipment. I can think of nothing else so cheaply and easily aquired that contributes more to the hunter's comfort and enjoyment. A great deal of trouble will be saved every time his clothing is donned or removed and when his gear is removed before he enters a cafe or other public place.

In many sections of the country, especially in the South and Southwest, one of the hunter's most constant and annoying problems of a more or less minor nature is the drastic temperature change during the course of the day. The hunter often sallies forth in bone-chilling weather before dawn and then finds himself yearning for the old-fashioned swimming hole about noon. It is simple enough to dress for either kind of weather, but the hunter often encounters both kinds in a single day. After struggling with this problem for years, we finally concluded that a shoulder-supported canvas knapsack is the most practical solution. We now dress for maximum comfort in the early dawn, deposit excess clothing in the sack as rising temperatures dictate its removal, then again put on what is needed as night begins to fall.

Items carried regularly in the knapsack are a wingbone turkey call, our Gunslinger sling, a plastic bag large enough to hold a heart and liver, a cheesecloth bag to protect our kill, a candy bar, an extra pack of cigarettes, and two large red bandana handkerchiefs. A thermos bottle and light lunch are added if we plan to be out all day, and the camera and light meter go along when photographs are wanted. When hunting in isolated areas or in areas with which we are not thoroughly familiar we add to our knapsack waterproofed matches, a small whetstone, a compass, additional ammunition for the hand gun (if carried), a heavy-duty flashlight, and a first-aid kit. In Mexico we also carry water-purification tablets, a snakebite kit, and a large quantity of insect repellent in both powder and liquid form. And plenty of ammo.

Items carried on or about the person will vary with the individual, so I can only tell you what I carry. My hunting license is pinned inside my cap or hat except when hunting in those states which require that the license be openly displayed on headgear or lapel. I carry a red bandana in each hip pocket, and in one of them a length of rolled-up toilet paper. In each side pants pocket I carry one and only one metallic object—a flint lighter in one and a tiny one-cell penlight-battery-operated flashlight in the other. My cigarettes and glasses case are carried in the breast pocket of my shirt. If there is snow on the ground I will find room for a string-type field cleaner, which will be needed if the rifle barrel becomes clogged with snow, and several books of safety matches will be stowed in various pockets at all times. A pencil stub, to fill out the tag, is usually carried in my watch pocket and I always wear a wrist watch.

Some hunters carry a length of twine with which to fasten the tag to their kill, but we always slice off a strip of deer skin for this purpose. Quite a few hunters, anticipating the possibility of a need to summon their partner at a time when no empty cartridge case is available, add a whistle to their list of personal items. You will note that we carry nothing, with the possible exception of gloves or mittens, in the pockets of our outer clothing. Our reason is that these garments are subject to being shifted between our backs and our knapsack, which is often deposited in a cache along the trail.

Few men, except those who travel unbroken wilderness as an occupational hazard, ever get lost—I mean *really* lost—more than one time. This harrowing experience will forever afterward keep a man constantly alert to his position in relation to camp or to a major trail which leads to it. Although I am subject to losing my sense of direction, I have never been seriously lost in all my days of tramping the wilderness. This paradox is easily explained—the fortunate early discovery of my weakness impressed on me the necessity of keeping acutely aware of my surroundings and of continually noting all landmarks, and this practice virtually precludes the possibility of my becoming lost. I have learned, as you must learn, that a compass will be of little help unless it is used properly and frequently during the day. When improperly used, a compass may cause you to become even more thoroughly lost. I seldom use a compass except when entering completely unfamiliar country relatively devoid of landmarks.

It is my considered opinion that the novice should never go anywhere alone in wilderness country where his safe return

depends upon the use of instruments. When the sky is overcast or threatens to become so, or when easily-identifiable landmarks are lacking, the beginner woodsman should venture
only a short distance from camp except in the company of a
person who knows the country well. A compass is of little value
unless it is fairly large and of good quality and is used in conjunction with a watch. Both must be used to check your travel
time and direction of travel at frequent and regular intervals.
Before ever leaving camp in strange territory, you should definitely establish the exact position of north in relation to the
camp and all visible surrounding landscape. A wilderness expedition composed entirely of novice hunters, none of them
familiar with the country to be hunted, would be the height of
folly.

A light or lantern will assist your nighttime progress only
when you are traveling a well-defined trail. Anytime you become confused as to the trail or your direction, a light will usually increase your confusion. For this reason I will not use a
constant light in traveling a trail at night unless on overcast
sky or thick overhead foliage robs me of all visibility. The
experienced woodsman will use his light very sparingly, flash-
ing it only on deeply-shaded spots and while negotiating rough
or treacherous terrain. When operating in rough, broken, or
precipitous country, a hunter should be in camp before the
last daylight has left the sky. It's tough to leave a promising
stand at the most potentially-productive period of the evening,
but that's the price that the wilderness hunter must sometimes
pay. Anytime I become the least bit uneasy as to my exact
bearing when wilderness hunting, I immediately begin to unravel my back trail, even if the time is high noon. And the
moment I become uncertain as to the direction to camp, I
couldn't be induced to take another forward step if guaranteed

it would take me within Bowie knife range of a grizzly bear. I intend to die at the age of ninety-nine on a comfortable sleeping bag in a cozy hunting camp, and not from despair and exposure while lost in some dark, frozen thicket.

Once when I was younger and stronger I became temporarily lost while deer hunting. A buck had been hit hard by Tom Junior, aged fifteeen, but had lived long enough to travel a great distance into rough country which was totally unfamiliar to us. The sky was overcast and I unknowingly became completely turned around in my sense of direction while engrossed in unraveling the deer's twisting trail. After gutting the buck, I hoisted it on my back and started up a rugged hill. Tom objected to my choice of direction, but I felt confident that our camp lay over this young mountain and foolishly discounted Tom's opinion because of his tender years. When I had reached the top of the hill, after a prodigious feat of strength and endurance, the sun burst out suddenly and I realized my great error. I was now so completely lost that I had to back-track laboriously by the scant blood trail left by the dripping carcass. Since that day I have always trusted Tom's innate sense of direction, which has never let us down.

Camping out under primitive conditions is a highly specialized project requiring the planning and supervision of a thoroughly-experienced person. The beginner should never attempt a camping expedition in the exclusive company of other beginners, but should arrange to join groups of veteran campers until he has mastered the art sufficiently to strike out on his own. Any reader who is not an experienced woodsman is urged to avail himself of a good book devoted to camp making, compass and map reading, and wilderness survival. A little knowledge being a dangerous thing, I hesitate to pursue this subject further, for fear of luring an incompetent person into attempting something far beyond his capabilities on the mistaken assumption that I have covered all the salient features. In fact, I haven't even scratched the surface.

All the general means and equipment for comfort and survival completely aside, the whitetail seeker should bring along several items peculiar to his role of hunter. At least some member of the party should have with him a spare rifle with ammunition, a cleaning rod with accessories, a can of oil, an alarm clock, a whetstone, and a small kit of hand tools consisting of a small pair of pliers, and two or three assorted-size screwdrivers. There should be at least one large complete first-aid kit and a supply of aspirin tablets and tablets for the relief of indigestion. Any ailing member who does not respond promptly to either of these remedies should be removed immediately to more suitable surroundings. It is a regrettable fact than an elderly man who is unaccustomed to the rigors and hardships of camp life will invariably sicken within a few days. We were once forced to interupt an expensive and elaborate elk hunt in the Rockies because a seventy-year-old companion sickened alarmingly in the ten-thousand-foot altitude. This man was strong and active and had never previously been sick a day in his life. On the other hand, persons not too advanced in age are almost invariably invigorated by the outdoor life, and a few days in the woods will make the average middle-aged man feel like a kid again.

Whenever a reasonable likelihood of rain exists, the hunter should bring along a raincoat, preferably one with a hood or cape. Though I seldom hunt in rain too heavy to be turned by normal outdoor clothing, I recall one ten-day hunt during which a slow rain fell almost incessantly. If we had chosen not to hunt in the rain we would not have hunted at all.

The camper's bed is such a personal item that it definitely

comes under the heading of hunting equipment. Forget all the glowing eulogies lavished on balsam-bough beds or that horrible contraption which is responsible for more twisted spines than is arthritis—the folding army-type cot. To avoid sleeping on one of those instruments of torture, I'd fight a rattlesnake and give him first bite. A full-size, well-insulated sleeping bag supported by a heavy-duty air mattress, both of good quality, is the only type of bed which the experienced camper will consider. Avoid the mummy-type bag, which is too restrictive, and bring along a square of waterproofed tarp, large enough to permit you to lay half of it under the bed, with at least eighteen inches of apron sticking out, and to fold the remainder over, to cover the entire bed. The heavy tarp will save the mattress from many thorn punctures and, when drawn over so as to completely cover the sleeper, will probably insure a good night's rest even if a storm should rip the tent and let in some water. When used in really cold weather, no sleeping bag can ever be too warm, so don't be afraid of the word "arctic" when used to describe a certain make. The hunter should also have two wool army blankets in his bedroll. These can be placed over the bed in bitter weather; and, should the weather turn unseasonably warm, the camper can sleep on top of the bag and use one or both of the blankets for cover. In a bed such as described, a sleeper wearing two pairs of heavy wool socks and a suit of insulated underwear should be able to spend a comfortable night at the South Pole.

We will devote little further discussion to the hunter's clothing, because such a wide difference in temperatures will be encountered in the various parts of the country at different seasons of the year that specific recommendations are not possible. In the high Rockies, the New England states, southern Canada, and the northen tier of border states, weather approximating that of the Arctic may be encountered. This is especially true during the late-autumn and early-winter hunting seasons. A beginning hunter should seek and *heed* the advice of qualified persons who have had experience in the area of the projected hunt. A reputable dealer in sportswear should also be able to make specific recommendations as to proper clothing.

Heavy socks, of not less than 80 per cent wool, are a necessity for the cold-weather sportsman. At least six pairs should be taken along and they should be changed frequently, thoroughly aired and dried, and rotated in use. Quilted, insulated underwear has become a must for the hunter, rendering all other types obsolete. I recommend the two-piece type over the one-piece. A reversible red-and-khaki vest of the same quilted and insulated construction is a highly desirable item. Remember to wear ordinary cotton underwear or shorts directly next to your lower body or the insulated underwear will chafe and gall you.

I have never hunted in the far north nor have I hunted in temperatures below zero; but I hesitate to make specific clothing recommendations even for regions familiar to me, because individuals vary so much in their sensitivity to cold. I often meet people, dressed just as I am, who express acute discomfort from cold while I feel comfortably warm. On the other hand, I have met persons who, though lightly dressed, were perfectly comfortable, while I, bundled up like an Eskimo, felt that the icy hand of death was surely upon me.

At all costs, the hunter must avoid clothing that is binding or restrictive in the chest or shoulder regions. He should also avoid excessive bulk in his covering of these regions. These prohibitions are necessary for the very important reason that there must be nothing to prevent or interfere with the free and easy mounting of the weapon. Many a chance at game has been lost because an over-bundled hunter could not properly raise his rifle to his shoulder.

I do not feel qualified to make clothing suggestions for sub-zero temperatures, but here is an outfit which has served me well in weather not colder than zero. First, a two-piece suit of cotton underwear topped by a two-piece suit of down-filled insulated underwear. My trousers are the olive drab, very heavy woolen type as issued by the Marine Corps for cold-weather service. A heavy woolen red shirt is topped by a red quilted vest, already mentioned. Next comes a heavy woolen waist-length jacket of Marine Corps pattern, and the outer garment is a hip-length, lightweight parka with an imitation fur collar that can be zipped up to form a hood. This parka is made of water-resistant poplin and has a quilted insulated lining. Because of the double offset fastening, no wind will penetrate, and there is a lacing in the hood by means of which the lower part of the face can be shielded. Unless the two last-named garments are red in color, a large red bandana should be safety-pinned or basted to the back shoulder area of each.

The hunting hat or cap should be red, and the cap should be worn whenever there is a probability that the protection of the hood will be needed. The hood's bulkiness will not permit of additional head covering, and the cap can be more easily stuffed into knapsack or pocket than a hat can. Keeping the hands warm is a major problem in sub-zero weather, and the double mitten-gloves developed by the military are the best that I know of, for extremely cold weather. In such extreme cases, we use felted-wool mittens designed with a split in the palm of the right, or trigger-hand, mitten. However, in my family we rarely use a mitten on our trigger-hand preferring, if possible, to keep it warm in our side pocket.

For really cold weather, either wet or dry, I know of nothing in the way of footwear to surpass the insulated rubber boot. These should be selected in a size large enough to hold a heavy felted inner-sole liner and still be sufficiently roomy to pull on easily when the foot is covered with a heavy wool sock. These boots are too warm for use in temperatures much above freezing, so the hunter should also take along a pair of low boots or high shoes, to be worn in more moderate weather. This footgear should have soft gum-rubber—or preferably crepe-rubber—soles, and should be amply large to permit two pairs of medium-weight wool socks to be worn when needed.

When the ground is dry and temperatures do not drop below sixteen degrees, I wear a pair of high-top gymnasium shoes, with one or two pairs of heavy wool socks. Although all my hunting companions agree that this combination is unsurpassed for quiet walking, I have made few converts. They refuse to believe that, with the exception of insulated boots, this is the warmest footwear I have ever discovered. When their feet are slowly freezing in heavy boots they simply cannot believe that my own, encased in canvas shoes, could be cozy and warm. I have even worn these shoes in light, wet snow without particular discomfort.

Although tennis or gymnasium shoes will seldom last more than one hunting season, their low cost makes them about the cheapest footwear obtainable. Unfortunately, few people have feet that will permit them to wear a soft, heelless shoe in comfort. The Good Lord did a much better job on the lower of my two extremities, giving me strong, high arches and feet free of corns, bunions, and ingrowing toenails. My manner of walking very lightly and placing my feet very carefully allows me to negotiate even rocky country without developing stone bruises. The average heavy-walking individual who seldom watches where he places his feet would be quickly incapacitated. Truly, one man's meat may be another's poison.

The typical indoor worker who drives a well-heated car, works and lives in the pleasant environment of central heating, and sleeps under an electric blanket will require twice as much clothing as is required by a man who works outside in winter weather and is inured to the cold. Again, a man who spends long periods of time watching trails, scrapes, or buck-runs, will need more clothing than the hunter who walks continually. Also, each mile-per-hour of wind velocity produces the same effect as lowering the temperature by almost a full degree. Thus a twenty-mile wind in twenty-degree weather will require a man to dress as warmly as he would need to do in calm zero weather. Therefore the whitetail hunter should not scorn the use of alcohol-burning hand and foot warmers whenever their need is warranted. I would like to suggest, however, that the hunter first be certain that he is otherwise properly outfitted before resorting to their use.

One last word on clothing—you should start out each day with thoroughly dry clothing, especially those garments worn next to the skin. Beginning the morning with damp clothing will leave you feeling clammy and cold all day.

As a young man, I considered myself a real he-coon and bull-of-the-woods—a worthy running mate for Daniel Boone or Pecos Bill. Scorning all luxuries unknown to Davey Crockett, I set about proving that I was man's man, come hell or high water. Now having proved my point, I gladly embrace all modern devices that actually reduce my labor and add to my comfort and enjoyment. Unfortunately, 99 per cent of all the new gimmicks designed for the hunter are completely useless, and most of the remaining one per cent pose more problems than they solve. Although I may provoke gasps of horror from the "progressive" school of gimmick-conscious shooters, it is my opinion that lightweight insulated boots and clothing are for the whitetail hunter the most beneficial development of the past fifty years. The one other important contribution is the development of non-corrosive, non-fouling ammunition.

And now—good-bye, good luck, and good hunting.

13———BOW HUNTING THE WHITETAIL DEER

Lying peacefully along a lonely stretch of the south-central Texas coast, not very far from the town of Victoria, is the famed Aransas Wildlife Refuge, winter home of the vanishing whooping crane and a variety of waterfowl, and the permanent home of such birds and mammals as the wild turkey, the whitetail deer, and the pitiably few Attwater's prairie chickens still surviving in this area. Here, the combination of mild winters, abundant rainfall, and lush semi-tropical vegetation, promotes such a rapid increase in the deer population that serious range depletion would quickly result if artificial means were not employed to remove the surplus and hold the herd in check. Until the mid nineteen-sixties, this was no problem; a well organized and highly efficient trapping operation provided plenty of animals for all the restocking programs in Texas plus all the deer that could be sold or traded to other states and foreign countries.

Gradually, however, the nation's effort to establish viable whitetail herds in all suitable habitats neared a successful conclusion, and the demand for deer-on-the-hoof dwindled to a trickle. It was then that the State Fish and Game Commission wisely inaugurated a special pre-regular-season archery hunt in the refuge. This precedent-setting move was greeted with unbridled enthusiasm, and the sport of bow and arrow hunting—in our part of the world—was given a tremendous boost. The "Hayes boys," like most other devout deer hunters hereabout, were caught up in the frantic rush to participate in this "new'" form of hunting, and, though we never acquired the shooting skill to supplant Robin Hood in the history books, we had a lot of fun, and we had the rare opportunity of observing the peak rutting frenzy.

In all forms of recreational hunting—as opposed to hunting for profit or survival—the primary goals should be: the healthful exercise provided, the enjoyment of observing and being a part of nature, and the personal pleasure derived from the *pursuit* of the quarry. Within this concept, recreational hunting with the bow and arrow can be every bit as rewarding as can any other manner of hunting. The fact that there are at least eight million bow hunters in this country attests to the popularity enjoyed by this rapidly growing hobby. The reader contemplating the adoption of this primitive sport should, however, be well aware of the limitations imposed on the practitioner, as well as the advantages already cited. This knowledge can best be imparted by direct comparisons between bow hunting and the more conventional hunting method embracing the use of firearms.

Firstly, even the most highly skilled archer must limit his attempts at deer to a range not greater than fifty yards, while the less skilled (or "average") archer must pass up all shots at ranges exceeding forty yards. Reasons for this range limitation will be given later.

Secondly, this severe limitation as to effective range demands a higher degree of patience, stealth, self-restraint, woodsmanship, and all-around deer "savvy." It virtually demands the use of first-class equipment and attire, as well as the judicious employment of camouflage.

Thirdly, the bowman must be ever mindful that his target area is limited to the animal's' lungs and heart. Unlike the high-power rifle bullet, which shatters bones, smashes, stuns, and numbs, the arrow kills almost exclusively by inducing hemorrhage. In other words, the fatally stricken animal bleeds to death.

Very seldom, if ever, will an arrow drop a deer in its tracks, and a lung-shot animal generally runs twice as far as would be expected of a bullet-shot deer with the identical shot placement. The bow hunter, therefore, should be highly skilled in the art of tracking wounded game. Incidentally, the arrow should never be used on dangerous game; it has virtually no "stopping" power, and even the properly hit animal—from the close range at which it would necessarily have to be shot—would undoubtedly live long enough to reach and maul the shooter.

The wealth of useful information regarding the white-tail's habits, traits, and behavior, together with the pertinent advice relating to the hunting of this animal—as contained in the preceeding chapters of this book—will have prepared the reader (as well as any book could possibly do) to find himself a deer, and to arrange matters in such a way as to ensure a clear shot within the limited range of the bow-launched arrow. The balance of this chapter, therefore, will deal principally with the selection and use of archery hunting equipment, and to the accessories and incidental items related to this sport.

The severe range limitation placed on the bow and arrow is due not so much to the weapon's lack of killing-power as to several congenital faults of a more serious nature; actually, the broadhead hunting arrow kills even large animals surprisingly well. The primary range-limiting factor is the "rainbow" trajectory of the missile that demands exacting range estimation coupled with exacting elevation compensation on the part of the bowman. At the maximum ranges we have discussed, this requires a very high degree of skill reinforced by considerable practice. Other major range-limiting factors include the arrow's pronounced tendency to veer off course from the effect of even a moderate wind, and the drastic deflection displayed upon striking even a tiny twig.

The bow hunter's clothing and footgear demand careful consideration and judicious selection. A head-to-foot camouflage outfit is earnestly recommended, including, most importantly, a see-through face screen. The true, Indian-style moccasin is the ideal foot gear, but dark sneakers will do very well. Camouflage netting is readily available, and several yards of this material, for the construction of a blind, should be carried in a camouflage knapsack. Camouflage clothing, of course, can be worn with safety only on private property or during bow-only seasons; it could prove fatal if worn where rifle hunting was also being practised.

When it comes to the selection of equipment, I strongly suggest that the beginner consult a reputable "pro" shop. In the event that the reader may be quite distantly removed from such a fountainhead of practical advice, I will attempt, briefly, to guide him away from the major pitfalls. The first item to be considered is the bow, and the person who hasn't kept abreast of developments in this device is due for a traumatic shock.

Fast fading from popularity is the classic long-bow, as typified by Robin Hood's legendary weapon, and this includes the latest models featuring composite (laminated) construction and recurved tips. Taking their place is the much more complex "compound" bow that was introduced in the mid-nineteen-sixties. Traditionally, the compound bow features a distinctly separate center section (called the "riser") that includes the pistol-grip handle and the arrow-rest. Short, powerful limbs of laminated construction are attached to the riser through intermediary metal frameworks, each containing ratchet gears and a protruding tie-point for the string.

The extremity of each limb supports an eccentrically pivoted wheel, called a "rolling cam" by some manufacturers, and somewhat below each of these cams is located another pulley or "wheel" The "string" is a slender, vinyl-covered steel cable of considerable length, and that is strung only with the assistance of a quite necessary accessory called a "stringer-destringer." The string is wound in a complex pattern around each of the cams and pulleys. The purpose of the aforementioned ratchet gears is to "tune" the limbs so that the eccentric cams rotate in agreement, and they also provide a means whereby the bow's draw-weight can be varied between 45 and 60 pounds, the usually encountered range. Some models can be set at 75 pounds pull, but all, as a rule, come set, from the factory, at the reasonable draw-weight of 50 pounds. Believe me, Robin Hood would turn over in his grave at a glimpse of one of these mechanized contraptions.

The general type of compound bow just described is called a "four wheeler," and the advantages (clearly not esthetic) include: adjustability of the draw weight, a definite increase in cast (speed imparted to the arrow) over the older, classic instrument now termed a "stick" bow, and a distinctly unique draw-force sequence that requires maximum force to be applied at some point *prior* to full draw, then suddenly relaxing (or letting off) so that only about one-half to two-thirds of the peak force is required to hold the arrow in fully drawn position. This feature is a tremendous boost to accurate shooting, and it particularly aids the deer hunter who must, if possible, draw his bow at such time as the movement can't be observed by his quarry, but who may then be forced to hold this position while awaiting an opportunity for the shot. This four-wheeler compound bow just described is not, however the type that I recommend to the hunter. At least as a hunting instrument, it has already been superseded.

In 1975 a simplified modification of the compound bow arrived on the scene. This later type dispenses with the two inner pulleys and the tie-points for the string, but it does retain the rolling cams on the ends of the limbs, thus accounting for the common term, *two-wheeler*. Having but one minor disadvantage as compared with the four-wheeler—a slightly less favorable resistance curve to the draw—the two-wheeler is lighter, less costly, less complicated, and less difficult to string. But, best of all, it requires no "tuning." And, as an additional bonus, the absence of some of the mechanical guts and "gizmos" helps somewhat to mitigate the congenital "unbeauty" of the thing.

Every bow of every type has an optimum flexing point called the "draw length," which requires matching length in the arrow if maximum results from the combination are to be realized. Inasmuch as every person's natural draw length is dependent on his physical dimensions, the prospective buyer must first determine his own draw length before selecting his bow. This figure is best obtained with the use of a trial bow, the measurement being done by an experienced archer. However, if you should wish to estimate your draw length, you may multiply your height, in inches, by the figure, 0.416. This works out, for the four arrow-lengths commonly available, as follows: height 5' 8", draw length 28"; height 5' 10", draw length 29"; height 6' 0", draw length 30"; height 6' 2", draw length 31".

Not only must the arrow's length be compatible with the associated bow, but its stiffness or "backbone"—called *spine*— must be just sufficient to withstand the terrific acceleration given the missile upon release of the bow string, but not more so. This requires that the arrows to be used with a given bow be selected with two particular specifications in mind: the spine rating, in pounds, and the length, in inches.

The hunting arrows currently available are made from hollow aluminum alloy or from cedar. I suggest that yours be of the anodized aluminum type featuring interchangeable points and replaceable nocks, and that the fletching be synthetic "feathers." These are more durable than real feathers, and, unlike nature's product, will withstand much more use and abuse, and are unaffected by rain or dew. Six such arrows, matched, are suggested for your initial purchase. And don't forget to buy a package of replacement broadhead points; almost every shot taken at game will result in a damaged or broken point (or a lost arrow), so repairs or replacements are continually in order. The replacement hunting points I recommend are called Bear Savora Super-S Hunting Heads.

The bow hunter will need a few additional convenience items and accessories, but I distinctly warn against his succumbing to a common affliction best described as "gadgetitis." If a person should undertake to buy even one of every gadget and gimmick available to the archer, he couldn't walk without staggering under the load. But there are two things he will need that may prove to be the best of his investments; a set of "field" points for target practice, and a target and target butt on which to practice—and practice—and practice.

An essential item for the hunter is a quiver, and I consider the type that attaches directly to the bow to be much the best for his purpose. Lightness, compactness, and speed of withdrawal, are most important; a large capacity isn't. But I strongly suggest that you select a model featuring a hood that covers the points. Broadhead points are easily damaged, but most importantly, they can injure you cruelly; they are deadly weapons that must be handled with the utmost care and caution.

Another bow accessory I unhesitatingly recommend to the tyro archer is a bow sight. Get the simplest model you can find, and calibrate it yourself to coincide with your own bow, arrows, and individual release.

Another needed accessory is an arm guard, and my personal preference is for a camouflage vinyl "snap-on" model. Other types are available, including a leather "lace on" model.

Bow shooting requires the use of special finger protectors to be worn on the arrow-releasing hand. There are two general types of these: finger tabs, and fingertip gloves. Opinion is definitely divided on these types. Of the three best bow hunters I know, two favor the finger tab, while the third (and myself) favor the shooting glove. This latter is truly a skeletonized affair consisting of three leather fingers connected to a slender wrist band by a narrow strip across the back of the hand.

A small repair kit containing, among other odds and ends, replacement nocks and cement, is a useful addition to the bow hunter's gear, and a stout bow case is a wise investment.

Most states now require all hunting arrows to be plainly labeled with the owner's name and address, so be sure to provide yourself with some small gummed labels, and stick one near the fletching on each arrow. And by all means get yourself a good, authoritative textbook devoted to the art of bow shooting.

Archery requires the use of muscles not ordinarily used in routine daily living, and the first-timer may make the painful discovery of muscles he didn't even know he had. Start with a few shots the first day, then gradually lengthen your practice sessions until your muscles are firm and strong. A weak or frail person should start with a low-priced beginner's bow, drawing about twenty-five or thirty pounds, and use this for a while.

When will you be ready to try for deer? Well, if you should draw a permit to hunt on Camp Hood, near Killeen, Texas, you would have to demonstrate that you could place four out of five arrows into a 9-inch paper plate from a distance of twenty yards.

14—SOUTH TEXAS TROPHY HUNTING

SOUTH TEXAS

A rolling ocean of thorny brush
As far as the eye can see . . .
A desolate, lonely, primitive place,
As wild as a land can be.
Where the hot wind's breath blows the kiss of Death
To the withered, sun-parched ground,
And coyotes howl on their nightly prowl
As darkness closes down.
Where all things tread in mortal dread
Of the fearsome rattler's bite,
And the rabbit's wail tells a gruesome tale
Of death in the dead of night.

After Tom Junior had become a prosperous family man, and had taken a fair share of run-of-the-mill bucks, he began the practice of leasing hunting rights in that particular section of the state (roughly embracing Webb and all adjacent counties)) known far and wide to serious whitetail hunters simply as "South Texas." I have never cared for this part of my state—much preferring the beautiful Hill Country—but when my grandson, Buck (Tom IV), grew old enough

269

to join in the hunting, I began making one or two annual pilgrimages to South Texas for a hunt with my boys.

The deer there are far from numerous except on a few posted and intensively patrolled ranches, and the thick, thorny, and ever-present brush makes off-road travel, afoot, both difficult and painful. Other inconveniences include a hot, stultifying climate—punctuated in late season by brief but bone-chilling "northers"—very little rainfall, and an abundance of diamond-back rattlesnakes, one of the most deadly venomous serpents in all the world. No prudent person walks through the brush without wearing high-top boots or cumbersome "snake leggings." I honestly believe South Texas whitetail hunting to be the most difficult, frustrating, time-consuming, and expensive, of any in the world.

You may now be wondering why anyone in his right mind would deliberately choose to hunt in such a place, and why whitetail buffs flock there in droves each hunting season. The answer is quite simple: South Texas whitetails are big—*really big*—and the huge antlers of the fully mature bucks are not exceeded in size by those of any other whitetails on Earth. This area is truly a mecca for serious trophy hunters, and, believe me, there are no more rabid sports enthusiasts to be found, anywhere, than Simon-pure "'trophy hounds."

Now, when I say South Texas whitetail hunting is expensive, I mean *expensive*. All land is in private hands, and the owners are well aware of the insistent demand for hunting privileges, and of the current cheapness of money. Hunting privileges are normally obtained in one of two ways: a ranch—or a specified portion thereof—is leased outright for one or more seasons, or, most usually, the hunter buys a "gun," which permits him to participate with other "guns" in the hunting on a specified piece of land. At this writing, a lease may cost anywhere from one dollar—the price we currently pay for 5,000 acres—to three dollars per acre.

"Guns," at present, range in cost from a possible low of $300 to as high as $650 for well-above-average hunting territory. Some outfits—often with a long waiting list—charge as much as $1,250 per "gun," and furnish prepared meals, bunkhouse privileges, transportation (if needed), deluxe tower blinds, superlative hunting, personnel to take charge of downed game, and various other conveniences. Some, no doubt, might even aid the "gun" in the aiming and discharging of his rifle if so requested.

I personally know men who spend up to $10,000 annually in their unceasing quest for a truly outstanding trophy, and who may not have fired a shot in the past several seasons. These men are completely disinterested in killing an ordinary buck; their goal is to garner a head so massive, so multi-pointed, and so symmetrical, that it will qualify as a "Boone & Crockett" trophy. Let me tell you, briefly, about the famous Boone & Crockett Club.

Back in the year 1887 Theodore Roosevelt—a dedicated conservationist and enthusiastic hunter—assembled a group of like-minded friends and formed a club that would promote quality hunting as opposed to *quantity* hunting, particularly as applied to big-game species. Continued through the years, this organization has become the universally acknowledged "official" standard setter, measurer, and recorder for American big game trophies. The club appoints "official" scorers in various parts of the country who personally examine, measure, and evaluate each candidate trophy. Application blanks and literature outlining the measurement procedure are available from your taxidermist. Incidentally, if the skull-plate base of the antlers should become cracked, or should the trophy be deemed not to have been taken in "fair chase," then the trophy will not be given recognition. Any obvious alteration of the trophy will also cause its disqualification.

The club's sphere of activity embraces this entire continent, and their interesting and informative publication—a book titled *North American Big Game*—is kept updated by revision from time to time. The latest edition—at this writing—is dated 1971. Among dedicated "head" hunters, having one's trophy listed in *Boone & Crockett* is just about the ultimate achievement ranking slightly below the Medal of Honor, but well ahead of the Nobel Prize.

The club recognizes all whitetails—with the sole exception of the little Coues deer of Sonora and southern Arizona—as belonging to a single group that is headed thusly: *"Odocoileus Virginianus* (and certain related sub-species)." Including both the Typical and Nontypical categories, there are, altogether, about 500 trophies listed. This may seem like a large number, on first thought, but when one considers the fact that this is an all-time accumulation, and furthermore, if one reflects on the matter of millions of hunters having devoted millions of man-hours to the delightful pursuit of these trophies, then the reasonable conclusion may be reached that the odds are greatly against any particular hunter connecting with one of these "super mossbacks." "Boone & Crockett" bucks are becoming quite scarce; the extreme hunting pressure, almost everywhere, permits precious few antlered whitetails to live for as long as five years, the minimum time required to grow a real trophy head.

North American Big Game lists trophies from every

section of the country, but the greatest numbers come from two rather well-defined areas: the far northern ranges, on both sides of the Canadian border, and the "South Texas" region of the Lone Star State. *Odocoileus virginianus borealis* attains the greatest size and weight of any whitetail, but old *o. v. texanus*—although he never puts on (or needs) much fat—grows almost as large a frame, and antlers that are just as massive. Those "little" Texas whitetails you may have heard about are the result of overcrowding, and are limited to certain local areas. All whitetails—excepting those inhabiting South Texas—are best hunted by the tactics, equipment, and methods previously outlined in this book. On the contrary, South Texas whitetails are most successfully hunted by methods and equipment peculiar to this part of the world. The importance of this statement should not be disregarded by any reader contemplating a hunt in this area.

Back in the middle of the past century when whitetails began their gradual invasion into the more typical pronghorn range of South Texas, nature helped them to adapt by inducing certain changes both in living habits and in physical characteristics. The extreme heat and humidity, coupled with the seasonal scarcity of surface water, and compounded by the relative absence of concealment, have combined to alter the deer's normal daily living pattern; the pressing need to conserve vital body moisture, and to escape detection by a host of predators, has turned them into predominantly nocturnal animals. And, like their desert mule deer cousins, South Texas whitetails have acquired the ability to subsist entirely without ever taking a drink of water. Watching a water "hole" will normally prove a waste of time.

Another trait that adds to the difficulty of harvesting these deer is their extreme wariness, caused principally by the relentless year-round poaching practiced by a sizable number of the local *residentes* who habitually carry a loaded rifle whether afoot, horseback, or driving a vehicle, and who blast away at every deer that offers a shot regardless of age, sex or offspring dependence. This is not done as a deliberate flaunting of the law; it is simply their way of life. An excessive number and variety of predators contributes to the deer's chronic state of super alertness; coyotes are ever present and they are quick death to any sick, weak, or severely injured deer, and they destroy approximately half of the annual fawn crop. Golden eagles are frequently seen here in the fall and winter, cougars are far from extinct, and even an occasional jaguar wanders in from Mexico.

These deer seem to have sharper vision than their original migrant ancestors. This development has probably come about because they must do a great deal of feeding and traveling over extensive stretches of low brush that leaves them well exposed to danger. This former pronghorn range has conditioned the deer to emulate the antelope's reaction to peril; they take notice of a moving enemy while it is still a very long distance away, frequently take flight at a distance of half a mile, and, like pronghorns, run until out of sight regardless of how far "out of sight" may be.

The great and prevailing obstacle to every human endeavor in South Texas is the overwhelming, ever-present, progress-stifling brush. Only since the introduction of modern off-road vehicles has it been practical for man to readily penetrate and freely circulate within this hostile barrier. A dependable off-road vehicle is almost essential to the hunter, and every serious hunter has one. A pickup truck equipped with positive-traction drive and puncture-resistant tires is about the minimum vehicle I can recommend, and the most nearly ideal conveyance, in my opinion, is one of the special hunting cars having 4-wheel drive as currently offered by several major auto makers. The British Land Rover and the American Jeep are typical examples, and nearly every vehicle used here is extensively modified.

Our Jeep is typical of the modified South Texas brush buggy, having a special elevated rear seat with hold-on rails, a "skid" plate welded to the frame below the motor and transmission, a tow yoke, a power winch on the front bumper, ball hitches fore and aft, special, very-heavy-duty tires containing liquid sealant, and steel brackets for the support of rifle scabbards.

Becoming somewhat popular are used (but retreaded) aircraft landing tires so stiff and heavy that they will support the vehicle even when uninflated. You won't be able to fully appreciate this innovation until you have experienced the curse of mesquite thorn punctures. These will be our next replacements.

A modification truly inspired is the addition of a ten-foot steel tower to the rear of the vehicle, equipped with a seat on top and hinges at the base for lowering to horizontal position when traveling the highway.

Generally speaking, South Texas bucks are shot from elevated blinds or towers provided with ladders. Placed at what is hoped to be a favorable location, the tower is mounted by the hunter who simply watches and waits. Since it is no longer illegal, here, to hunt from a vehicle on private land, the tower-equipped vehicle provides an infinite choice of locations. The hunter buying a "gun" may expect to find tower blinds that are permanently erected at experience-dictated locations, and that are available to all participating "guns" on a first-come basis; the leaseholder, on the contrary, must provide his own. Most hunters bring portable prefabricated blinds, widely advertised in Texas, having a swiveled seat at the top and a bar in front of the shooter for a rifle rest. Models are available in heights of from ten to twenty feet, with the option of an open chair seat or more sheltered seat featuring a top plus sides and back. This latter type—and all 20-footers—will require the attachment of guy wires. The hunter owning a tower-mounted vehicle is really in business.

Most permanent tower-blinds are constructed principally of lumber, and will probably be abandoned by the builder at the expiration of his lease. The succeeding leaseholder may therefore be provided with a windfall. More than a few wealthy ranchers and leaseholders engage a steel construction firm to design and fabricate massive, bolt-assembled towers up to fifty feet in height. These will be delivered and erected at the designated sites in the brush. A roomy cubicle at the top will be carpeted and provided with sliding glass windows on all sides which may be opened soundlessly. A gun rack, a shelf or two, a bottled-gas heater, and a well-padded swivel chair complete the contraptions.

I know two building contractors, each of whom has a specially designed *house,* of plain but conventional "shotgun" construction, dimensioned to fit the bed of a huge flat-bed trailer. These are hauled each season to the hunting lease by big tractor-trucks, where work crews unload and level them, clear and level a "yard" area, construct barbecue pits, hook up the electric power generators, connect coupling hoses to the water-tank trucks parked alongside, erect the TV antennas, dig septic tanks and lay flexible sewer lines, fill the ice trays, connect the butane tanks, and light the pilots on the water heaters, kitchen ranges, and room heaters. The work crews then haul each tower-blind to its designated location, prepare a foundation, then raise the structure (with the aid of power machinery) and securely guy it. Maybe it's a case of sour grapes with me, but I much prefer my hunting to be on a more traditional basis.

I so dislike sitting in a prepared blind that I seldom make use of one unless the weather is nasty. We have abandoned the practice of constructing permanent blinds, but keep several portable types on hand that are frequently employed through necessity. Still-hunting is virtually impossible in many areas of South Texas, and very difficult to practice in most others; so much so, in fact, that practically "everybody" pronounces it to be completely impractical. Perhaps I am just plain lucky, but I have managed to do quite well at it.

Fate, as we all know, doesn't always deal your cards from the top of the deck. Tom Junior, for example, has spent a small fortune in South Texas in quest of trophy bucks, while I, on the other hand, would rate my interest and investment as rather mild. Tom is also the most proficient hunter in our family, and although both he and Buck have collected several truly impressive trophies, I am the only one of us that the Red Gods have presented with a "Boone & Crockett" deer. Except for a quirk of Fate, Tom, rather than I, might have taken this animal. Briefly, I will tell you the story.

In scouting our hunting grounds, each of us had located areas used by big bucks, but, after several consecutive days of hunting, without success, we mutually agreed to trade hunting areas in an effort to break the monotony. You have guessed, of course, what happened on the very first morning following the exchange. When the rising sun had brightened the long gentle rise on the far side of the shallow draw I was facing, I began to move slowly along a route that would provide me with a commanding view of the opposite slope. I had progressed for about one hour and three hundred yards when something a bit out of the ordinary caught my eye; a small dead tree whose leafless branches bore an uncanny resemblance to a monstrous set of antlers. Adjusting my binoculars for a better look, I perceived—at a distance of 200 yards—the head, only, of a great deer that was watching me intently.

Had the animal been closer, or the huge body been visible, I might have lost my "cool," but with only the white throat patch for a target, and the great distance required for the shot, I forced myself to be calm and deliberate. Quickly scanning the ground near my feet, I found a small spot free of burr cactus on which I firmly planted my seat. Slipping my left arm into the sling, and bracing my elbows firmly over my knees, I placed the crosswires on that remote spot of white, pressed the trigger, and made local history. The 15-point head—made into a beautiful shoulder mount— scores 170 2/8 Boone & Crockett points. The deer field-dressed 180 pounds.

The rifle I used that day was a .300 Magnum although I usually hunt with a 7mm Magnum. Buck uses a 7mm Magnum also, while Tom favors his .300 Weatherby, keeping a .25/06 Remington in reserve. All our rifles are sighted-in to be dead-on at a range of 300 yards, and our scopes range in power from fixed 4 to variable 7. I believe that shooting opportunities average as far, here, as they do in any other section of the nation, 300 yards being a fair estimate. The calibers we use are typical, and together with the .270 Winchester represent the choice of most veteran hunters. Leave your pet .243 at home; it simply isn't dependable on these big, cactus-toughened deer at ranges exceeding 200 yards.

But don't forget to bring along your binoculars.

We have finally come to the conclusion that "horn rattling" is the most productive method of hunting South Texas bucks, and it is best done with a tower-equipped vehicle that is moved at half-hour intervals and parked in likely spots. One person sits atop the tower while the other walks a short way into the brush and "rattles up a storm." This method sometimes gets results in the middle of a hot day, a time when these deer seldom show themselves to a "watcher." Ordinarily, the deer move freely in daylight hours only during the "cold snaps" and "wet northers" of late December. This is so generally true that numbers of men refrain from hunting until the last two weeks of the six-weeks season.

I have finally given up scrape-hunting in South Texas, having watched heavily scraped areas for days on end—from crack of dawn until pitch darkness—and seeing no living thing, but finding, each morning, fresh and plentiful evidence of frenzied rutting activity. Perhaps, during hot weather, the sexual urge is stimulated only by the lower temperatures of night.

Any reasonably symmetrical head having a spread of 21 inches, and 10 points, is generally considered a "trophy." If you see one like this, and the points are long and the beam quite heavy, shoot! You are unlikely to ever get a better. Always strive for both a side view and a head-on view of the antlers; from the side, the tips should jut out even with the nose, and the head-on view should show the rack to be at least three inches wider, on both sides, than the tips of the animal's ears. Always try to determine the body size; mediocre antlers can appear very big on a small buck.